THE
MODERN
BUILDER'S
GUIDE

THE MODERN BUILDERS GUIDE.

BY M. LAFEVER.

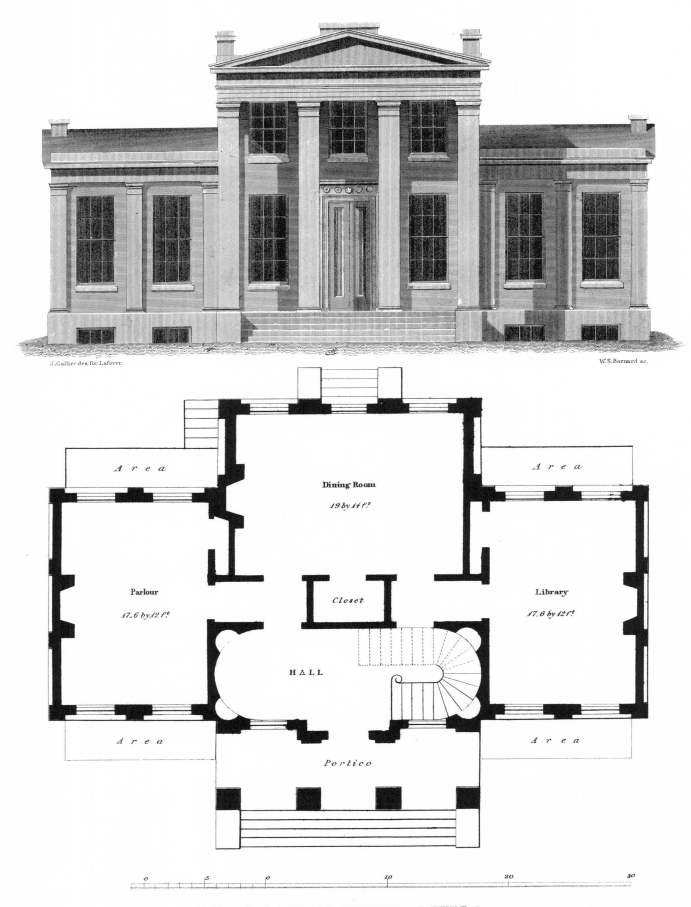

J. Gallier des. for Lafever.

W. S. Barnard sc.

Area

Area

Dining Room
19 by 14 f.

Area

Area

Parlour
17.6 by 12 f.

Closet

Library
17.6 by 12 f.

HALL

Portico

0   5   0   10   20   30

DESIGN FOR A COUNTRY VILLA.

New York. Published by Henry C. Sleight.

Plates Printed by Wm. D. Smith.

THE MODERN BUILDER'S GUIDE

by MINARD LAFEVER

A Reprint of the first (1833) Edition
with three additional Plates from the third Edition

With a new Introduction by
JACOB LANDY
The City College,
The City University of New York

DOVER PUBLICATIONS, INC., NEW YORK

Published in Canada by General Publishing Company, Ltd.,
30 Lesmill Road, Don Mills, Toronto, Ontario.
Published in the United Kingdom by Constable and Company, Ltd.,
10 Orange Street, London, WC 2.

This Dover edition, first published in 1969, is an unabridged and unaltered republication of the first edition as published by Henry C. Sleight,—Collins & Hannay in 1833, to which have been added three plates from the third (1846) edition, a new introduction by Jacob Landy, and ten illustrations of buildings by Minard Lafever.

The publisher is grateful to the George Peabody Branch, Enoch Pratt Free Library, Baltimore, Maryland, for making a copy of the first edition available for reproduction. The publisher also gratefully acknowledges the assistance of the Columbia University Libraries, which provided the copy of *The Architectural Instructor* from which five of the illustrations in the Introduction were photographed.

Standard Book Number: 486-22260-8
Library of Congress Catalog Card Number: 68-54518

Manufactured in the United States of America
Dover Publications, Inc.
180 Varick Street
New York, N. Y. 10014

INTRODUCTION

DOVER EDITION

THE MODERN BUILDER'S GUIDE was the second of five publications written by the New York architect Minard Lafever.[1] Extremely influential throughout the United States during the first half of the nineteenth century, such "builders' guide" books were basically eclectic compilations intended to be of immediate use to carpenters, masons, and others in the building trades. Included most often were sections on practical geometry and constructional techniques, the classical "orders" and decorative detail as illustrated in well-known Greek monuments, and "original" designs by the author for various types of structures and room interiors. In obtaining much of this material, it was accepted practice to borrow freely from similar books published in England.

As Lafever acknowledged in his Preface to *The Modern Builder's Guide*, the most popular source of information on construction was Peter Nicholson of London, whose books were no less influential in America than in England. Equally invaluable for examples of Greek architecture were the excellent plates in the four volumes of *The Antiquities of Athens* (London, 1762–1816), begun by the English architect-archeologists James Stuart and Nicholas Revett and completed by others. Occasionally, too, the advice of local talent was solicited. Again, Lafever indicated in the Pref-

ace that Mr. Joshua Coulter of Philadelphia made helpful suggestions in the "department of Hand-railing," while New York colleagues J. C. Brady and Martin E. Thompson expressed approval of the work as a whole.

Four of Lafever's books, including the present volume, are properly classified as "builders' guides." His last work, published posthumously as *The Architectural Instructor* (New York, 1856), falls into the category of "house pattern" books which became more popular after the mid-forties. Here most of the material consisted of plans and elevations for houses, which by the fifties embraced all the eclectic styles then current in architecture. Also included were suggested designs for other types of buildings, to which Lafever added descriptions and plates for some of his own executed works. It was the "builders' guides," however—Lafever's in particular—which were most significant in spreading Greek Revival ornament throughout the country during the pre-Civil War period.[2] Talbot Hamlin, in his enthusiastic accounts of Greek Revival architecture in America, repeatedly emphasized that while Lafever's detail was Greek-inspired, it was never a simple matter of archeological copying. More important than his obvious use

---

[1] For a complete listing of Lafever's publications and details of all their editions, see Henry-Russell Hitchcock, *American Architectural Books*, 3rd rev. ed. (Minneapolis, 1962), p. 58. *The Modern Builder's Guide* was issued first in 1833, and was reissued in 1841, 1846, 1849, 1850, 1853 and 1855. The present reprint is based on the first edition, but also contains three plates (Nos. 54, 55 and 89) which first appeared in the edition of 1846.

[2] Many specific examples are cited in Talbot Hamlin, *Greek Revival Architecture in America* (New York, 1944). This invaluable study was reprinted in 1964 by Dover Publications, Inc. See also Clay Lancaster, "Builders' Guide and Plan Books and American Architecture, from the Revolution to the Civil War," *Magazine of Art*, XLI (January, 1948), pp. 16-22. For a more concentrated study by the same author, see "Adaptations from Greek Revival Builders' Guides in Kentucky," *Art Bulletin*, XXXII (March, 1950), pp. 62-70.

of such Greek decorative motives as anthemia and rosettes, was Lafever's attempt to express Grecian qualities of delicacy and restraint in freely creative "American" inventions.

In his first publication, *The Young Builder's General Instructor* (Newark, 1829), Lafever's application of classical detail to modern architectural forms was still rather crude and clumsy. His second effort, *The Modern Builder's Guide*, profited from a more matured taste, while the third of his builders' guides, *The Beauties of Modern Architecture* (New York, 1835), contained highly polished and sensitive designs, decidedly personal in flavor.[3] It was for the strength of his creative power, blended with exquisite restraint, that Lafever was considered by Hamlin to have been "perhaps the greatest designer of architectural decoration of his time in America. . . . To him more than to any other one man is due the clear, inviting quality of the interiors of Greek Revival houses and the crisp, imaginative character of the wood and plaster detail that so frequently accents and beautifies them" (page 147).

Noteworthy in the Preface to *The Modern Builder's Guide* is Lafever's self-critical appraisal of his first book. Dissatisfied with its "defects and inaccuracies," he decided to withdraw *The Young Builder's General Instructor* from print and publish a "substitute" volume instead of a corrected second edition.

Following the Preface of the work here reprinted is a section (Plates 1–21) on geometry adapted to practical carpentry. Although the problems here were based on Nicholson's *The Carpenter's New Guide*, Lafever felt that his own explanations were better suited to the comprehension of carpenters. Continuing with practical matters of construction are topics on groin arches (Plates 22–25), roofing (Plates 26, 27), and staircases and hand-railing (Plates

28–42).[4] Some of the plates in the last group were based on the methods of Joshua Coulter. Also of a technical nature are Plates 56 and 84, the former dealing with window construction and the latter with angle bars and pediment moldings. Pages 102 to 146 of the text include definitions of terms used in carpentry, masonry, plastering, and architecture in general. These glossaries were taken from Nicholson's *The New Practical Builder* (London, 1823–25).

The next major section is on "Grecian Architecture," the text of which came from *The Antiquities of Athens*, by Stuart and Revett. The illustrations (Plates 43–53), from the same source, consist of details of the Greek orders as used in the Choragic Monument of Thrasyllus (destroyed in 1827), the "Temple of Theseus" (Temple of Hephaestus), the Parthenon, the "Temple on the Ilissus" (destroyed in 1778), the Erechtheum, and the Choragic Monument of Lysicrates. Many of these plates were signed by James H. Dakin (1806–52), a draftsman and, for a short time, partner in the New York architectural firm of Ithiel Town and Alexander Jackson Davis.

Since the text and plates in the sections on building construction and Greek architectural detail are largely derivative, the real significance of *The Modern Builder's Guide* for American architectural history rests in the "original" designs by Lafever, illustrated in the plates but not described in the text. Of these, Plates 54 and 55 show elevations and plans of a "Church in the Grecian Ionic Order" and a "Gothic Church . . . very similar to the New National Scotch Church London."[5] Of interest here is the evident influence of contemporary English "Regency Period"

---

[3]For an analysis of Lafever's artistic progress, with particular emphasis on his adaptations of Greek Revival detail, see Hamlin, *Greek Revival Architecture in America*, pp. 146-47, 347-55. The Da Capo Press has republished *The Beauties of Modern Architecture* (New York, 1968) with a new introduction by Denys Peter Myers.

[4]The same subject was dealt with in Lafever's fourth publication, *The Modern Practice of Staircase and Handrail Construction* (New York, 1838), taken from Peter Nicholson's *The Builder, and Workman's New Director* (London, 1824), except for the perspective views and plans of two original Greek Revival villa designs.

[5]These designs were first published as Plates 65 and 66, with descriptions, in Lafever's *The Young Builder's General Instructor* of 1829. Plates 54, 55,

FIGURE 1.

FIRST REFORMED DUTCH CHURCH. 1834-35. Joralemon Street, near Court
Street, Brooklyn (destroyed 1886). This Ionic structure was Lafever's earliest
building of significance in the New York area. Although his builder's guide
books were extremely influential in spreading Grecian motives throughout the
country, this structure is the only known example of his own practical use of
the Greek Revival temple form. *Photograph courtesy of The New-York Historical
Society, New York City*

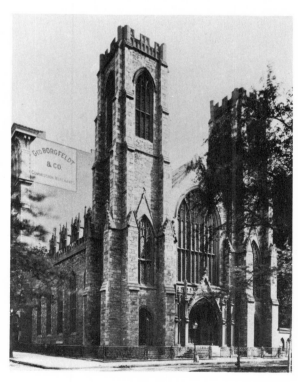

FIGURE 2.

NEW DUTCH SOUTH REFORMED CHURCH ON WASHINGTON
SQUARE. 1839-40. University Place and Washington Place,
Manhattan (destroyed 1895). Lafever's design for this first
in a series of Gothic Revival churches derives from that of
the National Scotch Church in London, which was also the
model for the "Gothic Church" project illustrated in
Plate 55 of *The Modern Builder's Guide. Photograph ca.
1890, courtesy of The New-York Historical Society, New
York City*

FIGURE 3.

FIRST UNITARIAN CHURCH. 1842-44. Pierrepont Street and
Monroe Place, Brooklyn. Dedicated as The Church of the
Saviour, this major work by Lafever was his most elegant
Gothic Revival construction. It still stands in Brooklyn
Heights, but the original Perpendicular center window seen in
this print of 1845 has since been replaced by one in the Deco-
rated style. *Photograph courtesy of the First Unitarian Church
Brooklyn*

FIGURE 4.

CHURCH OF THE HOLY TRINITY. 1844-47. Clinton and Montague Streets, Brooklyn (spire removed 1906). This magnificent Gothic Revival edifice in Brooklyn Heights, the product of Lafever's taste for rich decorative detail as well as the driving ambition of his patron, Edgar John Bartow, is seen here as illustrated by Lafever for his last book, *The Architectural Instructor* (1856).

FIGURE 5.

DESIGN FOR A MONUMENT TO GEORGE WASHINGTON IN NEW YORK CITY. 1847. With this colossal but unrealized Egyptian obelisk design for a Washington Monument, as depicted in *The Architectural Instructor*, Lafever expanded his eclectic repertoire by adding Egyptian motives to the Greek and Gothic. Typically, he shows greater concern for free invention than for archeological accuracy.

FIGURE 6.

BROOKLYN SAVINGS BANK. 1846-47. Fulton and Concord Streets, Brooklyn (destroyed 1936). Another aspect of Lafever's eclecticism is seen in his design, in *The Architectural Instructor*, for the old Brooklyn Savings Bank. Lafever personalized this example of the once fashionable Italian High Renaissance *palazzo* mode by appending some Greek Revival details.

buildings on the early development of Lafever as an architectural designer. The National Scotch Church was illustrated in the volume by James Elmes on *Metropolitan Improvements; or, London in the Nineteenth Century* (London, 1827), which Lafever could have seen in the library of his fellow-architect A. J. Davis. This Gothic Revival structure was later also the basis for Lafever's New Dutch South Reformed Church on Washington Square (1839–40). More eclectic in its borrowings was Lafever's design for the "Church in the Grecian Ionic Order," inspired in part by John Soane's Holy Trinity Church (1824–28), and by Robert Smirke's St. Mary's Church (1821–23), both in St. Marylebone, London.[6]

Further reflections of English Regency influence appear in Lafever's projects for "Country Residences." That in Plate 89 (first published as Plate 44 in *The Young Builder's General Instructor*) is very similar to the "rationalistic" design for a villa shown in Plate XXXIV of John Soane's *Sketches in Architecture* (London, 1798). Even more ambitious is the country residence depicted in Plates 72 to 79. Included are plans of the basement (72), main story (73), and second story of the center section (74), elevations of the façade (75) and side (76), and sectional views (77–79) taken at various points in the building. There are some slight discrepancies between the details of the plans and sections and the elevations. The front and rear porticoes shown in the plans of Plates 73 and 74, for example, have five columns, whereas that in the front elevation of Plate 75 is the more common tetrastyle version, with four columns in the Ionic order. In his design for the façade, Lafever again adopted one of the current English villa types in Regent's Park, London, this

time the "Grecian" villa of George Bellas Greenough (1822–24), by Decimus Burton, as illustrated in Elmes, *Metropolitan Improvements*. In both residences the Ionic center section was derived from the north porch of the Erechtheum. The Doric order was used in the distyle in-antis porches of the wings and also in the small tetrastyle porticoes at each end of the house.

The same temple-type house with wings, simpler in form, appears in the frontispiece of *The Modern Builder's Guide*. Free-standing, square, anta-type piers are used in the portico instead of the customary columns. This house type, popularized through Lafever's publications, was widespread throughout the United States. Since the elevation is signed "J. Gallier des. for Lafever," it may be that the design for this "Country Villa" was supervised by Lafever but actually created by his partner, James Gallier.[7]

Very important for an appreciation of Lafever's contribution to Greek Revival architecture in America is the group of remaining plates (57–71, 80–83, 85–88) in *The Modern Builder's Guide*. These illustrate for the most part a variety of fireplace mantels, front doors, and parlor details. All are based on Lafever's adaptations of Grecian decorative motives. (Some of the plates are signed by Dakin.) As mentioned above, the artistic quality here is far superior to that of comparable architectural forms in *The Young Builder's General Instructor* (1829), and is surpassed only by Lafever's superb Greek Revival designs in *The Beauties of Modern Architecture* (1835).[8]

---

and 89 of *The Modern Builder's Guide* did not appear in first or second editions, and are here reproduced from the third (1846) edition.

[6] The churches by Soane and Smirke were illustrated in Elmes's publication on London architecture. A detailed discussion of Lafever's Regency phase will appear in the author's forthcoming book on the architecture of Minard Lafever.

[7] An account of Lafever's partnership with James Gallier (1798-1868), from 1832 to 1834, is given in the latter's *Autobiography of James Gallier, Architect* (Paris, 1864), pp. 19-21. See also Talbot Hamlin's article on Gallier in the *Dictionary of American Biography* (New York, 1944), XXI, pp. 33-301.

[8] For extended analyses of individual plates of Lafever's "original" designs, see Denys Peter Myers, Jr., "From Carpenter to Architect: Observations on the Career of Minard Lafever" (unpublished M. A. thesis, Columbia University, 1947-48), especially pp. 19-39. See also Hamlin, *Greek Revival Architecture in America*, pp. 350-51.

In general, the drawings show Lafever's predilection for delicate and refined Ionic ornament. The repertoire of motives is illustrated in Plates 61 and 62. Tastefully applied to otherwise plain surfaces, framed with simple moldings, were rosettes (Plates 66, 80, 86, 88), anthemion bands (Plates 60, 66), consoles (Plates 57, 66, 81), anta capitals (Plates 70, 80, 87), and scrolled anthemia (Plates 69, 82). The three door designs by J. H. Dakin (Plates 63–65) have even more fanciful versions of the anthemion and acanthus scroll motive in the transoms. Variations of the Erechtheum door also appear (Plates 60, 66), as does the Ionic column (Plates 60, 80).

Lafever's contemporaries applied many of his Greek-inspired patterns to their own architectural designs. In New York, for example, the colonnaded opening between the front and back parlors in the Seabury Tredwell ("Old Merchant's") House, at 29 East Fourth Street, is similar to the sliding door arrangement shown in Plate 60 of *The Modern Builder's Guide*.[9] For the modern architect, the archeological value of these Greek Revival motives will, perhaps, be less meaningful than Lafever's sensitive and freely inventive adaptations to the domestic architecture of his day.

Lafever's popular builders' guides gave him national importance in the development of the Greek Revival movement in America. Of significance, too, was his own architectural practice, confined largely to New York, and representative of the various revival movements which flourished in the pre-Civil War period. Lafever's career exactly paralleled the English development from an early Regency phase into the Greek Revival, followed by an Early Victorian period which included Renaissance Revival efforts as well as continuous Gothic

Revival work. With Alexander Jackson Davis and Richard Upjohn, he was one of the pioneer eclectics in New York,[10] although he did not live long enough to practice in either the High Victorian Gothic or the International Second Empire modes.

Very little information about Lafever has been preserved, compared with the abundant material available for other New York architects like A. J. Davis, Upjohn, and Detlef Lienau. For his own work, a major source is Lafever's last book, *The Architectural Instructor*, published posthumously in 1856, which describes and illustrates six of his structures. Of these, the Church of the Holy Trinity and Packer Collegiate Institute, both in Brooklyn Heights, are still standing, whereas the Brooklyn Savings Bank and Munro Academy (Elbridge, New York) were destroyed in 1936 and 1929 respectively. Also included are the competition project for a Washington Monument in New York, which was finally chosen but never executed, and a design for a "Sepulchral Obelisk," which Lafever used for the grave monument of Ada Augusta Shields in Greenwood Cemetery, Brooklyn. One other project, a "Village Church," is comparable in its tower and spire to Lafever's Church of the Holy Apostles in New York.

Of Lafever's early work in the Greek Revival style, the only building known to be definitely by him was the First Reformed Dutch Church (1834–35) in Brooklyn (Figure 1). In designing its Greek Ionic temple form (octastyle amphiprostyle), he was assisted by his partner at the time, James Gallier. Clearly, Lafever's major contribution to the Greek Revival movement in America was through his builders' guides rather than his own architectural production.[11] His major significance

---

[9]This was pointed out by Hamlin, *Greek Revival Architecture in America*, p. 142, who also attributed the house to Lafever on the basis of the similarity of other details to designs in *The Young Builder's General Instructor* and *The Beauties of Modern Architecture*. The house itself was erected about 1832 by an unknown builder, but its interior was probably decorated several years later under the influence of Lafever's books.

[10]See Talbot Hamlin, "The Rise of Eclecticism in New York," *Journal of the Society of Architectural Historians*, XI (May, 1952), pp 3-8.

[11]It should be mentioned that Hamlin, in *Greek Revival Architecture in America*, p. 147, and in the *Dictionary of American Biography*, XXI, p. 480, attributed another Greek Revival building in New York to Lafever, St. James Roman Catholic Church (1835-37), in the Doric order, on James Street, near

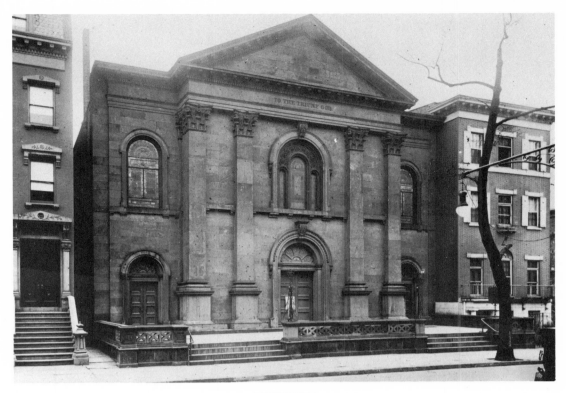

FIGURE 7.

REFORMED CHURCH ON THE HEIGHTS. 1850-51. Pierrepont Street, near Monroe Place, Brooklyn (destroyed 1936). While the domed interior of the Church on the Heights was supposedly inspired by that of the Church of the Madeleine in Paris, Lafever's design for the monumental façade was a mature interpretation of the Italian High Renaissance style, conveying some of the flavor of Palladio's Venetian churches. *Photograph courtesy of The New-York Historical Society, New York City*

FIGURE 8.

STRONG PLACE BAPTIST CHURCH. 1851-52. Strong Place and Degraw Street, Brooklyn. The exterior of Lafever's last Gothic church was his closest approximation to the spirit of English parish churches of the Decorated period, particularly in such features as lancet and quatrefoil openings, picturesque irregularity in plan and elevation, and an impressive corner tower planned originally with a tall spire. *Photograph courtesy of The Long Island Historical Society*

FIGURE 9.

PACKER COLLEGIATE INSTITUTE. 1854-56. Joralemon Street, between Court and Clinton Streets, Brooklyn. In the last year of his life Lafever was commissioned to design a school for girls, seen in this illustration from *The Architectural Instructor* as a Tudor Gothic composition in which Lafever again adapted a traditional style to modern use.

FIGURE 10.

DESIGN FOR AN ITALIAN VILLA. In *The Architectural Instructor* Lafever presented not only several of his executed public buildings but also many designs for cottages, villas, and mansions in the Italian (as in this sumptuous example), Tuscan, Gothic, Grecian, and Roman styles.

as an architect was in a series of Gothic Revival churches, the first of which was the New Dutch South Reformed Church on Washington Square (1839–40), New York (Figure 2).[12] As noted above, the design of this church, and the project for a church in Plate 55 of *The Modern Builder's Guide*, were based on the National Scotch Church in London.

Lafever's churches of the early forties contributed to the mature phase of the Gothic Revival in New York. They did not, however, share in the "ecclesiological" fervor or emphasis on archeological correctness of his contemporaries Richard Upjohn and James Renwick. Characteristic of the warm personal flavor and florid richness of his mature Gothic Revival style is Lafever's most impressive work, the Church of the Holy Trinity (1844–47), in Brooklyn Heights (Figure 4). Before this, however, he had designed three other churches in the Gothic mode, the First Baptist Church (1841–42), at Broome and Elizabeth Streets, New York, the sensitively conceived Church of the Saviour (1842–44; Figure 3) still standing in Brooklyn Heights but now known as the First Unitarian Church, and the Pierrepont Street Baptist Church (1843–44), which, before its destruction in 1877, was only one block away from the Church of the Saviour.

With other architects of the day, Lafever, in addition to the Greek and Gothic Revival styles, also practiced the various eclectic

modes which fostered "The Battle of the Styles" in New York. In the Egyptian manner were his designs, mentioned above, for a Washington Monument (1847) in New York (Figure 5), and the Shields Monument (1845) in Brooklyn. Both were in the form of obelisks. If the Whalers' Presbyterian Church (1843–44) at Sag Harbor, Long Island, is by Lafever, as is generally believed, it would add to his works in the Egyptian mode.[13] Variations of Italian Renaissance eclecticism appeared in Lafever's Church of the Holy Apostles (1846–48), still standing at Ninth Avenue and 28th Street, in New York,[14] and in the old Brooklyn Savings Bank (1846–47; Figure 6). The former was partially in the Tuscan Doric manner of the fifteenth century, and the latter in a reduced version of the High Renaissance "palazzo style." Possibly Renaissance in its original conception was Lafever's design, about 1847, for a stone archway and terrace, at the foot of Montague Street, in Brooklyn Heights, described by Hamlin as "a monument of true Greek simplicity."

In the late forties, Lafever returned to the Gothic style for the Church of the Neighbor (1848–50), which was at the corner of Monroe Place and Clark Street, in Brooklyn Heights, before it was demolished in 1964. Also Gothic was the First Presbyterian Church (1848–50) in Syracuse, New York. In the same city, Lafever continued the "Italian Style," however, for the First Baptist Church (1848–50) and the First Dutch Reformed Church (1849–50). For the Reformed Church on the Heights (1850–51), in Brooklyn (Figure 7), Lafever attempted a sixteenth-century Italian style in the manner of Palladio. His last contributions to the Gothic Revival were the Strong

Chatham Square. Although others have accepted the attribution, it is based only on stylistic evidence, since there is no documentary material available. Near by, at Oliver and Henry Streets, the Mariners' (Baptist) Temple (1844-45), an Ionic, and like St. James, distyle in-antis church, has often been incorrectly attributed to Lafever. The Mariners' Temple is illustrated in Ada Louise Huxtable, *Classic New York* (New York, 1964), p. 81, and St. James in Alan Burnham, *New York Landmarks* (Middletown,Conn.,1963),p.93,and Huxtable,p.76.

[12]Lafever is erroneously categorized as having been primarily a Greek revivalist who also worked in the Gothic idiom by James Early, *Romanticism and American Architecture* (New York, 1965), p. 40. Like Upjohn, Lafever gave up the Grecian mode by the end of the 1830's.

[13]See the illustration in Samuel M. Green, *American Art* (New York, 1966), p. 226, showing the steeple before its destruction in 1938.

[14]The Church of the Holy Apostles was the model for several churches outside New York City. By Lafever himself were the Reformed Protestant Dutch Church (1851-52) in Kingston, New York, and the Pearl Street Congregational Church (1851-52) in Hartford, Connecticut. Holy Apostles is illustrated in Burnham, p. 111.

Place Baptist Church (1851–52; Figure 8), Lafever's "particular delight," and Packer Collegiate Institute (1854–56; Figure 9), still serving its original purpose, both in Brooklyn. Similar to Packer in its Tudor Gothic detail, but more "provincial" in its simplicity, was his design for Munro Academy (1854), in Elbridge, New York.

A number of houses in the northeastern section of the United States have been attributed to Lafever, but these, as so many others throughout the country, were probably only influenced by the "temple-type" house patterns and the decorative detail shown in his several builders' guide books. The Seabury Tredwell ("Old Merchant's") House (1831–32) in New York has already been discussed.[15] Most often mentioned, too, are the Campbell-Whittlesey House (1835–37), Rochester; the Robert Bartow House (1838?), Pelham Bay Park, New York; the Richard Alsop House (1838–39), Middletown, Connecticut; and the Benjamin Huntting House (1845–46), Sag Harbor, Long Island. Some of these houses have also been attributed to other architects, but no documentary proof has yet been found to support definite authorship for any of these structures.

Unlike many of his colleagues, Lafever seems to have been entirely self-taught as an architect, although he was a well-trained carpenter and an experienced builder. Born August 10, 1798, near Morristown, New Jersey, Lafever at the age of nine moved with his parents to the Finger Lakes region of western New York State. In the following years, he assimilated the Late Colonial Georgian and Early Republican architectural traditions which prevailed in that area. After a brief stay in Newark, New Jersey, Lafever moved to New York about 1827 or 1828, where he took part in the great building boom of the late twenties and early thirties, and rapidly made the transition from carpenter to archi-

tect. Lafever's new status was confirmed in 1829 by his publication of *The Young Builder's General Instructor* and by his participation in the competition for the Albany City Hall. (His plans for this structure were not adopted.) His constant striving for self-improvement led him also to attempt what he felt were necessary changes in current building practice, particularly in domestic architecture.

Scattered references to his personality and professional career indicate that Lafever was an ambitious and strong-willed man, firm in his demands upon himself and others. This attitude is well expressed in the Preface to *The Modern Builder's Guide*. His construction techniques were conservative, as was his conscientiousness in superintending the erection of his buildings. Traditional materials, brick, stone, and wood, were used in all of his works, but Lafever's particular favorite was plaster. This material enabled him to adequately express his decorative exuberance, especially in the rich detailing of Gothic interiors. Lafever's "stylistic development" was largely a series of eclectic changes from one revival style to the next, as they were successively favored by current usage. In all of these, however, he did not mechanically "copy" traditional models, but rather grasped their basic characteristics and applied them to his own designs in a number of imaginative variations.

While not as well known today as his peers, Richard Upjohn and James Renwick, Lafever's professional reputation must have at least equalled theirs in his own lifetime. He was selected for a variety of commissions in and out of New York City, and he participated in several important competitions of the day. His works were described and often praised in contemporary newspapers and journals. An early member of the American Institution of Architects, Lafever undoubtedly would have been invited to join the American In-

---

[15]An interior view is illustrated in Burnham, p. 85. For the exterior, see Huxtable, p. 97. The house, threatened with destruction, has been designated a New York City Landmark by the Landmarks Preservation Commission. The few remaining buildings definitely known to be by Lafever should be similarly preserved.

stitute of Architects had he not died in 1854, three years before its founding. Of all Lafever's professional activities, probably most significant for the historical development of American architecture were his influential

November, 1968
New York City

builders' guides. Of considerable importance among these was *The Modern Builder's Guide*, here republished for the first time in over a century.

JACOB LANDY

THE
MODERN
BUILDER'S
GUIDE

PREFACE.

SEVERAL years have elapsed since I offered to the public a compilation entitled, "The Builder's General Instructer." Those who are aware how flattering a reception and how ready a sale that work met with, will be somewhat surprised perhaps to learn, that, instead of issuing a second edition of it, I have, at a considerable pecuniary sacrifice, entirely withdrawn the work from print. The truth is, though others seemed perfectly satisfied with the book, I myself was not. Subsequent investigation, and increased experience as an architect, enabled me to discover many defects and inaccuracies, which had at first escaped my notice; and though I might have issued a corrected edition, yet, as I had much additional matter that I wished to present, and as this new matter, together with the numerous alterations to be made in the old, would have materially changed the character and well nigh destroyed the identity of the original, I, on the whole, preferred to suppress that work, and prepare a substitute. That substitute, compiled with the utmost care, and at a great expense of time, labour, and money, I herewith present to the public.

From the tenor of some of the above remarks respecting my former work, it may perhaps be inferred, that I deem the present one faultless, and capable of safely bidding defiance to criticism. Such is not the fact. Faultlessness is scarcely to be looked for in any human production; and if it were, I should not presume to claim it as an attribute to the "MODERN BUILDER'S GUIDE." It is hoped, however, that no material error or glaring defect will be found in this work, and that excellences will be discovered, great and numerous enough to more than balance its imperfections.

Though there is considerable original matter in the following pages, and though a large portion of that which is not new, as to substance, is entirely so, as it regards manner and language, yet, taken as a whole, it claims to be no more than a compilation. Before concluding, therefore, it will be proper to specify the authors whom I have either consulted or made extracts from, as well as the other sources of aid that I have enjoyed, in compiling this book.

From the works of the justly celebrated Mr. Nicholson of London, I have derived a greater amount of aid than from any other source. His "Carpenter's New Guide," and his "New Practical Builder," (especially the latter,) are works which need no eulogium of mine; nor need I apologize for having, to an extent somewhat large, availed myself of his labours, to enhance the value of this compilation. On the following subjects, namely, Geometry as connected with practical Carpentry, Veneering, Arches and Groins, Niches, Coverings of polygonal and hemispherical roofs, Pendentives, Domes, Circular Sashes, and Hand-railing, I have freely consulted the "Carpenter's New Guide," and in many instances taken it as a model; while, on several topics connected with Joinery, Masonry, and Plastering, I have made copious extracts from the "New Practical Builder."—The Glossary of Technical Terms is from the same work.

The only other *authors* to whom I owe acknowledgments, are Messrs. Stuart and Revett, of London; from whose highly valuable and popular work entitled, " The Antiquities of Athens," I have borowed the article relating to the ancient Orders of Architecture.

To Mr. Joshua Coulter, an eminently skilful and experienced stair-builder residing in Philadelphia, I am indebted for several valuable suggestions and improvements in the department of Hand-railing. These have, in their appropriate place, been severally pointed out, and duly accredited. I have also consulted several able and experienced architects in this vicinity; especially Mr. J. C. Brady (now deceased) and Mr. Martin E. Thompson, of this city. The plan of this work was some time since submitted to the inspection of these two gentlemen, and they were pleased to say, that it met with their entire and cordial approbation.

The publication of this work has, of necessity, been delayed much beyond the period originally announced; but this delay is the less to be regretted, inasmuch as it has been the means of considerably enhancing the value of the work.

In the preparation of it, I have all the while acted under a strong conviction, that something of the kind was imperiously demanded by the wants of carpenters and builders in general, but especially by the wants of such as are commencing the study and practice of the building art. For these tyros in the art, rather than for the experienced architect, this work is chiefly designed; and, in preparing it, I have made the benefit of these my principal aim. At the same time, it is believed that the work will prove a valuable auxiliary to those builders, who, though well versed perhaps in the practical part of their profession, have little or no acquaintance with its theory, or with the scientific principles which lie at its foundation. In submitting the result of my labours to these two classes, and to the public at large, I indulge the hope, that, so far as those labours are calculated to subserve the purpose for which they were bestowed, they may be appreciated and rewarded; and that if, in the following pages, any thing of an opposite tendency shall be discovered, it will be generously overlooked, or at least regarded with an indulgent eye.

MINARD LAFEVER.

New York, Sept. 1833.

GEOMETRY

ADAPTED TO

PRACTICAL CARPENTRY.

As Geometry is the foundation on which practical Carpentry is based, it is considered important, in compiling this work, to introduce such geometrical problems as will be most useful to operators. The problems will be accompanied by diagrams, or figures, such as are common in Carpentry, and will be explained in such a manner that a workman, even if not thoroughly acquainted with Geometry as a science, will be able to understand them, and when necessary, make a practical application of them.

The problems introduced in this work, are much the same as in Mr. Nicholson's new " Carpenter's Guide." The most of these are correct, and well adapted to the purposes for which they were introduced. The explanations, however, are not, as it seems to me, sufficiently clear, or suited to the comprehension of carpenters of limited scientific attainments. To such, the explanations contained in this work, will, it is believed, prove exceedingly useful.

DEFINITIONS.

I.
A point has position, but not magnitude. (Plate I. Fig. 1.)

II.
A line is length, without breadth or thickness. (Fig. 2.)

Note.—Lines and points are constantly made use of in Carpentry, and without them, no figure can be described.

IV.
A superficies has length and breadth only. See *a b c d*, (Fig. 4.) Thus, the face of a board is a superficies.

V.
A solid has three dimensions—length, breadth, and thickness.

A solid may be formed in the following manner. Let *a b c d*, (Fig. 4.) be the under side; *e f g h*, one of the vertical sides; *i j k l*, the other vertical side; and *m*, the upper side, or surface. Now suppose *i l* moved to *b c*, and *e h* to *a d*; then raise *j k* perpendicular to *b c*, and *f g* perpendicular to *a d*, and turn *m* directly over *a b c d* : a solid will be formed.

VI.

A curve line is continually changing its direction.   (Fig. 5.)

A curve is produced in various ways ; as with a compass, trammel, intersecting lines, &c. ; and, except when made by means of a trammel, will be a true curve.

VII.

Parallel lines, whether straight or curved, are always equally distant from each other.   (Fig. 6.)

NOTE.—Two elliptical lines cannot be drawn parallel to each other, by means of a trammel, or intersecting lines.

VIII.

Oblique lines change their distance, so as on one end to approach, and on the other to recede from each other.   On the side where they approach they would meet, if continued.   (Fig. 7.)

IX.

A tangent is a straight line, touching a curve, without cutting it when produced. (Fig. 9.)

X.

An angle is the inclination towards one another of two straight lines, having different directions, but meeting in a point, and being in the same plane. (Fig. 10.)

XI.

A right angle is that, which is made by a straight line perpendicular to another straight line   (Fig. 8.)

XII.

An oblique angle is one, that is either greater or less than a right angle. If greater, it is an obtuse angle. (Fig. 12.)   If less, it is an acute angle. (Fig. 11.)

XIII.

Rectilineal figures are those, which are contained by straight lines.

XIV.

Trilateral figures, or triangles, are bounded by three straight lines.   (Fig's. 13, 14, &c.)

XV.

Quadrilateral figures are bounded by four straight lines.   (Fig's. 17, 18, &c.)

XVI.

Multilateral figures, or polygons, are bounded by more than four straight lines.

XVII.

Of three sided figures, an equilateral triangle is that which has three equal sides (Fig. 13.)

XVIII.

An isosceles triangle has only two sides equal.   (Fig. 14.)

XIX.

A scalene triangle has all its sides unequal. (Fig. 15.)

XX.

A right-angled triangle has one of its angles a right angle. (Fig. 16.)

XXI.

An obtuse-angled triangle has one of its angles an obtuse angle. (Fig. 15.)

XXII.

An acute-angled triangle has all its angles acute angles. (Fig. 13.)

XXIII.

A rectangle is a four sided figure, having all its angles right angles. (Fig's. 17 and 18.)

XXIV.

An equilateral rectangle is one that has all its sides equal. (Fig. 17.)

XXV.

An oblong rectangle, or an oblong, has all its angles right angles, but has not all its sides equal. (Fig. 18.)

NOTE.—An oblong has its opposite sides equal.

XXVI.

A rhombus has its four sides equal, but its angles are not right angles. (Fig. 21.)

XXVII.

A rhomboid has four sides, of which the opposite ones are equal to each other, but its angles are not right angles. (Fig. 22.)

XXVIII.

A trapezium is a quadrilateral figure, having none of its sides parallel. (Fig. 20.)

XXIX.

A trapezoid is a quadrilateral figure, having only two of its sides parallel. (Fig. 19.)

NOTE.—Figures having three angles, as triangles, are called trigons ; four, tetragons ; five, pentagons ; six, hexagons ; seven, heptagons ; eight, octagons ; nine, nonagons ; ten, decagons ; eleven, undecagons ; twelve, duodecagons ; and so on.

XXX.

A circle is a figure bounded by a curve line, called the circumference, which is every where equi-distant from a certain point within the circle, called the centre. (Fig. 23.)

XXXI.

A diameter of a circle is a straight line drawn through the centre, and terminated both ways by the circumference. (Fig. 23.)

XXXII.

A radius of a circle is half of a diameter, or a straight line drawn from the centre to the circumference. Thus, from 1 to 4, (Fig. 23.) 1 to 2, or 1 to 3, is a radius.

XXXIII.

An arch of a circle is any portion of the circumference ; as at 1, 3, 2, (Fig. 24.)

XXXIV.

The chord of an arch is a straight line joining the extremities of the arch ; as 1, 2 (Fig. 24.)

XXXV.

A segment of a circle is any portion of the circle, bounded by an arch and its chord. (Fig. 24.)

XXXVI.

A semicircle is half a circle, or the segment cut off by a diameter. (Fig. 25.)

XXXVII.

A sector of a circle is any part of the circle, bounded by an arch and two radii drawn to the extremities of that arch.   Thus, 1, 2, 3, (Fig. 26.) is a sector.

XXXVIII.

A quadrant is a quarter of a circle.   Thus, 1, 2, 3, (Fig. 27.) is a quadrant.

XXXIX.

The altitude of any figure is a perpendicular, let fall from its vertex upon the opposite side, or base.   Thus, *a b*, (Fig. 28.) is the altitude of the triangle.

NOTE.—When several angles are at one point, as at 1, (Fig. 29.) any one of them is expressed by three letters ; of which, the letter that is at the angular point, is put between the other two letters, and one of these two is placed somewhere upon one of the straight lines that contain the angle, and the other upon the other line. Thus, the angle which is contained by the straight lines 3, 1, and 4, 1, (Fig. 29.) is named the angle 3, 1, 4, or 4, 1, 3.   But if there be only one angle at a point, it may be expressed by a single letter placed at that point ; as the angle at A, (Fig. 30.)

N. B. To measure an angle, a circle is so described that its centre shall be the angular point, and its circumference shall cut the two lines which contain the angle. The arch between these two lines is called a *measure* of the angle.   Thus, the arch *b c*, (Fig. 30.) is a measure of the angle.

PROBLEMS—PL. 2.

TO ERECT A PERPENDICULAR TO A GIVEN LINE 1 3 2, (PLATE II. FIG. 1.) FROM A GIVEN POINT 3, IN THE SAME.

On each side of the point 3, take any two equal distances, as 3 1, 3 2 ; from the points 1 2 as centres, with the distance 1 2 as radius, and on the same side of the given line, describe two arcs of circles intersecting each other at 4 ; join 3 4 : the line 4 3 will be the perpendicular required.

UPON A BASE SIX FEET IN LENGTH, TO ERECT A PERPENDICULAR THAT SHALL BE EIGHT FEET LONG.

Let the line 12 (Fig. 2.) be the given base; from one end, as 1, of this line, with the distance ten feet for radius, describe an arc of a circle ; from the other end 2, of the base, draw a perpendicular 2 3, (see preceding problem,) so as to cut the arc : the perpendicular 2 3 will be eight feet long.

FROM A GIVEN POINT, TO LET FALL A PERPENDICULAR UPON A GIVEN STRAIGHT LINE.

Let 1, (Fig. 3.) be the given point, and 2, 3, the given straight line; from 1 as a centre, describe an arc so as to cut the given line in two points, as 2, 3 ; from the points 2, 3, as centres, with the distance 2, 6, or 3, 5, for radius, describe two arcs cutting each other at 4 ; join 1, 4 ; 1, 4 will be the perpendicular required.

FROM ONE EXTREMITY OF A GIVEN STRAIGHT LINE, TO ERECT A PERPENDICULAR TO THAT LINE.

Let 3, 1, (Fig. 4.) be the given straight line, and 1 that extremity from which it is required to erect a perpendicular ; take any distance, as 1, 4, and from 4 as a centre, with 4, 1 for radius, describe an arc 3, 1, 2, meeting the given straight line at 1 and 3 ; join 3, 4 and produce the line 3, 4 to 2 ; join 1, 2, and 1, 2 will be the required perpendicular.

TO BISECT, OR DIVIDE A GIVEN LINE INTO TWO EQUAL PARTS.

Let 1, 2, (Fig. 5.) be the given line ; from the points 1, 2, as centres, with any distance greater than half 1, 2 for radius, as 1, 4 and 2, 3, describe arcs of circles cutting each other at 5 and 6 ; join 5, 6 : the line 1, 2 is bisected at 9.

TO BISECT AN ANGLE.

Let 3, 1, 2, (Fig. 6.) be the given angle : it is required to bisect it. From the point 1 as centre, with any distance, as 1, 2, for radius, describe an arc so as to cut the sides containing the angle ; from the points of intersection, 3, 2, with any radius, describe arcs cutting each other, as at 4 ; join 4, 1 : the angle 3, 1, 2, is bisected by the line 1, 4.

AT A GIVEN POINT IN A GIVEN STRAIGHT LINE, TO MAKE AN ANGLE EQUAL TO A GIVEN ANGLE.

Let 4 6, (Fig. 8.) be the given straight line, and 4 the given point, and 2 1 3, (Fig. 7.) the given angle ; from the point 1, as a centre, with any distance, as 1 3, for radius, describe an arc 3 2, meeting the lines 1 3, 1 2, at 3, 2 ; on the given straight line 4 6, take the same distance, and from 4 as centre, describe an arc 6 5, equal to the arc 3 2 ; join 5 4 : the angle 5 4 6 is equal to the angle 2 1 3.

PL. 3.

UPON A GIVEN STRAIGHT LINE, TO DESCRIBE AN EQUILATERAL TRIANGLE.

Let 1 2, (Plate III. Fig. 1.) be the given straight line ; from the points 1, 2, as centres, with the distance 1 2 for radius, describe arcs of circles cutting each other at 3 ; join 3 1, and 3 2 ; the triangle 1 3 2 is equilateral.

TO DESCRIBE A SQUARE UPON A GIVEN STRAIGHT LINE.

Let 1 2, (Fig. 2.) be the given straight line ; from the points 1, 2, as centres, with the distance 1 2 as radius, describe arcs of circles, 1 3 and 2 4 ; from the point 5 where they intersect, with half the distance 5 2, that is, with 5 6 for radius, describe the arcs 6 3, 7 4 ; through the points 3, 4, draw the straight lines 3 2, 3 4, 4 1 : the quadrilateral figure, described upon the straight line 1 2, is a square.

A SIDE OF A POLYGON OF ANY NUMBER OF SIDES WHATEVER BEING GIVEN, TO DESCRIBE THE POLYGON OF WHICH IT IS A SIDE.

Let 1 6, (Fig. 5.) be a side of a polygon of six equal sides; from 6, as centre, with the given side for radius, describe a semicircle; divide the semicircle into as many equal parts as the polygon is to have sides, viz. in this case, six, and through the points of division 2, 3, 4, draw the straight lines 6 9, 6 8, 6 7; draw also the radius 6 5; from the point 1, with the side 1 6 for radius, describe an arc, and from the point 9, in which it cuts the line 6 9, with the same radius, describe an arc cutting 6 8 in 8; do the same from the points 8 and 7; join 1 9, 9 8, 8 7 and 7 5 : 1 9 8 7 5 6 is the polygon required.

THROUGH A GIVEN POINT IN THE CIRCUMFERENCE OF A CIRCLE, TO DRAW A TANGENT TO THAT CIRCLE.

Let 2 (Fig. 7.) be the given point in the circumference; draw the radius 1 2, and through 2, draw 3 4 at right-angles to 1 2 : 3 4 is the tangent required.

A TANGENT TO A CIRCLE BEING GIVEN, TO FIND THE POINT WHERE IT TOUCHES THE CIRCLE.

Let 1 2 (Fig. 8.) be the given tangent; take any point, as 2, in 1 2, and from 2 draw a straight line 2 3 to the centre of the circle; bisect 2 3 in 4, and from 4, with 4 3 or 4 2 for radius, describe an arch cutting 1 2 in 5 : 5 is the touching point required.

TO FIND A MEAN PROPORTIONAL BETWEEN TWO GIVEN STRAIGHT LINES.

Let 1, 2, (Fig. 9.) be the two given straight lines; place 1, 2 in one straight line 3 4 5, 3 4 being equal to 1, and 4 5 to 2; bisect 3 5 in 6, and describe the semicircle 3 7 5; from the point 4 draw 4 7 at right angles to 3 5 : then 3 4 is to 4 7 as 4 7 is to 4 5; that is, 4 7 is the mean proportional required.

THROUGH ANY THREE POINTS TO DESCRIBE THE CIRCUMFERENCE OF A CIRCLE.

Let 2, 3, 4 (Fig. 10.) be the three given points; join 2 3 and 3 4, and from 3, with any radius, as 3 7, describe an arc 7 6 5 8; from the points 2 and 4, as centres, with the same radius, describe arcs, cutting the first-described arc in the points 6, 7, and 5, 8; through the points of intersection draw the straight lines 8 5, 7 6, and produce them till they meet : a circle described from the point 1, in which they meet, will have the points 2 3 and 4 in its circumference.

TO FIND THE LENGTH OF ANY GIVEN ARC.

Let 1 2 3 (Fig. 11.) be a given arc; draw the chord 1 3; bisect the given arc in 2, and from 1, as a centre, with the distance 1 2 as radius, describe the arc 2 6; produce the chord 1 3 so that 6 4 shall be equal to 1 6; divide 3 4 into three equal parts, and produce the straight line 1 4 so that 4 5 shall be equal to one-third of 3 4 : the straight line 1 5 is the length of the arc 1 2 3.

PL. 4.

TO CONSTRUCT A TRIANGLE OF WHICH THE SIDES SHALL BE EQUAL TO THREE GIVEN STRAIGHT LINES.

Let 12, 34, 56, (Plate IV. Fig. 1.) be the three given straight lines; from one extremity, as 2, of the line 1 2 for a centre, with the distance 3 4 for radius, describe an arc, and from the other end 1 of the same line, with 5 6 for radius, describe another arc so as to cut the first-described one; from the point of intersection 7, draw the straight lines 7 1, 7 2: 1 2 7 is the triangle required.

NOTE.—Of the three given straight lines, the length of any two taken together must be greater than that of the remaining one.

TO MAKE A TRAPEZIUM EQUAL TO A GIVEN TRAPEZIUM.

Let 1 2 3 4 (Fig. 2.) be the given trapezium; divide it into two triangles by joining two opposite angles, as 2, 4; draw a straight line 5 6 (Fig. 3.) equal to 2 3 in Fig. 2., and at the points 5, 6, in the straight line 5 6, make (See Prob. VII.) the angle 6 5 7 equal to the angle 3 2 4, and the angle 5 6 7 equal to the angle 2 3 4; at the points 5, 7, in the straight line 5 7, make the angle 7 5 8 equal to 4 2 1, and the angle 5 7 8 equal to 2 4 1: the trapezium 8 5 6 7 is equal to the trapezium 1 2 3 4.

ANY IRREGULAR POLYGON BEING GIVEN, TO MAKE A POLYGON EQUAL AND SIMILAR TO THE ONE GIVEN.

Let 1 2 3 4 5 (Fig. 4.) be the given irregular polygon; divide it into three triangles by the straight lines 1 3, 1 4; draw a straight line 1 2 (Fig. 5.) equal to 1 2 in Fig. 4. and as in the preceding problem, upon 1 2 (Fig. 5.) make the triangle 1 2 3 equal to the triangle 1 2 3 in Fig. 4; upon 1 3, the triangle 1 3 4 equal to 1 3 4; and upon 1 4, the triangle 1 4 5 equal to the triangle 1 4 5 in Fig. 4: then will the two polygons be equal and similar.

A TRIANGLE BEING GIVEN, TO MAKE A RECTANGLE EQUAL TO THE TRIANGLE.

Let 1 2 3 (Fig. 6.) be the given triangle, and from the angle at 1, let fall the perpendicular 1 4 upon the opposite side; bisect 1 4 in 5, and through 5 draw the straight line 6 7 parallel to 2 3; draw 3 7 and 2 6 at right angles to 2 3: the rectangle 2 3 7 6 is equal to the triangle 1 2 3.

TO MAKE A SQUARE EQUAL TO A GIVEN RECTANGLE.

Let 1 2 3 4 (Fig. 7.) be the given rectangle; produce one of its sides, as 1 4, so that the part produced 4 8 shall be equal to the side 4 3 of the rectangle; bisect 1 8 in 9, and from 9, with 9 8 or 9 1 for radius, describe the semicircle 1 7 8; produce the side 4 3 till it meets the semicircle at 7, and upon the straight line 4 7 describe the square (See Prob. IX.) 7 6 5 4: the square 7 6 5 4, is equal to the rectangle 1 2 3 4.

TO MAKE A SQUARE EQUAL TO TWO GIVEN SQUARES.

Let 1, 2 (Fig. 8.) be the two given squares; place them so as to touch, and so that one side of one square shall be at right angles to one side of the other, as 3 5, 5 4 in the Figure; join 3 4, and upon the hypothenuse 3 4 of the right-angled triangle 3 5 4 describe the square 3 6 7 4: the square 3 6 7 4 is equal to the two squares 1, 2

PL. 5.

TO MAKE AN ELLIPSIS WITH A THREAD OR STRING.

Let 1 2 (Plate V. Fig. 1.) be the longest diameter of the required ellipsis, and let 4 3, at right angles to 1 2, be half of the shortest diameter; from the point 3, as centre, with half 1 2 for radius, describe arcs cutting 1 2 at the points 5 and 6; at these two points place pins, and, holding a pencil at the point 3, put a thread or cord round the two pins and the pencil, so that, when round them, it shall be stretched or *taut;* move the pencil round, keeping the string stretched, and an ellipsis will be described.

TO MAKE AN ELLIPSIS BY A TRAMMEL.

Let 1 3, 2 4 (Fig. 2.) be the axes or diameters of the required ellipsis; let 6 7 8 be a trammel, 6 being the place for a pencil, and 7, 8 places for pins to move in grooves; make 6 7 equal to half the shortest diameter, that is, to 4 5, and 6 8 equal to half the longest, that is, to 1 5; move the pencil round, and an ellipsis will be described.

AN ELLIPSIS BEING GIVEN, TO FIND ITS CENTRE AND ITS TWO AXES.

Let 1 4 7 2 5 8 (Fig. 3.) be the given ellipsis; draw any two parallel lines, as 1 2, 1 2; bisect those lines in 3, 3, and through 3, 3, draw the straight line 4 5; bisect 4 5 in 6, and from 6, as centre, with any radius, describe an arc so as to cut the circumference of the ellipsis, as 7 8; join 7, 8, and through 6 draw 9 10 parallel to 7 8, and through the same point draw 11 12 at right angles to 9 10: 6 is the centre, 9 10 the conjugate axis, and 11 12 the transverse axis, of the given ellipsis.

ONE DIAMETER OF AN ELLIPSIS BEING GIVEN TO DESCRIBE AN ELLIPSIS, SUCH THAT ITS TWO DIAMETERS SHALL BE PROPORTIONAL TO THE DIAMETERS OF ANY GIVEN ELLIPSIS.

Let 8 6 (Fig. 4.) be one diameter, as for instance the conjugate of the required ellipsis, and let 1 2 3 4 be a given ellipsis, 1 3 being its conjugate and 2 4 its transverse diameter; about the ellipsis 1 2 3 4 describe the rectangle 9 10 11 12 by drawing straight lines through the points 1, 3, parallel to 2 4, and through the points 2, 4, parallel to 1 3; draw the diagonals 12 10, 11 9; through the point 8 or 6, and parallel to the transverse axis 2 4, draw the straight line 13 16 or 14 15 so as to meet the diagonals; through the points in which they meet the diagonals, and parallel to the conjugate axis 1 3, draw the straight lines 16 15, 13 14; the part 7 5 of the straight line 2 4, cut off by the lines 16 15, 13 14, is the transverse axis of the required ellipsis; describe

(See Prob's. XXII. and XXIII.) the ellipsis 5 8 7 6 : the diameters of this ellipsis are proportional to those of the ellipsis 1 2 3 4 ; that is, 8 6 is to 7 5 as 1 3 is to 2 4.

TO DESCRIBE AN ELLIPSIS ABOUT A GIVEN PARALLELOGRAM, SO THAT ITS LENGTH SHALL HAVE THE SAME RATIO TO ITS WIDTH, THAT THE LENGTH OF THE PARALLELOGRAM HAS TO ITS WIDTH.

Let 1 2 3 4 (Fig. 5.) be the given parallelogram ; draw the diagonals 1 3, 2 4, and through the point 1 7 in which they intersect, draw 1 5 1 4 parallel to 1 2 or 4 3, and also 6 1 6 parallel to 1 4 or 2 3 ; from the point 1 7 where the diagonals intersect, with half the width of the parallelogram for radius, describe the quadrant 6 7 ; bisect the arc 6 7 in 5, and through 5, draw the straight line 8 9 parallel to the line 1 5 1 4 ; draw the lines 6 9, 9 1 4, and through the point 2 draw 2 1 2 parallel to 9 6, and 2 1 1 parallel to 9 1 4 ; produce the line 1 5 1 4 till it meets 2 1 1 in 1 1, and produce the line 1 6 6 till it meets 2 1 2 in 1 2 ; 1 7 1 2 will be half the width, and 1 7 1 1 half the the length of the required ellipsis ; make 1 7 1 0 equal to 1 7 1 1, and 1 7 1 3 equal to 1 7 1 2, and describe the ellipsis 1 0 1 2 1 1 1 3 : its length is to its width as the length of the parallelogram 1 2 3 4 is to its width.

TO DIVIDE A GIVEN STRAIGHT LINE INTO PARTS THAT SHALL BE PROPORTIONAL TO THE PARTS OF A GIVEN DIVIDED STRAIGHT LINE.

Let 1 4 (Fig. 6.) be a straight line divided in the points 2, 3, and let 1 5 be the line given to be divided ; place the lines 1 4, 1 5 so as to make any angle whatever, as 4 1 5 ; join the other extremities by the line 4 5, and through the points 3, 2, draw 3 6, 2 7 parallel to 4 5 ; the straight line 1 5 is divided in the points 6, 7, so that 5 6 is to 6 7 as 4 3 is to 3 2 and 6 7 is to 7 1 as 3 2 is to 2 1.

ANOTHER METHOD OF DOING THE SAME THING.

Let 1 4 (Fig. 7.) be a straight line divided in the points 2, 3 ; upon 1 4 describe the equilateral triangle 1 6 4, and if, as in this case, the line to be divided be shorter than the divided line, place it within the triangle and parallel to the divided line, as 7 5 ; join 6 2, 6 3 : the line 7 5 is divided by the lines 6 2, 6 3, so that its parts are proportional to the parts of the given divided line 1 4.

NOTE.—If the line to be divided be longer than the divided one, produce two sides of the equilateral triangle beyond the base and until the said line can be placed between them parallel to the base. In both cases, the length of the line to be divided, measured from the vertex on the two sides, will give the points in which the said line will cut those sides.

TO INSCRIBE AN EQUILATERAL AND EQUIANGULAR OCTAGON IN A GIVEN SQUARE.

Let 1 2 3 4 (Fig. 8.) be the given square ; draw the diagonals 1 3, 2 4, and from the points 1, 2, 3, 4 as centres, with half of either diagonal for radius, describe arcs of circles meeting the sides of the square in the points 5, 8, 7, 10, 9, 12, 11, 6 ; join 12 5,

6 7, 8 9, 10 11 : an equilateral and equiangular octagon 12 5 6 7 8 9 10 11 has been inscribed in the given square 1 2 3 4.

PL. 6.

THE LENGTH AND HEIGHT OF A SEGMENT OF A CIRCLE BEING GIVEN TO DESCRIBE THE SEGMENT.

Let 1 2 (Plate VI. Fig. 1.) be the length, and 5 1 3 the height of the segment to be described ; bisect the line 1 2 in 1 3, and from the point of bisection draw the straight line 1 3 8 at right angles to the line 1 2 ; draw the chord 1 5 ; bisect that chord, and through the bisecting point draw the straight line 1 0 8 perpendicular to 1 5 ; the point 8 where the two perpendiculars meet is the centre of the circle of which the required segment is a part ; from 8, with 8 5 as radius, describe the arc 1 5 2, and you have the segment required.

THE LENGTH AND HEIGHT OF A SEGMENT OF A CIRCLE BEING GIVEN, TO DESCRIBE THE SEGMENT BY MEANS OF RODS.

Let the line 1 2 (Fig. 2.) be the length, and 3 4 the height, of the required segment ; take two rods 5 3, 6 3, each equal in length to the line 1 2, and make such an angle with them that when the angular point is at 3, the rods will meet the extremities of the line 1 2 ; secure them at that angle by the cross-piece 7 8 ; at the points 1, 2 fix pins, and through a hole in the rods at the point 3 put a pencil ; move the pencil round, keeping the rods pressed against the pins, and the segment 1 3 2 will be described.

TO DO THE SAME THING BY MEANS OF A FLAT TRIANGLE.

Let 4 3 (Fig. 3.) be the length, and 1 2 the height, of the required segment ; join 3 2, and through 2 draw 2 5 parallel to 4 3 and equal to 2 3, and join 5 3 ; place pins at the points 2, 4, and with a pencil at the vertex of the triangle, move the vertex round from 2 to 4, as in Figure 4 ; take up the pin at 4, and place it at 3 ; then move the vertex from 2 to 3, and the required segment will be described.

THE TWO AXES OF AN ELLIPSIS BEING GIVEN, TO DESCRIBE THE ELLIPSIS.

Let 4 6 (Fig. 5.) be the transverse and 1 3 the conjugate axis of the required ellipsis ; through 6 draw 6 7 parallel and equal to 2 1 ; bisect 6 7 in 8, and draw 8 1, 7 3 cutting each other at 9 ; bisect 1 9, and from the bisecting point draw a straight line perpendicular to 1 9 ; produce that straight line and the axis 1 3 till they meet at 1 2 ; draw 1 2 7 cutting the axis 4 6 in 1 5 ; make 2 1 7 equal to 2 1 5, and produce 3 1 so that 2 1 3 shall be equal to 2 1 2 ; draw 1 2 1 4, 1 3 1 8, 1 3 1 6, and from the points 1 2, 1 3 as centres, with the distance 1 2 1 or 1 3 3 for radius, describe the arcs 1 4 9 1 8 1 6, and from the points 1 7, 1 5, with 4 1 7 or 6 1 5 for radius, describe the arcs 1 4 18, 9 1 6 : 1 6 3 4 is the ellipsis required.

TO DO THE SAME THING BY MEANS OF ORDINATES.

Let the line 1 2 (Fig. 6.) be the length, and the line 4 9 half the width of the ellipsis to be described; on the length 1 2 describe the semicircle 1 8 2; divide the semicircle into any number of equal parts, as for instance sixteen, and through the points of division 1, 2, 3, &c. and at right angles to the transverse axis 1 2, draw the ordinates 1 1, 2 2, 3 3, &c.; draw 1 3 perpendicular to the transverse axis, and equal to 4 9, and join 4 3; take in the compass that part of the straight line 7 7 which is cut off by the lines 1 4, 3 4, that is, take 7 1, and on both sides of the transverse axis, and at each end of the same, cut off the length 7 1 on the straight line 1 1; take 6 2 and cut off the same length on 2 2, on each side of the transverse axis; on 3 3, cut off the length 5 3; on 4 4, the length 4 4, intercepted between the lines 1 4, 3 4; on 5 5, the intercepted length 3 3; on 6 6, the intercepted length 2 2; and so on: the circumference of the required ellipsis will pass through the points in which the straight lines, or ordinates, 1 1, 2 2, 3 3, &c. were cut off.

PL. 7.

TO FIND THE SECTION OF A SEMI-CYLINDER, WHEN IT IS CUT BY A PLANE THAT IS PERPENDICULAR TO THE PLANE COINCIDING WITH ITS FLAT SIDE, BUT IS NOT PARALLEL TO ITS ENDS OR BASES.

Let the semicircle 7 6 8 (Plate VII. Fig. 1.) represent one end of a semi-cylinder, the four-sided figure 7 8 10 9, a portion of its length, and the line 9 10, the edge of a plane cutting the semi-cylinder perpendicularly, but not parallel to the plane 7 6 8; divide the arc 7 6 8 into any number of equal parts, as for instance twelve, and from the points of division 1, 2, 3, &c. draw perpendiculars to the line 7 8, and produce them till they meet the line 9 10; from the points 1, 2, 3, &c. where they meet 9 10, and at right angles to the same, draw the lines 1 1, 2 2, 3 3, &c. each equal to the line of the same name in the semicircle 7 6 8; describe the curve 9 6 10 passing through the extremities of those lines: the figure B is the section required.

AN ACUTE ANGLE BEING GIVEN, TO CUT A SEMI-CYLINDER IN A DIRECTION OBLIQUE TO THE DIAMETER OF THE BASE, AS BEFORE, AND BY A PLANE MAKING AN ACUTE ANGLE EQUAL TO THE GIVEN ONE WITH THE PLANE WHICH COINCIDES WITH THE FLAT SIDE OF THE SEMI-CYLINDER.

Let the semicircle 7 a 8, the four-sided figure 7 8 10 9, and the straight line 9 10, represent the same things as in the preceding problem, and let the angle b a f at C, be the given acute angle; at C, draw d e at right angles to d a and equal to the radius a b or 8 b of the base; through e draw e c parallel to d a; produce a f till it meets e c in c, and from c let fall the perpendicular c b; in 9 10 take any point, as e, and from e draw e f at right angles to 9 10, and equal to a c at C; produce f e so that e g shall be equal to a b at C; through g draw g d parallel to 7 8, and join d f; produce the radius a b to d, and through g draw g h parallel to d a, and join h b; divide the arch 7 a 8 into any number of parts, and through the points of division draw straight lines, as 1 2, 3 4, 5 6, parallel to $h\,b$; from the points in which those lines meet the line 7 8, draw lines at right angles to 7 8 to meet the line 9 10, and through the points in which they meet 9 10, draw straight lines parallel to $d\,f$, and equal to their corresponding lines in A; describe a curve passing through the extremities of the parallel lines in B, and you have the required section.

AN OBTUSE ANGLE BEING GIVEN, TO CUT A SEGMENT OF A CYLINDER IN A DIRECTION OBLIQUE TO THE DIAMETER OF THE BASE, AND SO THAT THE PLANE CUTTING IT SHALL MAKE AN OBTUSE ANGLE EQUAL TO THE GIVEN ONE WITH THE PLANE THAT COINCIDES WITH THE FLAT SIDE OF THE SEGMENT.

Let the angle $b\,a\,f$ at C (Fig. 3.) be the given obtuse angle; from the point a draw $a\,d$ at right angles to $a\,b$ and equal to the radius $a\,b$ of the base 7 a 8; through d draw $d\,c$ parallel to $a\,b$, and produce $a\,f$ to meet $d\,c$ in c; in 9 10 take any point, as e, and from e draw $e\,f$ perpendicular to 9 10 and equal to $a\,d$ at C; from $e\,f$ cut off $e\,g$ equal to $d\,c$ at C, and through g, and parallel to 7 8, draw $g\,d$ to meet 9 10 in d, and join $d\,f$; from d let fall upon 7 8 the perpendicular $d\,b$, and through g draw $g\,h$ parallel to $d\,b$, and join $h\,b$; in A draw any number of lines parallel to $h\,b$, and from the points in which they meet 7 8, and at right angles to the same, draw straight lines to 9 10; through the points where they meet 9 10, draw straight lines parallel to $d\,f$, making each equal to the line of the same name at A; through the extremities of these parallels trace a curve, and the required section will be described.

NOTE.—In looking at these figures, we must imagine A to be a plane standing at right angles to the plane 7 8 10 9, and B another plane making with 7 8 10 9 whatever angle is specified in the problem. That the learner may better perceive the *why* and *wherefore* of what is done, and the correctness of the result obtained, it will be well for him to draw these figures on some stiff kind of paper, and then cut them out, and bend the parts A and B so as to make them form, with 7 8 10 9, the angles required. A must, in all these figures, stand at right angles to 7 8 10 9, but in the first of them, B must form a right-angle with that plane; in the second, the acute angle $b\,a\,f$; and in the third, the obtuse angle $b\,a\,f$. By making the planes A and B form the required angles, the learner will see that if planes were made to pass through the parallels in A, they would, if produced, pass through the parallels in B, the plane belonging to each parallel in A, passing through the corresponding parallel in B.

PL. 8.

TO FIND THE SECTION OF A SEMI-GLOBE, WHEN IT IS CUT BY A PLANE AT RIGHT ANGLES TO ITS BASE, OR FLAT SIDE.

Let the circle $a\,d\,f$ (Plate VIII. Fig. 1.) represent a semi-globe with its flat side uppermost, and let the straight line $c\,d$ represent the edge of a plane cutting the semi-globe at right angles to its flat side; bisect $c\,d$ in 1, and from 1, as centre, with 1 c or 1 d for radius, describe the semicircle $c\,g\,d$; $c\,g\,d$ is the section required.

ANOTHER METHOD OF DOING THE SAME THING.

Let the circle *a d f* (Fig. 1.) and the line *c d* represent the same thing as before; draw the diameter *a b*, and from the centre *e*, with the distance from *e* to the centre of the line *c d*, that is, with *e* 1 for radius, describe an arc 1 1, so as to meet 1 *d* and *e b;* from the same centre with different radii, describe concentric arcs, as 2 2, 3 3, &c. to meet the same lines 1 *d*, *e b*, and from the points 1, 2, 3, &c. in which the arcs meet the semi-diameter *e b*, draw perpendiculars, as 1 1, 2 2, &c. to the circumference; from the points in which those arcs meet the line 1 *d*, draw the perpendiculars 1 1, 2 2, &c., equal in length to those of the same name on *e b;* through the extremities of the perpendiculars on 1 *d*, and those that may by a similar process be erected on 1 *c*, describe the curve *c g d: c g d* is the section required.

NOTE.—The learner will see that the semicircle *c g d* represents that face of the piece *a c d f*, or of the piece *c h d*, which is made by cutting through the semi-globe at *c d* in a direction perpendicular to the flat side of the semi-globe. A moment's reflection, without any demonstration, will convince him that whenever a semi-globe is cut at right angles to its flat side, the face produced by the cutting will be a semi-circle, of which the straight line that designates the place of cutting, will be the base, or diameter. When, therefore, this straight line is given, (as it always is,) the learner has only to describe a semicircle upon it, to find the shape and size of the face required. That he may clearly perceive the accuracy of the second method, let him imagine the semi-globe to be cut through, perpendicularly to its flat side, at *a b* as well as at *c d*, and the quarter-globe *a f b* to be turned up at right angles to the face *a h b*: he will then see that the lines 1 1, 2 2, &c. on the face *a f b* are the perpendicular distance of the points 1, 2, &c. in the spherical surface from the flat side of the semi-globe; and that since the points 1, 2, &c. in *c d*, are at the same distance from the centre *e* as the points 1, 2, &c. in *a b*, the perpendiculars from 1, 2, &c. in *c d* to the spherical surface must be of the same length with the perpendiculars from 1, 2, &c. in *a b* to the spherical surface; in other words, that the lines 1 1, 2 2, &c. on the face *c g d*, must be equal in length to 1 1, 2 2, &c. on *a f b*.

The required sections in Figures 2. 3. and 4. are found by the second method of the preceding Problem. In Figure 3. the solid to be cut is supposed to have a circular base, but an elliptical elevation; and A at Figure 4. represents an ogee standing on a circular base, and from it B is found by the method just mentioned.

A SEMI-GLOBE BEING CUT BY A CYLINDRICAL SURFACE AT RIGHT ANGLES TO ITS FLAT SIDE, TO FIND THE FORM AND SIZE OF A VENEER, OR COVERING, TO BE BENT ROUND THE SECTION.

Let the circle *a b d c* (Fig. 5.) represent a semi-globe, and the arc *a b*, a cylindrical surface cutting the semi-globe at right angles to its flat side; draw the diameter *c d*, and bisect the arc *a b* in 1; from *e* the centre of the globe, with *e* 1 for radius, describe the arc 1 1. and enlarging the radius, describe also the arcs 2 2, 3 3, &c.; from the points 1, 2, &c. in which the arcs meet *e d*, draw to the circumference of the circle the perpendiculars 1 1, 2 2, &c. ; obtain the length of the arc *a b*, and place it in a straight line *a b* at B, and divide the straight line *a b* so that if bent round the arc *a b*, its divisions would correspond with those made in that arc by the arcs 1 1, 2 2, &c. ; from 1 in the straight line *a b*, corresponding with 1 in the arc *a b*, draw the perpendicular 1 1, equal to 1 1 at A ; from 2, the perpendicular 2 2, equal to 2 2 at A ; and so on ; trace a curve through the extremities of these perpendiculars, and you will have the required covering, or veneer.

TO FIND THE RIBS OF A GOTHIC NICHE, WHEN THE PLAN AND THE FRONT ELEVATION ARE GIVEN.

Let 2 6 8 (Fig. 6.) be the plan, and *a b c* the front elevation of a Gothic niche ; at H, I, J and K, draw the bases 1 3, 1 4, 1 5, 1 6, respectively equal to the bases 1 3, 1 4, 1 5, 1 6 in the plan ; divide the base 1 *a* (Fig. 6.) into any number of equal parts, as 6, and from the points of division 1, 2, &c. erect the perpendiculars 1 1, 2 2, &c. ; divide the bases at H, I, J and K into as many equal parts as 1 *a* was divided into, and from the points of division erect the perpendiculars 1 1, 2 2, &c., each equal to the perpendiculars of the same name on 1 *a ;* through the ends of these perpendiculars, trace curves, and the ribs for half the niche will be completed.

PL. 9.

TO DRAW THE LINING OF A CYLINDRICAL SOFFIT CUTTING PERPENDICULARLY INTO A FLAT WALL WHICH DOES NOT STAND PERPENDICULAR TO A HORIZONTAL BASE.

Let the line 4 1 (Plate IX. B.) be a horizontal base, or the level of the ground ; at the point 1, make the angle 4 1 2 equal to the inclination of the wall, and make the line 1 2 equal to the radius of the cylindrical soffit, and from 2 let fall the perpendicular 2 3 ; with 1 2 at B for radius, describe the semicircle *f* 4 *e*, (Fig. 1.) and on the diameter *f e*, with the distance 3 1 at B for the width, describe (either by means of ordinates, as in the Figure, or by any of the methods pointed out in this book) the semi-ellipsis *f g e ;* divide the arc *f* 4 *e* into any number of equal parts, as eight, and from the points of division 1, 2, &c. let fall upon *f e* the perpendiculars 1 *d*, 2 *c*, &c. and produce them to the curve line *f g e ;* take that part of the perpendiculars which is intercepted between the straight line *f e* and the curve *f g e*, and in the straight line 4 1 at B, make 4 5 equal to the intercepted part *d d* at Fig. 1. ; 5 6 equal to *c c ;* 6 7 equal to *b b ;* and 7 8 equal to *a g ;* from 2 draw 2 4 at right angles to 2 1, and from the points 5, 6, 7, 8 in the line 4 1, draw the perpendiculars 5 12, 6 11, &c. to meet the line 4 2 ; take the stretchout or length of the arc *f* 4 *e* at Fig. 1. and place it in a straight line *a b* at C, and make divisions in *a b* corresponding with the divisions in *f* 4 *e ;* from the points of division *d, c, b,* &c. erect the perpendiculars *d d, c c, b b,* &c. and make *d d* equal to 4 12 at B ; *c c* equal to 12 11 ; *b b* equal to 11 10, and so on ; do the same with the other half of *a b*, and through the ends of those perpendiculars describe the curve *a a b*.

THE BASE OR PLAN AND ONE OF THE COMMON RIBS OF THE ROOF OF A HEXAGON BEING GIVEN, TO FIND THE ANGLE OR HIP RIBS, AND THE COVERING OF THE ROOF.

Let the hexagon 5 6 7 8 9 10 (Fig. 2.) be the given plan, and let the part B of Fig. 2. be the given common rib, of which the line *o* 5 is the base; divide the rib B into any number of equal parts, as four, and through the points of division 1, 2, &c. and parallel to the side 6 7 of the hexagon, draw the lines 1 2, 2 3, &c. to meet the base 5 7 of the angle rib to be found; from the points 2, 3, &c. in which the parallels meet 5 7, erect the perpendiculars 2 1, 3 2, &c. making 2 1 equal to 2 1 in B, 3 2 to 3 2 in B, and so on; trace the curve 7 1 2 3 4 through the ends of the perpendiculars, and the required angle rib is found. To find the form of the roof-boards, produce the base 5 *o* of the rib B to 4, and make *o* 4 equal to the stretchout or length of the rib B, and divide it into as many equal parts as you did B, viz. four; through the points of division 1, 2, &c., and parallel to the side 6 7, draw the lines 1 1, 2 2, &c. making 1 1 on each side of *o* 4 at D equal to 2 2 between the bases *o* 5, 7 5; 2 2 on each side of *o* 4, equal to 3 3 between those bases; and so on; through the ends of the parallels 1 1, 2 2, &c. trace the curve lines 7 4, 6 4 and the figure 6 4 7 at 10 is the covering for one side of the hexagon roof.

AN ARCH OF ANY FORM BEING GIVEN TO DRAW ARCHES FOR GROINS WHETHER RIGHT OR RAMPANT, THAT SHALL BE SIMILAR TO THE GIVEN ARCH.

Let *o* 4 8 (Fig 3.) be a given arch of a Gothic form; bisect it in 4, and draw the chord *o* 4; divide *o* 4 into any number of equal parts, as four, and through the points of division 1, 2, &c., and from the centre *p* of the base *o* 8, draw the lines *p* 7, *p* 6, &c. to meet the arc *o* 4; from *o*, and at right angles to *o* 8, draw a straight line *o* 3 of any length, and through the points 7 6, &c. in which the lines *p* 7, *p* 6, &c. meet the arc *o* 4, draw from the vertex 4 the lines 4 1, 4 2, &c. meeting the perpendicular *o* 3 in 1, 2, &c.; take any base *o* 8 at A, and bisect it in *p*, and from *p* draw the perpendicular *p* 4 equal to *p* 4 in Fig. 3.; from the extremities of the base *o* 8 erect the perpendiculars *o* 3, 8 3, and divide them so that the parts *o* 1, 8 1, shall each be equal to *o* 1 in the perpendicular at Fig. 3.; the parts 1 2, 1 2, equal to 1 2 in the perpendicular at Fig. 3.; and so on; from the points of division in the perpendiculars *o* 3, 8 3, draw the lines 1 4, 2 4, &c. to the point 4, and join *o* 4, 8 4; divide the straight lines *o* 4, 8 4 into as many equal parts as the chord *o* 4 in Fig. 3. was divided into, viz. four, and through the points of division 1, 2, &c. in these lines, draw from *p* the lines *p* 7, *p* 6, &c. to meet the lines 1 4, 2 4, &c.; through the points 7, 6, &c. in which they intersect these lines, trace the curves *o* 4, 8 4, and the arch *o* 4 8 at A is similar to the given arch *o* 4 8 at Fig. 3.

In the same manner may the rampant arch at B be drawn, with this difference only, that the lines *o* 3, *p* 4, 8 3 are drawn perpendicular, not to the base *o* 8, but to a horizontal base.

The heptagon at Fig. 4. represents the plan of a heptagon roof; A is a common rib having the line *o* 5 for its base; B is an angle rib drawn from A in the same manner as the angle rib in Fig. 2.; and C is the covering for one side of the roof, and is found as in Fig. 2.

D is also a covering of the same dimensions with C, and may be formed in the same manner.

TO FIND THE COVERING OF A HEMISPHERICAL DOME.

Let the circle 1 6 5 (Fig. 5.) represent the base of the dome; at F draw the line 5 4 equal to the width of any board which you would make a part of the covering; bisect 5 4 in *o*, and from *o* erect the perpendicular *o* 4 equal to the length or stretchout of a quarter of the circumference 1 6 5; on 5 4 describe the semicircle 5 4 4, and divide the quarter-circumference 5 4 into any number of equal parts, as four, and from the points of division 1, 2, &c. let fall upon *o* 4 the perpendiculars 1 1, 2 2, &c.; divide the line *o* 4 into as many equal parts as you did the arc 5 4, viz. four, and from the points of division 1, 2, &c. erect the perpendiculars 1 1, 2 2, &c. making each equal to the perpendicular of the same name in the semicircle on 5 4, viz. 1 1 to 1 1, 2 2 to 2 2, &c.; from the same points erect perpendiculars of the same length on the other side of *o* 4, and through the ends of the perpendiculars on both sides, trace the curve lines 4 4, 5 4: the board F has the requisite length and shape for a part of the covering of the hemispherical dome of which the circle 1 6 5 is the base.

Note.—If, as in this Figure, the width of each board be made equal to a fourth part of the stretchout of the arc 1 5 or 6 5, then sixteen boards will just cover the dome.

TO FIND THE COVERING OF A DOME HAVING A CIRCULAR BASE, BUT AN ELLIPTICAL ELEVATION.

Let *o* 7 (Fig. 5. C) be the height of the dome, and let the arc 6 7 represent half of the elliptical surface; draw the chord 6 7, and on the diameter 6 1 make 6 3 equal to half the width of a given board, and from 3 draw 3 4 at right angles to 6 1, and so as to meet the chord 6 7; take the straight line 1 3 at D equal to twice 6 3 at C, that is, equal to the width of the given board, and, bisecting 1 3 in 2, erect the perpendicular 2 4 equal to the stretchout of the arc 6 7 at C; from the line 2 4 at D, cut off the part 2 *a* equal to the perpendicular 3 4 at C, and with 2 *a* for the height and 1 3 for the length, describe (See Plate VI. Fig's. 1. 2. 3.) the segment 1 *a* 3; divide the arc 1 *a* into any number of equal parts, as four, and from the points of division let fall upon 2 4 the perpendiculars 1 1, 2 2, &c.; divide the line 2 4 into the same number of equal parts, viz. four, and from the divisions 1, 2, &c. and at right angles to 2 4, draw the lines 1 1, 2 2, &c. equal to the corresponding lines in the segment 1 *a* 3, that is, 1 1 equal to 1 1, 2 2 to 2 2, &c.; do the same on the other side of 2 4, and trace curves, and you will have in D the length and form of one board for the covering

In the same manner may be found the covering of a dome having a circular base and an ogee elevation.   See B and E, Fig. 5.

PL. 10.

WHEN, IN A CHURCH OR OTHER BUILDING, THE TOP OF A WINDOW HAVING A SEMICIRCULAR HEAD, RISES ABOVE THE LEVEL OF THE CEILING, SO THAT TO ADMIT LIGHT THROUGH THIS TOP, AN OPENING MUST BE MADE IN THE CEILING, TO FIND THE FORM AND DIMENSIONS OF AN OPENING FOR THIS PURPOSE.

Let the semicircle *a d e* (Plate X. Fig. 1.) represent the head of a window; bisect the arc *a d e* in *d*, and from *d* let fall upon the base *a e* the perpendicular *d f;* from *d f* cut off *d g* equal to the distance that the top of the window rises above the ceiling, and through *g* draw the chord *b c* parallel to *a e;* produce the straight line *d f* to 7, and make *g* 7 equal to *b* 7 at G; divide *g d* into any number of equal parts, as six, and through the points of division 1, 2, &c. draw the chords 1 1, 2 2, &c. parallel to *b c;* divide *g* 7 into as many equal parts, viz. six, and through the divisions 1, 2, &c. draw the straight lines 1 1, 2 2, &c. parallel to *b c*, and make 1 1 on each side of *g* 7 equal to 1 1 on either side of *g d;* 2 2 on each side of *g* 7, equal to 2 2 on either side of *g d;* and so on; through the ends of these parallels trace the curve lines *b* 7, *c* 7, and you have in the figure 7 *b c* the form of the aperture to be made.—To find the ribs of this aperture, on the base 1 1 of the rib A, with the part 1 *d* of *g d* for the height, describe (See Plate VI. Fig's. 1 2. &c.) the segment 1 *o* 1; on 2 2 at B for the length, with the part 2 *d* of *g d* for the height, describe the segment 2 *o* 2; and so on, omitting, at every step downward, one division more of the line *g d*, till for the height of the lowest segment 5 *o* 5, you have left only the highest division of *g d*, viz. 5 *d*: the arcs 1 *o* 1, 2 *o* 2, 3 *o* 3, &c. constitute the inner or concave edge of the ribs A, B, C, &c. the outer edge of which may be bounded by a curve, or by straight lines, as in the figure.

Another and perhaps a shorter way of finding the ribs, is to take *f a* or *f e* for radius, and from the ends 1, 1 of the base 1 1 at A, describe arcs cutting each other and the line *g* 7 at 8; the point 8 will be the centre, and *f a* or *f e* the radius, for describing the arc 1 *o* 1, that is, the rib A. From the ends of the other bases, 2 2, 3 3, &c. and with the same radius, make intersections of arcs on *g* 7, or *g* 7 produced, and you will find the centres for describing all the other arcs, 2 *o* 2, 3 *o* 3, &c.

TO DRAW AN ELLIPTICAL RIB BY MEANS OF A QUADRANT.

Let 6 6 (Fig. 2.) be half the length, and 6 7, at right angles to 6 6, half the width, of the ellipsis of which the required rib will be a part; with half the length 6 6 as radius, make at A the quadrant 6 6 7; divide the base 6 7 into any number of equal parts, as six, and draw the perpendiculars 1 1, 2 2, &c.; divide the base 6 7 in Fig. 2. into as many equal parts, viz. six, and from the points of division 1, 2, &c. ·erect the perpendiculars 1 2, 2 2, &c. making 1 1 equal to 1 1 at A, 2 2 equal to 2 2 at A, &c. and through the ends of the perpendiculars trace the curve 6 7: the curve 6 7 is the concave edge of the required rib.—If the rib is to be backed, that is, have a portion of one edge hewed off so as to make it range with some other edge, and if 7 8 (Fig. 2.) be the width that is to be taken off, from the points in which the perpendiculars already drawn meet the arc 6 7, draw other perpendiculars 1 1, 2 2, &c. each equal to 7 8, and through the ends 8, 1, 2, &c. trace the curve 8 6, which will give the rib as required.

TO DO THE SAME THING BY MEANS OF THE COMPASS.

Let the line *a* 3 (Fig. 3.) be half the length, and *a b* half the width, as in the preceding Problem; with *a b* for radius, describe from *a* the arc *b c*, and divide the difference between *a b* and *a* 3, viz. *c* 3, into three equal parts, and make *c l* equal to one of those parts; produce 3 *a* to *d*, and make *a d*, *a e* each equal to the four parts 3 *l*; from *d* and *e* as centres, with *d e* for radius, describe arcs cutting each other at *f*, and through *f* and *e* draw a straight line *f g*, unlimited towards *g*: *f* is the centre and *f b* the radius for describing the arc *g b*, and *e* the centre and *e* 3 the radius for describing the arc 3 *g*.—If the width 3 4 is to be taken off to make the rib range with A, make *e i* equal to 3 4, and through *f* draw *f h* parallel to 3 *a* and equal to 3 4; through *h* and *i* draw *h k*, unlimited towards *k*: *h* and *i* are the centres and *h m*, *i* 4 the radii for describing the arcs *k b*, *k* 4.

Figure 4. is drawn in the same manner with Fig. 3. and therefore needs no explanation.

PL. 11.

ONE RIB OF AN ELLIPTICAL DOME, THE PLAN OF AN OBLONG OPENING OF A STAIRCASE, AND THE PLAN OF AN ELLIPTICAL OPENING AT THE TOP FOR A SKY-LIGHT, BEING GIVEN, TO FIND THE OTHER RIBS, AND ALSO THE SPRINGING CURVE ON EACH SIDE OF THE OPENING OF THE STAIRCASE FOR THE RIBS TO STAND UPON.

Let the arch at F, (Plate XI.) having its base and height each equal to half the width of the ellipsis *e f g h*, be the given rib, of which the part over 5 *j* is all that is wanted; let the oblong *a b c d* represent the opening of the staircase, and the small ellipsis at A, the opening at top for a sky-light, and let the lines that converge towards A represent ribs. To find any one rib, as I, take the height of F, that is, the distance *h* A or *f* A for half the conjugate axis, and the distance between the point where the required rib is to meet the ellipsis *e f g h* and the point A, that is, *d* A, for half the transverse axis, and describe (See Plate V. Fig's. 1. 2 &c.) the quarter of an ellipsis; from the point *m* in which the base *d* A meets the small ellipsis, erect a perpendicular and produce it so as to meet the arch of the quarter-ellipsis: the part over *d m* is all that is wanted of this rib. In like manner for any other rib, describe a quarter-ellipsis with *h* A for its width, and the distance from the point A to where the rib meets the ellipsis *e f g h* for its length, and the part that is perpendicularly over that portion of the base intercepted between one side of the oblong and the circumference of the small ellipsis at A, will be the part that is wanted of the rib. Thus G is a quarter-ellipsis having the distance *h* A for its width, and the distance *g* A or *e* A for its length, and the part over 4 *k* is all that is wanted of it. H is the same with G. D corresponds with I, and J with F. B and C represent the ribs of one side and end of the oblong opening, with the springing curves on which they stand, and the plate at the base of the sky-light into which they enter. To find the springing curves, take half the width of the oblong opening, viz. *b* 4 or *c* 4, and with it for radius describe the semicircle at C for the springing curve on that or the opposite side ; and for the springing curve on the side *a b* or *d c* of the opening, describe the quarter-ellipsis at B, having the same height with the semicircle at C, and a length equal to that of the opening.

NOTE.—If any learner should fail to obtain a thorough knowledge of the problem from the foregoing explanations, and from an examination of the figure, let him imagine an elliptical dome to rest upon the ellipsis *e f g h*, such that its base or flat side exactly fills up or corresponds with that ellipsis, and that its altitude is just equal to half the width of its base, so that a curve line drawn from *h* to *f* on the dome and through the top, of it shall, with a straight line joining those points on the base, make a semicircle ; let him also imagine curve lines, corresponding with the straight ones in the Figure, to be drawn on the elliptical elevation, cutting each other at the top or vertex ; and he will see, that while the curve drawn from *h* to *f* is a semicircle, the curve drawn from any other point whatever to its opposite point, is a semi-ellipsis. Hence the propriety of making the rib F or J a quadrant, and every other one a quarter-ellipsis having the same height with F. Next let the learner imagine a piece cut off from the top of the elliptical dome, and the face made by the cutting may be considered the base of the sky-light. Then let him suppose curves similar to those at B and C drawn on the sides, and ends of what is left of the dome, and he will see the reason why parts only of the different ribs found are taken, and why such parts are taken as are, rather than others. If the student finds all this too great a task for his imagination, let him with his knife make a small elliptical dome, such as I have described, and let him draw the curve lines on it for ribs, and cut off the piece, and describe the springing curves, and he will at once obtain a satisfactory and an accurate knowledge of the Problem.

PL. 12.

THE BODY AND SIDE ARCHES OF AN UNDER PITCH GROIN BEING GIVEN, TO FIND A MOULD FOR THE INTERSECTING RIBS.

Let E (Plate XII. Fig. 1.) represent the body arch, and F the side arch, of an under pitch groin, and A, B, C, and D, the piers on which the arches rest; bisect the arch F in 4, and divide the half towards B into any number of equal parts, as four; from the divisions 1, 2, 3, 4, let fall perpendiculars upon the base 8 9 of the arch F, and produce them at pleasure; from the same points 1, 2, &c. draw the lines 4 4, 3 3, &c. parallel to the base 8 9, and meeting *a b* produced, in the points 4, 3, &c.; from *o* as centre, with *o* 1, *o* 2, &c. for radii, describe arcs so as to cut 8 9 produced, and from the points where they cut it, and parallel to the base *a b*, draw straight lines to meet the arch E ; from the points 4, 3, &c. in which they meet that arch, let fall perpendiculars upon *a b*, and produce them till they meet the perpendiculars from the divisions in F, through the points of intersection 1, 2, 3, &c. trace the curve 1 4 for the place of the intersecting ribs upon the plan ; through the intersections of corresponding ordinates from E and F, continue the curve 1 4 to the pier D, and on each side of this curve describe another parallel to it, for the thickness of the rib upon the plan ; bisect the inner curve in 4, and from 4 draw chords to the extremities of the curve, and parallel to these chords draw two straight lines so as to touch the outer curve, and the distance between these parallels will be the width of plank, or other stuff, necessary for the required ribs ; from the points 1, 2, &c. in the curve 1 4, let fall perpendiculars upon the chord 1 4, and produce them to the points 1, 2, &c. making the part produced 1 1 equal to 1 1 at F ; 2 2 equal to 2 2 at F, &c. ; through the ends of these perpendiculars, trace a curve line : G is a mould for the intersecting ribs. H is the same as G, and found in the same manner.

TO FIND THE ANGLE MOULD, OR A MOULD, WHICH, WHEN BENT UNDER THE INTERSECTING RIBS, WILL GIVE THE TRUE PLACE OF THE ANGLE UPON THE PLAN.

Obtain the stretchout or length of the under or concave edge of G, and place it in a straight line *o* 4; (Fig. 2.) divide *o* 4 into as many equal parts as half the arch F is divided into, viz. four, and from the points of division draw straight lines perpendicular to *o* 4, and respectively equal to the straight lines at I intercepted between the curve 1 4 and the chord 1 4 ; that is, make 1 1 in Fig. 2. equal to 1 1 at I ; 2 2 equal to 2 2 at I ; and so on ; trace a curve through the ends of the perpendiculars on *o* 4, and the required mould is found.

TO RANGE THE RIBS, SO THAT THEY WILL STAND PERPENDICULARLY OVER THE PLAN.

From the points 1, 2, &c in which the straight lines from the arch E meet the base 1 4 of H, and perpendicular to that base, draw the dotted lines 1 1, 22, &c. and make them respectively equal to those of the same name at F ; through the ends of these dotted perpendiculars, describe the curve *o* 4, and it will show how much is to be pevelled off from the rib H. The ranging of G is found in the same manner.

J and K are angle ribs, and are like G and H, except that they are drawn as already bevelled off. Fig. 3. shows the different parts of Fig. 1. in a more connected form, as well as some other parts belonging to an under pitch groin. The body arch E will stand perpendicularly over *n*, and the side arch F will stand over *m*. L is a part of the arch E, and will stand over *o*, and be connected with the angle ribs. The parallel rows of double lines in E represent the lath beams of the arch. *a*, *b*, and *c*, are jack ribs, and their places are at 1, 2 and 3 in Fig. 3. The jack ribs *e*, *f*, *g* and *h* belong over the letters of the same name between the angle ribs.

PL. 13.

TO FIND THE RIBS OF THE HEAD OF A NICHE, WHEN THAT HEAD IS TO FORM SOME PORTION OF A HOLLOW SPHERE, AND WHEN THE GROUND-PLAN AND THE FRONT RIB ARE GIVEN.

Let the segment of a circle at Fig. 1. (Plate XIII.) represent the ground-plan or base of the head of a niche, and let the semicircle at Fig. 2. be the elevation or front rib; draw the straight line *o* 3 (Fig. 3.) equal to the radius *w x* or *w y* at Fig. 1. and on *o* 3 set off *z* 3 equal to *z x* at Fig. 1.; at the point *z* in the line *o* 3, erect a perpendicular of unlimited length, and with *o* 3 for radius and *o* as centre, describe an arc so as to cut the perpendicular and the base *o* 3 : the part 3 *x*, intercepted between the base and the perpendicular, is the inner edge of the rib that will stand over *z x* in Fig. 1.—To find the rib that will stand over A (Fig. 1.) take the same length *w x* for base, and from it cut off 1 3 (Fig. 4.) equal to 1 3 at A; erect a perpendicular, as before, and with the same radius *w x* or *o* 3, describe an arc to cut the perpendicular and also the base : the arc 3 1 is the concave edge of the rib belonging over A. In the same manner find any rib whatever for the head of the niche.—For the bevel of the rib that is to stand over A, take 1 7 at A and place it at 1 7 in the base of Fig. 4., and a perpendicular erected at 7 will cut off the part required. Proceed in the same way in the bevelling of the other ribs.—The middle curve in the semicircle at Fig. 2. is drawn to show the ranging of the front rib, and the figures 1 2, 1 2 show where the ribs (Fig's. 4. and 5.) will be joined to the front rib.

PL. 14.

THE PLAN OF A NICHE IN A CIRCULAR WALL BEING GIVEN, TO FIND THE FRONT RIB.

Let the arc 5 *o* 5 (Plate XIV. Fig. 1.) represent a part of the circular wall, and let the crescent-like figure bounded by the arcs 5 *o* 5 and 5 *x* 5 be the base or plan of the niche; divide half the arc 5 *x* 5 into any number of equal parts, as five, and from the points of division 1, 2, &c. let fall upon the base 5 *s* 5 the perpendiculars 1 1, 2 2, &c.; from the point *s* as a centre, with the distance *s o* for radius, describe the quarter-circumference *o* 5, and divide it into as many equal parts as you did the arc 5 *x*, viz. five; from the divisions 1, 2, &c. and parallel to 5 *s* 5; draw the straight lines 1 1, 2 2, &c. to intersect the perpendiculars from 5 *x*, and through the points in which corresponding perpendiculars meet, trace the elliptical curve 5 *o* ; take the stretchout of the arc 5 *x* 5 and place it in the straight line 5 *o* 5 at Fig. 3. and make divisions in each half of 5 *o* 5, corresponding with those in the arc 5 *x* (Fig. 1.); at the divisions 1, 2, &c. in 5 *o* 5, erect perpendiculars respectively equal to the straight lines *a* 1 *b* 2, &c. intercepted between the face of the wall, 5 *o*, and the elliptical curve 5 2 *o* that is, make *a* 1 in Fig. 3. equal to *a* 1 in Fig. 1., *b* 2 to *b* 2, &c., and through the ends of the perpendiculars trace the curve 5 *d c b a o*, and so on the other side of the point *o*; parallel to 5 *o* 5 draw the straight line 5 6 for the thickness of the rib at the ends and middle, and you will have a mould (Fig. 3.) for finding the front rib and its place over the plan.—When this mould is bent under the front rib, its curved side will coincide with the front edge of the rib, that is, with the curvature of the wall.   Fig's 4. 5. and 6. are the back ribs, belonging over B, C, and D, in Fig. 1, and are found in the same manner as in the preceding problem.   Fig. 2. represent the front rib, with the back ribs attached to it.   Its curvature, as also that of the back ribs, is the same with that of the springing curve H, in Fig. 1. To obtain a just and clear conception of the position of the front rib, when elevated, let the learner imagine it laid upon the spring-ing curve H, so as to coincide with that curve in every part, and then, while H remains in a horizontal position, let him suppose the front rib, its ends turning on the ends of H, to be raised up till the front edge comes into an exact range with the bend of the wall, that is, with the arc 5 o 5.   In this position, the opening between this rib and the plane on which it stands, will be an elliptical opening, though the rib itself has the curve of a semicircle; and this explains why, in the process of finding a mould for the front rib, some of the curves described are elliptical ones.   If the front rib were to be raised so as to stand perpendicularly over the chord 5 s 5, it is evident that the back ribs, standing as they will on the springing-curve H, would not shoot far enough over to come in contact with the front rib; and it would therefore be necessary to let this rib fall back towards a horizontal position till it came in contact with the back ribs.   This *falling back* is represented by the dotted lines $s\,u$ and $p\,o$ in Fig. 4.   The short line $z\,t$ represents the front of the rib, when it is cut so as to range with the bend of the wall; and $z\,u$ represents it when so cut as not to range with the wall. The junction of the front with the back rib is at $v\,w$.   To know at what angle to bevel the ends of the mould, (Fig. 3.) from o, and perpendicular to the line 5 o 5, draw the line $o\,s$ equal to $o\,s$ in Fig. 1.; join s 5, and at right angles to s 5 draw a straight line, 5 6, of any length : the line 5 6 gives the bevel of the end of the mould.   If you would have the front rib of an equal thickness all round, erect perpendiculars at the points 1, 2, &c. in the straight line 5 5, (Fig. 3.) or at the same points in the line 5 6, and on that side of 5 5, or of 5 6 which is opposite the curved side of the mould; make these perpen-diculars equal, each to each, to the straight lines intercepted between the front ellip-tical line 5 2 o (Fig. 1.) and the dotted line above it; that is, at o, (Fig. 3.) or at the point directly over o, erect a perpendicular equal to $o\,z$ in Fig. 1.; at 1 in Fig. 3., a perpendicular equal to 1 1 in Fig. 1.; and so on; a curve traced through the ends of these perpendiculars will be parallel to the curved side, 5 $d\,c\,b\,a\,o$, of the mould.

PL. 15.

TO FIND THE RIBS OF THE HEAD OF A NICHE, THE PLAN AND ELEVATION OF WHICH ARE
GIVEN SEGMENTS OF CIRCLES.

Let the segment $a\,c\,b$ (Plate XV. Fig. 1.) be the plan, having the point e the centre of the circle of which it is a segment, and let the segment $a\,c\,b$ (Fig. 2.) be the eleva-tion, having f for the centre of the circle to which it belongs; through the centre e, and parallel to the chord $a\,b$, draw the diameter $b\,d$, and complete the semicircle $b\,c\,d$; from the centre e draw the straight line $e\,f$, at right angles to the diameter $b\,d$, and equal to $d\,f$ in Fig. 2, and from f (Fig. 1.) as a centre, with the distance $f\,b$ or $f\,d$ for radius, describe the arc $b\,i\,d$: the arc $b\,i\,d$ has the same bend or curvature that the back ribs will have. To know what part of this arc is wanted for the different ribs belonging over A, B, C, and D, (Fig. 1.) either proceed in the same way as in the two preceding problems ; or from e as a centre, with the distances $e\,1$, $e\,2$, $e\,3$ and $e\,4$ for radii, describe arcs so as to meet the diameter $b\,d$; from the points in which these concentric arcs meet $b\,d$, and at right angles to $b\,d$, draw straight lines to cut the arc $b\,i\,d$: of the arc $b\,i\,d$, $b\,8$ is the part required for the rib that belongs over A in the the plan ; $b\,6$, the part part wanted for the rib belonging over B, and so on. The bevel of the ribs is found in the same way as in Plate XIII. The line 9 10 (Fig. 3.) shows the bevel of the rib that is to stand over A in the plan. The bevelling of the front rib (Fig. 2.) is shown by the short lines $b\,i$, $c\,g$. A and B (Fig. 2.) represent the front studs or joists.

PL. 18.

THE PLAN AND ELEVATION OF THE HEAD OF A CIRCULAR-HEADED SASH, STANDING IN A CIRCULAR WALL, BEING GIVEN, TO FIND A MOULD FOR THE RADIAL BARS.

Let the parallel curves 1 3, 2 4, (Plate XVI. Fig. 1.) represent the curvature and thickness of the circular wall ; the curve $E\,s\,E$, the inner or concave edge of the base or plan of the sash head ; the arc $E\,x\,E$, (Fig. 2.) the elevation of the sash head ; the converging lines 1, 2, 3, &c., the places of the radial bars ; and F, the arch bar to which the radial bars are joined ; parallel to E E, draw the tangent line $w\,w$; divide the radial line $1\,s$ (B. Fig. 2.) into any number of equal parts, as six, (they may be equal or unequal, at discretion,) and from the divisions 1, 2, &c. let fall upon E E perpendiculars, and produce them till they meet the arc $E\,s\,E$; at the points of division 1, 2, &c. in the radial line $1\,s$, erect perpendiculars, and make them respectively equal to the straight lines intercepted between the tangent line $w\,w$ and the arc $E\,s\,E$; that is, make 1 1 equal to 1 1, 2 2 equal to 2 2, &c.: a curve traced through the ends of these perpendiculars will give one edge of a mould for the radial bar belonging at B. Proceed in the same way for the mould D of the radial bar belonging at C. As the bar belonging at 3 (Fig. 2.) will be straight, no mould is needed for that ; and as A, the mould for B, will serve for the bar belonging at 1, and D for the one belonging at 4, the two moulds A and D are all that are wanted in this case. If more radial lines are given, find the moulds for the bars by the same method.

METHOD OF FINDING THE FACE MOULD FOR THE HEAD OF THE SASH.

Let the arc $w\,s\,z$ (Fig. 3.) represent the plan or base of the sash head ; the arc $1\,x\,2$, the elevation of the same ; and the arc $o\,s\,o$ at D, the arch-bar ; divide half the arc $1\,x\,2$, that is, divide $1\,x$ into any number of parts, as six, and from the points of division let fall upon the chord $w\,z$ the perpendiculars $x\,7$, $v\,6$, &c. ; draw the chord $w\,s$ of half the arc $w\,s\,z$, and parallel to $w\,s$ draw the tangent line $w\,x$; at the intersections of the perpendiculars $x\,7$, $v\,6$, &c. with the tangent $w\,x$, erect the perpendiculars $x\,x$, $v\,v$, &c., and make $x\,x$ equal to $x\,x$, intercepted between the arc $1\,x\,2$ and the chord

1 x 2; $v\,v$ equal to $v\,v$; and so on; trace the curve o 1 2 o x, and you will have the concave edge of the face-mould required.

NOTE.—The distance between the parallels $w\,s$ and $w\,x$ (C. Fig. 3.) shows what thickness of stuff will be necessary for making the sash-head.

METHOD OF FINDING THE VENEER OF THE ARCH-BAR.

Divide half the arc $o\,s\,o$, viz. $s\,o$, into any number of parts, as six, and from the divisions, let fall perpendiculars upon the plan $h\,h$ of the arch-bar; at E draw the straight line $o\,s\,o$, equal to the length or stretch-out of the arc $o\,s\,o$, and in the straight line $o\,s\,o$ make divisions, each way from s, corresponding with those in the arc $o\,s\,o$; at these divisions erect perpendiculars equal, each to each, to those intercepted between the convex side of the arc $w\,s\,z$ and the line $h\ h$: a curve traced through the ends of these perpendiculars will give the required veneer. When this veneer, or covering, is bent round the arch-bar, its edges will coincide with those of the bar, and the letters and figures belonging to it, will stand perpendicularly over those of the same name in the plan $h\,x\,h$

METHOD OF FINDING THE MOULDS FOR GIVING THE FORM OF THE SASH-HEAD, SO THAT THE FRONT EDGE SHALL BE PERPENDICULARLY OVER THE PLAN.

Obtain the stretch-out of the upper or convex edge of half the sash-head, and place it in the straight line w 7; (Fig. 4.) produce w 7 to 1, and make the part produced, 7 1, equal to the stretch-out of the concave edge of half the sash-head; in the line w 1 make divisions corresponding with those in each half of the sash-head, and at the divisions erect the perpendiculars 7 s, 6 t, &c., making them equal, each to each, to the perpendiculars of the same name in the plan (Fig. 3.); trace the curve $w\,u\,t\,s$ and its continuation on the other side of 7 s, and also the parallel curve 3 10 3, and you will have the required moulds. If the mould on the left of the line 7 10 be bent round the convex edge of half the sash-head, and the one on the right, under the concave edge of the same, the sash-head, being cut by these moulds, will have the requisite form; so that when executed, every part of it will coincide with the bend of the wall, or, in other words, will stand perpendicularly over its plan.

PL. 17.

TO DRAW AN OPEN GROIN ARCH.

Let the oblong A B C D (Plate XVII.) be the plan of the arch, of which the corners A, B, C, and D, are the butments; and let Fig's. 1 and 2 represent the elevations, and the diagonals A C, B D, the bases over which the angle ribs are to stand; within the oblong A B C D, and parallel, respectively, to the sides A B and B C, draw the double lines L, M, N, O, P, (making the number of double lines equal to the number of jack-ribs required,) and produce them so as to intersect the diagonals A C, B D; from the points of intersection, 1 2, 1 2, &c let fall perpendiculars upon the sides A B, B C, of the oblong, and produce these perpendiculars so as to cross the elevations at Fig's. 1. and 2.; through the points where they meet the elevations, draw the chords L, M, N, O, P : the respective arcs subtended by these chords, shew the length and curvature of the jack-ribs required for the arch, and when the jack-ribs and angle-ribs are placed perpendicularly over their bases in the plan, they will intersect each other in the points 1 2, 1 2, &c. Fig. 3. represents an angle-rib. A scale of inches is likewise attached to the plate. The student will observe, that that part of the perpendiculars, which crosses the elevations, shews the cuts for the jack-ribs, the dotted line being the cut for the longest side of the ribs.

PL. 18.

CIRCULAR DOMES.

As the common method of finding the centres for describing the boards to cover a horizontal dome will be found in practice very inconvenient, for those boards which come near to the bottom ; I shall in this place show how to remedy that inconvenience.

TO FIND THE SWEEP OF THE BOARDS ON THE TOP. FIG. A.

Divide round the circumference of the dome into equal parts at 1, 2, 3, 4, 5, 6, &c. each division to the width of a board, making proper allowance for the camber of each board ; draw a line through the points 1, 2, to meet the axis of the dome at x ; on x, as a centre, with the radii x 1 and x 2 describe the two concentric circles, it will form the board G ; in the same manner continue a line through the points 2 and 3 at C, to meet the axis in w ; then w is the centre for the board C ; proceed in the same manner for the boards D, E, and F.

Now suppose F to be the last board that you can conveniently find a centre, for want of room ; on t its centre, and the radius t 5, make from t on the axis of the dome t a, equal to t 5 ; through the points 5 and a draw the dotted line 5 a b, to cut the other side of the circumference of the dome at b ; from the points 6, 7, 8, 9, 10, 11, draw radial lines to b, to cut the axis of the dome at i, k, l, m, n, o ; also through the points 6, 7, 8, 9, 10, 11, draw the parallels 6 c, 7 d, 8 e, &c. then will each of these parallel lines be half the length of a chord line for each board ; then take c 6 from Fig. A, which transfer to No. 1, from c to 6 and 6 ; make the height c i, at No. 1, equal to c i, at Fig A ; and draw the chords i 6 and i 6 ; then upon either point 6, as a centre with any radius, describe an arch of a circle 0 1 2 ; divide it into two equal parts at 1, and through the points 6 and 1 draw 6 q ; bisect i 6, in p ; draw p q perpendicular ; then i 6 is the length, and p q the height of the board G, which may be described as in Fig. 4, Plate V, of the Geometry. The reader must observe, that the length of the board is of no consequence so as the true sweep is got, which is all that is required. Proceed in the same manner with No. 2, by taking d 7 from Fig. A, and place it at No. 2, on each side of d at 7 and 7, and take d k, from Fig. A, and make d k at No. 2, equal to it ; draw the chords k 7 and k 7, and bisect k 7 at n ; draw n a perpendicular ; upon the other extremity at 7, as a centre, describe an arch 0 1 2, and bisect it at 1, and through the points 7 and 1 draw the line 7 a, to cut the perpendicular *n a* at *a ;* but if the distance *k* 7 is too long for the length of a board, bisect the arch 0 1 at *b ;* through 7 and *b* draw 7 *t,* and draw the little chord *a* 7, and bisect it at *t ;* draw *t u* perpendicular to intersect 7 4 at *u ;* and with the chord 7 *a* and the height *t u* describe the segment H.

In the same manner may the next board *I* be found, and by this means you may bring the sweep of your board into the smallest compass, without having any recourse to the centre.

SUPPOSE IT WERE REQUIRED TO DRAW A TANGENT FROM 8 AT NO. 3, WITHOUT HAVING RECOURSE TO THE CENTRE.

Bisect the arch 8 *ı* 8 at *l ;* on 8 as a centre, with a radius 8 *l,* describe an arch *e l t,* make *l t* equal to *l e ;* draw the tangent *t* 8.

GIVEN THREE POINTS IN THE CIRCUMFERENCE OF A CIRCLE, TO FIND ANY NUMBER OF EQUIDISTANT POINTS BEYOND THOSE THAT WILL BE IN THE SAME CIRCUMFERENCE.

Fig. K. Suppose the three points *a, b, c,* to be given ; to one of the extreme points *a* join the other two points *b* and *c* by the lines *a b* and *a c ;* with the radius *a b,* and the centre *a,* describe the arch of a circle *b* 1 2 3 ; then take *b* 1, and set it from 1 to 2, and from 2 to 3 ; through the points 2 and 3, draw *a d* and *a e ;* then take *b c,* put the foot of your compass in *c,* and with the other foot cross the line *a d* at *d ;* with the same extent put the foot of your compass in *d,* and with the other foot cross the line *a e* at *e ;* in the same manner you may proceed for any number of points whatever.

PL. 19.

Fig's. 1 and 2, Elevation and Plan of a niche, standing in a wall, with its ribs, for practice, which are obtained thus : draw the given rib A, a quadrant of a true circle, which is equal to the height of the niche in the curve at 6, 8, in Fig. 1, and equal to the depth 6, 7, on the plan Fig. 2.   B and C, jack-ribs, which are both the quadrant of an ellipsis, and have for their plans B C in Fig. 2 ; the two latter is described with a trammel, as represented in C.   The bevel 1, 2, and 4, 5, in B and C is the same as 1, 2, and 4, 5, in B C, Fig. 2.

NOTE.—The two last ribs will serve as patterns for the two on the opposite side, and save the expense of making expressly for that purpose.   For taking distances, and moving the trammel, refer to Fig. 5, Plate XXI.   This, however, is guided by pins moving in grooves, which is represented by the large lines in the cross at the rib C.

HIP-ROOFING, FIG. 3.

To obtain the height, length, and backing of the hip-rafter H, *a b f e* being a plan of the right angled ends, let *e c f* be the seat of the common principal rafters, *c d* the height of the roof, and *e d* and *d f* will be the length of the common rafters ; raise *g c* equal to *c d*, the given height, perpendicular from *a c*, the seat of the hip-rafter, draw *a g*, and the line *a* H *g* will be the length of the hip-rafter. To obtain the backing, draw *x z y* at right angles to *a c*, the seat of the hip, place one point of the compass on *z* and describe a circle to touch the rafter, draw *w x y* to intersect the circle and seat *a c* at *w*, and *x w y* will be the plans or backing of the rafter, D will be the shape, and one end of the rafter required.

TO GET THE CUTS OF THE PURLIN TO THE HIP-RAFTER, AND LIKEWISE THE JACK-RAFTERS TO THE HIP-RAFTERS.

Place the purlin I, at any place in the principal rafter, and at right angles to it, take any distance in the points of the compass, and from the point *h* describe the circle *p s r q*, drop *h s* square from the rafter at the upper side of the plate, drop *p n, s m, h i, r k*, and *q l*, parallel to the wall-plate *f b*, draw *k b* at right angles* to *r k*, and *q l*, draw *i l*, and F will be the side bevel to cut that part *h* 3 and 1 2 of the purlin to fit to the rafter ; draw *m n* to intersect the seat at *m*, draw *n i*, and the angle round G will be the down bevel to cut the sides *h i* and 2 3 of the purlin; and when thus applied to the end of the purlin, and cut accordingly, it will make a perfect joint to the hip-rafter ; turn *a* at the end of F down to the dotted line *z*, and *z i l* will be the side bevel for the jack-rafter to the hip. The bevel A will be the down bevel for the same or jack-rafters.

All that is necessary to say in relation to the opposite end of this plan is, that it is of a parallelogram form, and terminated at its extremities by two obtuse, and two acute angles, which consequently require the lines *g l, r k, h i, s m, p n, l, k*, and *n m*, parallel to the side walls *b f*, and *b j a*, in place of at right angles as in the square end. The irregular end has the same letters, and is performed by the same process, but will require it on both rafters, and on both sides of them.

TO DESCRIBE A SEGMENT OF A CIRCLE, FIG. 4, AT TWICE UPON TRUE PRINCIPLES BY A FLAT TRIANGLE.

Let the extent of the segment be *a b*, and its height *c d*; let *a d* of the triangle be a hypothenuse line to one half the segment, *a e* a parallel line to *c b*; place a pin at *a d* for the triangle to slide against, place a lead pencil at *d*, then move the triangle from *d* down to *a*, and one half the segment will be described ; and the same process on the other half will complete the segment.

TO DESCRIBE A SEGMENT WITH THREE STRIPS TO ANY LENGTH AND HEIGHT.

Make two rods *e d*, and *d f*, to form an angle *e d f*, so that each may be equal to *a d* and *d b* ; let *c d* be the height—place pins at *a b*, the extremities—place a pencil

---

* It will only answer at right angles when the plan is square, which is proved at the upper end of the plan, which are made parallel to the wall-plates.

at *d*, then move *d* round each way from *a* to *b*, and the segment will be complete. A segment of this description may be drawn to a great extent with rods, by describing it at twice, as in Fig. 4.

TO DESCRIBE AN OCTAGON, AND RAISE AN ELEVATION FROM IT, AS FIG'S. 7 AND 8.

Draw a geometrical square, as at *a b c d;* place one point of the compass on *a*, extend the other point to the centre *e*—let *a* stand, and describe a quadrant of a circle ; proceed thus at each corner, and the plan of the octagon will be at *f f f f*, &c. This method of raising the elevation will be understood by only noticing that the dotted lines are raised from the windows *g g g*, and angles *f f f f*, to the same in Fig. 6.

FIG. 8, TO FIND THE CENTRE OF A CIRCLE, WHOSE CENTRE HAS BEEN LOST.

Let *a b* be the curve ; take any distance, *c d*, and at any place on the curve *a b*, in the compass, and describe the circles *c d e, c d e*, and their intersections *f f* will be direct to the centre, and at the intersection of the two radiating lines at *g*, will be the centre required ; and may be proved by setting one point of the compass in *g*, and sweeping it round from *a* to *b*.

FIG. 9, TO FIND THE MITRE OF A MOULDING IN AN OBTUSE AND ACUTE ANGLE.

Let the plan or shape of the pannel be *a b c d*, draw the inner line of the moulding, which is of the same width all round ; draw *d f* to cross at the out and inside angles of the moulding, and *d f* will be the obtuse mitre ; and the same process at *a e* will make the acute mitre. The two bevels will be the cut for the templets or mouldings.

PL. 20.

NOTE.—As the term envelope, is not generally used by practical mechanics, it will be omitted in the explanation of these problems, and use the term stretchout of the soffit, as is now more generally in use.

PROBLEM 1, FIG. 1.

Let A B C D, be the plan of a wall in which a window or door is to be executed, and F the given circle of the window or door head, and L the circle of the head, (which is a semi-ellipsis, reversed to that of Fig's. 2 and 3,) on the convex side of the plane of the wall : then, in order to obtain the stretchout of the soffit J, to bend under F and L, draw the line A B and D C, parallel to the splay of the jambs, (which is A B and D C,) until they intersect at G ; then divide the given circle F, from A to D, into eight equal parts, or any other even numbers, and drop them perpendicular to the cord line A D, of the plan E, and from thence extend them until they all intersect at G ; then to produce the circle L, to correspond with the given circle F, draw the cord line L *a*, tangent to the convex line B C, of the plan E ; then take the heights 1 1, 2 2, 3 3, 4 4, &c. in F, the given circle of the window or door, and transfer them to the circle L, which will produce it when traced at those points. To produce the soffit to bend under the two circles F and L, precisely to cover the plan E, from A B to C D, (which is the base of the arch,) place one point of the compass on the letter G, and extend the other out to A; let G stand, and turn the point A round to D, across K; then take the distance 1 2 3 4, &c. to 8, on the curve of F, and transfer them to the curve line A D, across K, which will be the stretchout of the given circle; then take the distances 1 1 1—2 2 2—3 3 3—4 4 4, &c. across H and E, and transfer them to the same letters across I J; and then by turning round in 1 2 3 4 5 6 7 and 8, from A to D, and B to C, in J, the soffit J will be described as required, to make a perfect one to bend under F and L, and form under them two lines that will correspond with the two lines A D and B C, in the plan E.

NOTE.—This mould as it lays on the plate between the two lines that run from A to D and B to C, will answer for a pattern to cut the arch stone by, or for a veneering to the same surface; and may be obtained by another process, which is as follows :

Draw lines from 1 2 3 4, on the curve line A D, of the plan E, parallel to the cord line A D, of the plan, to intersect the splay of the jamb, which is the line A B G; then place one point of the compass on G, and extend the other point to 1, on the line A B G; let G stand and turn 1 round to 1, on the line A D, in which it will be observed to intersect the line A B, on 1 1 1 G. This one transfer explained is sufficient; for 2 3 4 is precisely the same in effect.

This last method is not as simple as the former; therefore it is not as expedient for practical use.

PROBLEM 2, FIG. 2,

Is also a circular head and a circular base, with its given curve on the convex side of the plan, and requiring a soffit, as in the above problem, which is described as follows :—

First, determine the splay of the jambs A B G and D C G; then draw the cord line *g h* of the given circle M, a tangent to the convex line B C, of the plan E, and transfer the distances 1 1, 2 2, 3 3, 4 4, &c. in M, to the same figures in E, the curve of the concave side of the arch; then trace round by 1 2 3 4, &c. to 8, and F will be semi-ellipsis; then to describe the width, length, and curve of the soffit J, take the distances 1 2 3 4, which is one half of the span of the given circle M, and place it between G and H, perpendicular to G B A, with their parts divided the same as they are on the cord line of M; then to determine the one half of the soffit J, which is to the centre line 4 4, H I, through K, take a compass and place one point on G, extend the other point 1, on the concave line A D, of the plan E; then take up the compass with G 1 between its points, and place the point G on 3, in the line G H; then take the distance A 1, on the circumference of the ellipsis F, and let the point in A stand and turn 1 round until it will meet the point 1 of the compass that is extended from 3 in the line G H, as above described; then the distance A 1, on the line A D, of the soffit J, will be that part of the stretchout of F, which is the head of the arch, and likewise determine the line 1, 1, 1, 3, from the line A D, of the soffit, to the line 6 4.   Then to obtain the point 2, on the line A D, of the soffit, take the distance G 2, on the line A D, of the plan E, and transfer it to the line 2, that extends from the line G H, to the line A D, of the soffit; minding particularly to have the distance 1 2, of the soffit, the same distance of 1 2, in the curve line of F, which will be the stretchout of that much of F, as above noticed at A 1; and by proceeding thus to the centre line 4 4, H I, one half of the line A D, the stretchout of the soffit will be obtained; and for the other half, take the lines and distances of the half already obtained, and transfer them to the lines 5 5 5 1, &c.   But before the transfer can be made, the line H 1 2 3 4, out to N must be determined, which is done thus : Take a compass and place one point on H between 1 1, and extend the other point to G ; let H stand, and turn G round to N, which will form the circle G I N ; then take the compass and place the two points on G and I, and let I stand, and move round until it meets the circle G I N, at N, and N will be the point required for the line H N, which is the same distance of H G.   The distances 1 1, 2 2, and 3 3, are transferred by turning 3 over to 3, &c.   As the explanations thus far only show the stretchout A D, of the soffit, the width is yet required, which is obtained thus :

Take the distances 1 1 1, across the plan E, and transfer them to the same figures in the soffit J, and so on with 2 2 2, 3 3 3, &c. from E to J, and the soffit required to bend under the arch directly over and parallel to the plan E, will be produced at J. It will be observed, that if a window should be executed in a wall that has one of the sides straight and the other circular, as at A D, and *g h*, in E, the same lines A D, and *g h*, in J, will cover or envelope the same.   But if the walls are both curved, as in A D, and B C, in E, the plan, the same letters in J will serve them.

PROBLEM 3, FIG. 3,

Is a circular head with splayed jambs standing in a straight wall, and has the same figures, letters, and explanations as that of Fig. 2 ; therefore the student will refer to Fig. 2 for its explanations.

AN ELLIPTICAL DOME, WITH ITS TIMBERS AND COVERING.

Fig. 1, Is the plan of an elliptical dome, which has for its given height at the transverse line B F, a semi-circle, and for its larger span D F, at right angles to F B, a semi-ellipsis, the height of which is obtained thus : Draw Fig. 7, the given circle rafter or rib of the dome at F, in Fig. 7, directly over the wall-plate F, in the plan Fig. 4, to join on the plate T of the sky-light, which causes the dome to fall a trifle under *s*, (T is an elevation of the Plate C on the plan Fig. 4,) draw the line from *t* in the curb Plate T out to *r* parallel to the base of Fig. 7, then place the points of the compass on *g* and *r*, let *g* stand, turn *r* round to *u*, and *u g* will be the height of the elliptical ribs in Fig. 5, next determine the location of the purlin at C in F, Fig. 7, and transfer it to Fig. 5 in the same manner as at *g r u*, and the location will be determined at G in Fig. 5.   To determine the solid and shape of the purlin plate A, in Fig. 4, as at

C C in Fig's. 5 and 7, draw *o o* through the centre of the plate A in Fig. 7, through C, then draw a line from *o* on the outer side of the rib and in the middle of the plate, to intersect it at the underside of the rib and plate; for the upper side, draw from *o*, the middle of the plate, at the under side of the rib to intersect its uppermost side at 2, and the solid and shape will be contained between the letters *o* 2 and *o* 2; and to produce the shape at the elliptical rib in Fig. 5, transfer the letters 2 *o* 2, round to the same letters at C, in Fig. 5, and where they intersect the upper and lower sides of the rib, will be the corners, form and solid of C, at that place. Here it will be seen it is not in square angles, as at C, in Fig. 7, which is caused by the ribs being of different circles. Next is to work the plate into its proper shape as at C C, in Fig's. 5 and 7: drop lines from *b c* in Fig. 7, down to *b c* at X in A, the plate at Fig. 4, which determines the plate A at X, then take the distance *b* 2 at C, Fig. 4, and transfer it to *b* 1 at X in A, at Fig. 4, which will determine the upper outside angle at X, when worked—and for the under angle, take the distance *a* 2 at C and apply it to *b* 2 at X, for the two middle angles *o o*, set a guage to the middle of the plate, when in form of *a b c d*. To obtain the angles at D in the Plate A, Fig. 4, noticing that the plate is wider at D than at X, (which is produced by the plan being of an elliptical figure,) drop lines from *b c* at C, Fig. 5, to D, which will determine the width of the plate at D; and for the upper angle on the plate, take the distance *b* 2 at C, and transfer it down to *b* 2 at D, which will produce the upper angle; and for the lower angle, take the distance *a* 2 at C, and transfer it to 2 *a* at D, in Fig. 4, the upper and lower angles will be at 2, and *a* at D, Fig. 4. As the angles of an elliptical plate cannot be described by a guage, as one could of a true circle, it will be understood that they must be struck with a trammel.

NOTE.—The plate A, in Fig. 4, in the first operation, is worked out square, as *a b c d* at C C in Fig's. 5 and 7, and then if worked off as above described, will form the solid and angles precisely as *o* 2, *o* 2. E G in Fig. 4, is a seat of an intermediate rib.

It may be useful to observe, that this method will work the bar of a sash, if required, in a sky-light.

TO OBTAIN THE COVERING FOR ONE FOURTH PART, WHICH WILL SERVE THE OTHER THREE PARTS.

First: Draw the given rib at Fig. 8, which is described at the letters A B 6; divide the curve of the rib from B to 6 into any number of equal parts, say six; and drop ordinate lines from thence perpendicular to the base line A B; take the base line A B, and transfer it to the seat line B 1 2 3 4 5 6 A, in Fig. 4; then draw the line B C, the base of Fig. 9, perpendicular to the seat A B, and transfer 1 2 3 4 5, to the seats C A, E A, and F A, parallel to B C, C D E, and E F, which will determine the seats of all the same figures in Fig's. 9, 10, and 11, when bent over the domes in their practical forms, and are obtained thus:

Take the distances 1 2 3 4 5 6, on the curve line B 6, of Fig. 8, and transfer them to the same letters in the perpendicular line of Fig. 9; then draw the lines 1 2 3 4 5, in

Fig. 9, parallel to the base line B C ; then raise lines from 1 2 3 4 5, on the seat line C A, in Fig. 4, to intersect 1 2 3 4 5, on the curve line C 6, in Fig. 9 ; then Fig. 9 will be the covering for that part on the plan Fig. 4, between the letters A B C, and also the stretchout of the same.   No further explanation will be required for Fig's. 10 and 11, as they have the same figures, and are produced by the same process as that of Fig. 9, except to describe the ribs which are at Fig. 8, and are as follows :

The curve C 6, next to B 6, in Fig. 8, is the seat of an intermediate rib, over C A, the plan in Fig. 4 ; and the line C 6, of Fig. 10, is the stretchout of the same ; D 6, in Fig. 8, is the intermediate rib E, in Fig. 5 ; of which D A and C E, in Fig. 4, is the seat.   E 6; in Fig. 8, is the rib that passes over E A, in the plan Fig. 4, of which the lines E 6, in Fig's. 10 and 11 are the stretchout, and will bend and joint over the same in practice.   F 6, in Fig. 8, is the rib D, in Fig's. 5 and 7 : and F A, or A D D D is the seat of it.

PL. 21.

DRAWINGS FOR RAKING MOULDS—RULES FOR CUTTING THEIR JOINTS, AND COVERINGS FOR DOMES.

This plate exhibits a drawing for a raking moulding, to mitre with a horizontal moulding, (for instance, the cymatium or crown moulding of an eave cornice ;) and likewise one of the same nature to mitre round a modillion, mutule, or any thing of the like nature suspended to the inclined cornice of a pediment, or any square body like a pedestal, where it may be necessary to mitre a moulding round it in an oblique direction ; a rule for making a templet, or mitre-box, for cutting the different joints to inclined mouldings, and likewise a method of obtaining the ribs and coverings to oblong, square, and oblong polygonal domes.

The above method of cutting the mitres of a moulding round a modillion or mutule, (although I believe it has not heretofore been explained,) is a subject of importance to every executor ; for in all pediments, even where the modillion is omitted, the same rule is required to cut the mitre of the inclined moulding at the lower end, which joins to the horizontal one, that is required on the lower side of a modillion.   I have considered it a problem of the utmost use, and consequently have made it a part of this plate, as will be seen in the following references and explanations.

REFERENCES TO THE FIGURES.

Fig. 1, a raking or inclined moulding, mitring to a level one.

Fig. 2, a moulding mitred round a modillion, mutule, or any square body, in an oblique direction.

Fig. 3, a templet or mitre-box, to show and cut the mitres of Fig. 2.

Fig. 4, a section of Fig. 3, with the moulding applied in order to cut the mitre.

Fig. 5, a section or end of Fig. 6, with the mouldings A C, in Fig. 2, applied for sawing.

Fig. 6, a templet or mitre-box, stretched out at A C, in Fig's. 5 and 2.

Fig. 7, an oblong polygonal dome, with its covering attached to it.

Fig. 8, the ribs for Fig. 7, as will be explained hereafter.

Fig. 9, an oblong square dome, with its ribs and coverings.

To draw a raking moulding to mitre with a level one, as in Fig. 1, draw the horizontal mould 1 5 6 3 2, as at A; then draw the horizontal ordinate lines 1, 10 10, 9 9, 8 8, 7 7, 5, 4, 6, and 2, 3, which will represent all the extreme points necessary for transferring and drawing B C; then draw the lines 1 10 9 8 7 4 6 3, according to the rake or inclination of the pediment, up through the moulds B C; then take a divider and apply the two points to 10 10, in A, and transfer it to the figures in B and C, and so on until 2 3, in A, is transferred up to B C, which will give all the same points according to their respective situations that there are in A, the horizontal and given mould; hence it will readily be seen that B is the size and shape of the raking mould required to mitre on to A, the given mould. C shows the shape of B at the joint of the two inclined mouldings, which is not important in practical drawings.

In the ovalo which is crowned by a projecting square, there will be a quirk produced by the relief of the ovalo under the square, which will be seen at 4 6, in A, and is also horizontal; but in B, the raking mould, it will be seen at 4 6 to be beveled, and is evidently necessary to be so, to mitre with 4 6 in A, the given mould.

NOTE.—The same mitre that is explained in Fig. 3 to cut C in Fig. 2, will also cut A in Fig. 1.

TO DRAW FIG. 2.

Let B be the given moulding that passes up the pediment, and C A, those that return from the front to the rear of the modillion, and mitres with the one that passes in the front, and the rear piece that extends from one modillion to the other, which are both the same. B being the given moulding, it will be only necessary to say that the distances *e e, e e, e e, &c.* in B, are transferred to the same letters in C A, in the same manner the distances 10, 10, &c. are to B C, in Fig. 1; and that the line 6 *a*, in B, is drawn perpendicular or square to the rake line *f f*, which is according to the pediment; and that the line *b a*, in A, and *c d*, in C, are drawn perpendicular to a horizontal line.

TO WORK THE MOULD C, TO FIT THE ANGLE PRODUCED WITH THE MODILLION AND UNDER SIDE OF THE CORONA OR FACIA BETWEEN THE MODILLION AND CYMATIUM OR CROWN MOULDING OF THE PEDIMENT.

First: It will be observed that the angle is an acute one, as at *d;* consequently the piece out of which the moulding C is to be worked, will be contained between the letters *d c f a;* and after the piece is thus worked, the executor will work his moulding precisely according to the curve of *b e e e e e a*, and C will be precisely the moulding required to mitre with the given moulding B.

TO WORK THE UPPER MOULDING A, TO MITRE WITH B, THE GIVEN MOULDING.

In this it will be observed that the angle a, is an obtuse angle, directly reverse to that of d, in C, but is obtained by the same process ; and the next thing that necessarily follows in practice, is the cutting of the joints, which is as it follows after the references to the letters A B C, in Fig. 3.

REFERENCES TO A B C, IN FIG. 3, A TEMPLET OR MITRE BOX.

A, Is the bottom of the templet, the same as A in the section at Fig. 4.

B, Is the side of the templet turned down.

C, Is the upper edge of the side B, when turned up in the form of Fig. 4, the same as C.

TO OBTAIN THE CUT OF THE MITRE OF THE LOWER AND UPPER END OF THE GIVEN MOULDING B.

First : lay down the projection of B, the given mould in Fig. 2, on the bottom of the templet at A, in Fig. 3, which is $g\,k$, and $h\,k$; then take the distances $c\,f$, and $b\,f$, at the upper and lower end of B, in Fig. 2, and apply them to $g\,l$ and $h\,l$, on the line between A B, in Fig. 3, which is their projections in their inclined positions ; then extend the dotted lines $l\,i$ and $j\,i$, out to the dotted lines $i\,k$ and $k\,i$, which is the projection of the given mould B, Fig. 2, as will readily be seen already applied at B, in the templet Fig. 4 ; then draw the lines $g\,i$ and $h\,i$, which will be the mitre of their respective inclinations, agreeable to the pediment.

As this is not a square mitre or angle of forty-five degrees as it lays on this plate horizontally, it is evident that the plum-cut will not be so to the bottom A, of the templet, as will be seen at the cuts $b\,h$ and $c\,h$, on the side B of the templet, which may be obtained as follows.

First : It must be understood that the cuts $b\,g$ and $c\,h$, in B, Fig. 3, is the same as $b\,g$ and $c\,h$, in Fig. 2 ; and also that they are the same distances, which will consequently show, that when the templet Fig. 3 is in a parallel line with $f\,f$, in Fig. 2, that the cuts $b\,g$ and $c\,h$, in Fig. 3, will also be parallel to the same letters and sides of the modillions in Fig. 2 ; hence it will be understood that if B, in Fig. 3, is turned up edgeways, (speaking after the manner of mechanics,) it will form a templet, of which Fig. 4 will be a section or end ; showing at the same time the given moulding B, in Fig. 2, applied to the templet in its proper form for sawing its joints. When the side B, is turned up as above described, it will form on its top the letter C, which is the same as C, in the section Fig. 4 ; then the line $f\,f$, in C, will be parallel to $g\,i$, in A, the bottom; $a\,a$, will also be parallel to $h\,i$, in A, the bottom : therefore it will be understood that if the given moulding B, in Fig. 2, is applied in the templet, as at B, in Fig. 4, and cut or sawed according to the lines $g\,i$ and $h\,i$ in Fig. 3, it will be in a proper shape for jointing to the moulds C and A, in Fig. 2, which are cut as described in the templet Fig. 6. It will likewise be understood that the same templet or mitre box will cut the moulding between the modillions; for it is precisely the same in its cuts.

TO DRAW AND CUT THE MITRES IN FIG. 6.

First: Draw the section or end of the templet Fig. 5, which is drawn precisely the shape of the modillion Fig. 2 in its elevation, and also right under it, in order to make it easily understood, together with the mouldings C and A, in Fig. 2, mechanically applied for cutting or sawing, which is transferred to the bottom A, in Fig. 6, by placing one point of the compass in b, and extending the other point to a, on the dotted line, which is the bottom of the templet or box, the same as $a\,a$, in Fig. 5, in its proper position; and then the point a, is moved round to c, in Fig. 6, which will produce the bottom A in Fig. 6 on a horizontal plane; and consequently it will be observed that $b\,c$ in A, Fig. 6, is the same as $a\,a$ in B, Fig. 5, which is the bottom, and $b\,e$ in B, Fig. 6, when turned up in due form, will form the side $a\,d$ in D, Fig. 5, and then as a matter of course, it will be observed, that C, in Fig. 6, will be the top of B in Fig. 6, and D in Fig. 5, and $j\,j\,j\,j$ in C, Fig. 6, will be the cuts across the side, and bottom A at $h\,h\,h\,h$; therefore the lines $h\,i,h\,i$, will be the side cuts, and at tne same time it will be seen that $e\,f$ in C, Fig. 6, will be the same as $d\,e$ in D, Fig. 5. Now according to the horizontal plane, Fig. 6, it will appear to cut mitres to form an angle of 45 degrees when put together on a horizontal plane, but when Fig. 6 is put together in the form of Fig. 5, it will be observed to cut the mouldings A A in Fig. 5, which is the same as A C in Fig. 2, to mitre mechanically to B the given mould in Fig. 2, as above explained.

TO DRAW FIGS. 5 AND 6 TEMPLETS OR MITRE-BOX, TO CUT THE MOULDINGS A AND C IN FIG. 2.

First draw Fig. 5, a section or end of the mitre-box, Fig. 6, in the same bevel with the modillion, Fig. 2, in order to produce the proper shape and bevels of the sides and bottom of the box, Fig. 6, to correspond with the rake and plumb lines in the modillion Fig. 2. B in Fig. 5, is the bottom of Fig. 6 at A, and is the same distance from a to a that it is from b to a, on the dotted lines starting at b from B in Fig. 6, which is transferred to the bottom A in Fig. 6, by setting one point of the compass on b, Fig. 6, and extending the other point down in a, then let the point on b stand, and move the point a round to c in Fig. 6, which shows the inclined bottom B of Fig. 5 transferred to Fig. 6, which lays here in a horizontal position, but will have the same surface, and be the same shape or bevel of B, in Fig. 5. B B in Fig. 6, are the sides of the box, and are of the same shape and size of D D in Fig. 5. C C in Fig. 6 is the upper edge of B B, when turned up in the form of D D in Fig. 5, and the distances $d\,g$ and $e\,f$, in $c\,c$, Fig. 6, is the same as $g\,c$, and $d\,e$ in D D, Fig. 5; $h\,h$—$h\,h$ across A, in Fig. 6, represents the mitres the same as in a common box; $h\,j$, &c. in B represents the side cuts; $j\,j$, &c. in $c\,c$ represents the cross cuts, which when turned up in the form of D D in Fig. 5, will correspond with $h\,h$, &c. in A, Fig. 6, which will complete the templet required to cut the mouldings A C in Fig. 2, and likewise applied at A C in the section of the box at Fig. 5.

Note.—The same rule that will cut the joint of the moulding C in Fig. 2, will cut the joint of A in Fig. 1. This rule I have not seen explained in the publications that have fell in my way, although it may be understood by many.

FIG. 7, TO OBTAIN THE COVERING FOR A POLYGONAL DOME.

The plan of the polygon is represented at the letters *n o p r q s*, and the covering at A B C, and obtained as follows :

Take the base line 0 4 in F, at Fig. 7, and transfer it to 0 4 in Fig. 8, then describe the circle 4 0, which will be a true circle, and one half of the given rib, then divide the back, or circumference of Fig. 8, from 0 to 4 into any number of equal parts, say 4, then drop ordinate lines from 1, 2, 3, 4, perpendicular to 1, 2, 3, 4, on the base line —then transfer the distance 0 1—1 2—2 3—3 4 to the same and corresponding figures on the base line at Fig. 7, then describe the dotted lines 1, 1, 1,—2, 2, 2,—3, 3, 3, at right angles across the base in F, Fig. 7, to intersect 1, 2, 3, in the same line, which is directly under the same figures on the back of the given rib at Fig. 8.

To describe the covering A of the part contained in the letter F, Fig. 7, take the distances 0, 1, 2, 3, 4, on the back of the given rib at Fig. 8, which is the stretchout of it, and transfer them to 0, 1, 2, 3, 4, in A, the covering, then draw the lines 1, 1, 1, —2, 2, 2,—3, 3, 3, in A, across the stretchout line of the back, and at right angles to it, then raise the lines 1 1—2 2—3 3 from the angular lines, or seat of the angular ribs, each side of F to intersect 1 1—2 2—3 3 at each extremity of A, the covering, then describe the lines *u* 4 and *p* 4 at the two extremities of A to intersect at the letters 1, 2, 3, 4, and the coverings for that part of the dome will be complete. Therefore the executor will understand, that in covering this dome, the boards, copper, or any other material, may be cut by the mould or pattern A, any width, the same as on any straight surface. The same process will produce B and C. The angle rib for E and B in Fig. 7, is represented at *p* 4 in Fig. 8, and for D C, Fig. 7, at *q* 4 and *r* 4, Fig. 8; *r* 4 is the angle rib, and *q* 4, the body on the same figures in D. From the above explanations, it will be understood that the coverings A B C will bend over their respective planes F E D, and also will answer for the opposite sides of the polygon.

Fig. 9 is a right-angled oblong dome, and the covering is obtained precisely by the same process, and is figured with the same figures: consequently it will not require any further explanation than to explain the different parts: A is half of the given rib, and is described by a true circle ; B is a body rib, and got by transferring the distances 1 1—2 2, &c. from A to the same figures in B, or otherwise with a trammel, by taking the distances 4 4, and 4 0, in the trammel as described in Plate XXI, at Fig. 5; C is an angle or hip rib, got by the same process. It will be seen that the perpendicular or vertical lines 4 4, of A B C, are all of an equal height, and the base lines 4 4—4 0—4 0, of A B C, are all of different spans, they will, notwithstanding, range when mechanically reared over their respective seats or bases. For the jack ribs, the student will refer to the letters E and H, in Plate XXV, where the cutting and fitting of the jack ribs are clearly explained. Z is the covering over one quarter of the dome at B, and the line 0 4 in Z, is equal to the stretchout of 0 4, the curve or back of the rib B; X is the covering over the side C, and the line 0 4 in X is the stretchout of the curve or back of the given rib A, consequently the line 0 4 in X will bind over the back of the given rib A in execution. The boarding for this dome may be cut as directed in Fig. 7.

PL. 22.

Explains the construction and method of executing a series of groin arches, resting upon an inclined plane, the widest opening, or body range having its descent in the direction of the inclination of the plane; the transverse ranges are therefore level. The ribs in both directions are set in vertical planes. The ribs in the body-range are a semi-ellipsis; those of the sides will also be semi-ellipses, but will not have their axes in a vertical and horizontal position.

REFERENCES TO THE FIGURES.

Fig. 1, Is the plan.

Fig. 2, Elevation of the transverse openings with their centres, and likewise a section of each body-rib at 1 2 3 4, &c.

Fig. 3, Section of the body-range at right angles, to the plane of its inclination.

Fig. 4, Moulds for describing the angles, at the intersection of the body-range and transverse ribs.

Fig. 5, Is an elevation of the centre in the body-range, and likewise a section of the transverse ribs, (see the Fig's. 1 2 3 4, &c.) which are the sections.

TO DRAW AND CONNECT THE ANGLE AND JACK-RIBS.

First, draw the body-rib, Fig. 5, by the same method as that of Fig's. 5 and 9, in Plate XXV, then draw the dotted ordinate lines $f o$, &c. from Fig. 3 through Fig. 5, to intersect the lines A L and M B in the plan Fig. 1, which are the seats of the angle ribs; from thence draw the dotted lines out of the curve of the rib in Fig. 2, making the distance at each ordinate the same distance of the ordinates in Fig's. 3 and 5.

TO DRAW THE MOULD, FIG. 4.

Draw the ordinates from the surface of the transverse rib in Fig. 2, perpendicular to the inclination of the plane, then draw the line 1 2, then take the stretchout of $d t f$ in Fig. 3, or 5, and transfer it to $v w$ in Fig. 5, hence it will be understood that the line $v w$ wraps over one half of the body-range: now it is necessary to produce the angle on the boarding of the body-range; first, it will be understood that the body-range is covered entire with boards, as may be seen in Fig. 5, marked with Fig. 12: now, to produce the angles, take the moulds 4 and 5, in Fig. 5, and apply the letters $z q r y$ to the letters $z i k y$, at the pieces in Fig. 2, and bend them over the boarding of the body-range, and they will produce the angle required for the boarding of the transverse-range to join on the boarding of the body-range.

NOTE.—If any part of this inclined plane should not be clearly explained, I will refer the student to the horizontal plane in Plate XXIV, which is in every respect more practically explained, and is also precisely the same as this in every process, and no difference prevails only in their planes.

The above is a design of groin arches for brick or stone.   The two following are lathed and plastered groin arches.

REFERENCES TO THE FIGURES.

Fig. 6, Plan of the apertures and piers, (see the letters A B C D E F G H, the plan of the piers.)

Fig. 7, Elevation of the body-rib.

Fig. 8, Elevation of the transverse-rib, drawn to correspond with the body range.

Fig. 9, Elevation of the transverse-rib, drawn to show the practical application to the angle ribs in Fig. 11.

Fig. 10, An angle-rib, drawn agreeable to the inclination of the plane, to correspond with Fig's. 7 and 8.

Fig. 11, Geometrical plan of the hip or angle-ribs, with the body and transverse ribs mitred to them.

REFERENCES TO FIG. 12, AN UNDER PITCHED GROIN.

Fig. 12, Plan and elevation of an under pitched groin.

Fig. 13, Section of the body-range.

Fig. 14, Section of lunettes or under pitched vaults, mitring into a large vault, raising to a greater height.

Fig. 15, Section of the angle-rib.

EXPLANATION TO THE PLANS AND ELEVATIONS OF THE INCLINED PLANE.

First, locate the piers A B C D E F G H at their proper distances for the apertures, then the inclination of A B, then determine the body-rib, Fig. 7, which is a semi-ellipsis, divide the concave of Fig. 7, into any number of equal parts 1 2 3 4 k 5 6 7 8, then drop ordinate lines from thence perpendicular to the base line x x, then extend the same in dotted lines until they intersect the seat of the groin o p, raise the dotted lines p 2 3 4 v 5 6 7 8 from the seat of the groin perpendicular to the line, x x, until they meet their corresponding figures on the inclined line A B, and the concave of Fig. 8; hence it will be understood by the student that Fig. 8 is got by taking the distances 2 2, 3 3, &c. in Fig. 7, and transferring them to the corresponding figures in Fig. 8, which will produce a corresponding curve in Fig 8 to Fig. 7.   The curve will be traced bending a slip of wood to the Figures 1 2 3 4, &c.

TO DRAW THE ANGLE-RIB, FIG. 10.

Draw the ordinates p 2 3 4 v 5 6 7 8 perpendicular to the seat of the groin o p, across to the corresponding figures in the concave of the rib, Fig. 10, then take the height q r, in the inclining line AB, which is the height it raises passing over one opening and apply it to o s from the seat of the groin, then the curve is produced in the same manner as Fig. 8.

TO SHOW THE APPLICATION OF THE JACK-RIBS TO THE GROIN OR ANGLE-RIBS.

Fig. 14, Is a plan of the angle and jack-ribs. In Fig. 9, it will be seen that 1 2 is equal 1 2 in Fig. 14, and so on; 3 4, 5 6, 7 8, in Fig. 9, are equal to the same figures in Fig. 14—and consequently they will correspond with each other, and form a complete groin.

EXPLANATION TO FIG. 12, AN UNDER-PITCHED GROIN CEILING.

First it must be understood that f o g is the seat of the groin-ribs; A D and A D the seat of the body-ribs C B; and 1 2 3 4 5, &c. the seat of the beams of 1 2 3 4 5, &c. in the body-rib C B. The beams are straight, and lathed the same as straight or horizontal ceilings.

TO DRAW THE ANGLE-RIB, FIG. 15.

Extend the opening of the body-range out to A D, then draw a semi-circle at Fig. 13, equal to the dotted arch line C B under the beams; also draw the dotted lines o o, n m and h h, y z, equal to the lunettes or projection of the under-pitch opening, which is the distance of o i at Fig. 14; then describe the angle or seat of the groin or hip at g o f, then raise the line o 2 equal to n m in Fig. 13, and i h in Fig. 14, the height of the under-pitch, perpendicular to the angle o g, then transfer the ordinates p q, &c. as in the preceding examples, and the curve of Fig. 15 will be produced.

NOTE.—The lathing in this example is bent under the beams, which is not the case where the jack-ribs mitre or join on to the hip or groin rib, when at right angles to the sides or butments of the groin.

PL. 23.

Represents two windows or doors; the first standing in an oblique wall, and the latter in a circular wall.

Fig. 1, Plan and elevation of an oblique window or door; the elevation is composed of the circle G H B—the plan of the oblique parallel lines A B C D.

Fig. 2, Soffit, obtained by taking the distances from the lines G B, to the lines A B, and D C, in Fig. 1.

To obtain Fig. 2, draw the line B G F, at right angles to the sides or jamb lines B C, and A D. To produce the stretchout of the line or head G H B, in Fig. 1; place one foot of the compass on B, and extend the other out to G; let B stand, and move G round to I ; then draw I J, touching the circle at B, and H J will be one half of the stretchout of the circle G H B ; take H J in the compass, and step it twice from G out to F, which will be the stretchout of the soffit.   Place the compass to 1 2, in Fig. 1, and transfer it to 1 2, Fig. 2, and 2 3 to 2 3, 3 4 to 3 4, &c. ; then take 2 2, across the plan Fig. 1, and transfer it to 2 2, in Fig. 2, and thus through from A D to B C, and F E ; then trace round by the figures 2 2, 3 3, 4 4, &c. out to F E, and the surface contained between the lines D A, E F, will be the soffit required.   This soffit is equal in length to the circular head G H B, and will bend under it and be in range with the plan A B C D.

Fig. 3, is a circular head and circular base, with a soffit drawn at Fig. 4.   The process of drawing is precisely the same as Fig's. 1 and 2.   A B C D, is the plan and shape of the wall ; A D E F, is the construction and size of the soffit when stretched out.   This soffit, when practically applied and bent under the line A H B, will correspond precisely with the plan A B C D.

NOTE.—The figures 1 2 3 4 5 6 7, &c. on the lines A H B, in Fig's. 1 and 3, are the corresponding figures with the figures on G F, in Fig's. 2 and 4, and likewise in plans and soffits.

PL. 24.

Exhibits a plan of groin arches, designed for brick or stone materials, resting on twelve piers, which are represented by the letters A B C D, &c.

It is often the case, that in architectural studies, the student labours under disadvantages at the first examination, for want of references to the different parts engaged in the problems which he wishes to learn ; therefore I shall continue to give them in all intricate drawings.

REFERENCES TO THE DIFFERENT PARTS.

A B C D E, &c. plans of the piers.

Fig. 1, Elevation of the centring of the elliptical range, and likewise a sectional view of the semi-circled centres.

Fig. 2, Sections of the covering, or boarding to the elliptical range ; (see o o o o o, the ends of the boards.)

Fig. 3, Sections of the semi-circle range, and likewise the given height of the groin.

Fig. 4, Is a sectional view of the elliptical centring, and an elevation of the given centre.

Fig. 5, Is a mould or pattern for determining the groin, or angle of the two ranges.

Fig. 6, Is an elevation of the given rib, or centre, and likewise three jack-ribs.

Fig. 7, Mould or pattern for forming the angle or groin in connection with Fig. 5.

To erect a number of groin arches, the first thing necessary, is to determine the opening and height thereof.   For the height, in this example, I have taken a semi-circle for the summit, or given height : now as the given height is of a semi-circle, and much less span than that of Fig. 2, it follows that 2 must necessarily be of an ellipsis; to obtain this ellipsis, the student will refer to Plate XXV, and he will obtain the necessary particulars therein at Fig. 5.

In the execution of a brick or stone groin arch, it is necessary to erect an entire range of centres, either one way or the other. (In this, I have taken those of the greatest span, which is considered most practical.) It will be seen that one of these openings are covered with boards, and the other has only the plan of the centres, (see *m n o p q*, &c. the plans of the centres,) on which the elevation *l* under Fig. 1 stands The opening between the piers A B E D G H I and K, which is boarded over is also timbered the same as the opening between the opposite piers and letters, it being understood that the body ranges or openings are covered with boards or plank entire, from one end to the other. It is next necessary to cover the lesser openings, consequently it will be necessary to obtain the seat of the angle on the covering, to correspond with the angles on the plan at the letters *a b c d*, for which proceed thus: Divide Fig's. 2 and 3 into as many distances as there are boards or plank to cover the same, then drop dotted lines from each joint or board perpendicular to the lines *a b* and *c*, and from thence continue the same line to the diagonal line *a d c* and *a b d*, which has the same figures as those on the circular line at Fig's. 2 and 3, and are likewise the seat of the groin or angle.

To obtain the seat of the angle on the covering of the elliptical range, get the stretchout of Fig. 2, from *a* to *b*, and place it at any convenient place, say Fig. 5, (see the line *a b* in Fig. 5, which is the stretchout) then take the distance *e d* from the line *a b* from one pier to the other of the capital letters A and B, and set to *e d* in Fig. 5, 5 5, 9 9, &c. and transfer them to the corresponding letters in Fig. 5, and then strike a line through all of those points, and it will produce the necessary line for the seat of the angle on the covering. It will be proper to observe that those parts in the line *a b* Fig. 5, are just equal to the width of the boards in the circle at Fig. 2, for *a b* in 5 is the stretchout of 2

To apply Fig. 5 to the covering, first, it is understood that Fig. 2 is the covering: accordingly it will be proper to suppose Fig. 2 standing on the level *a b*, and also underboarding; hence it is evident that if the pattern at the letters *a c b d* are bent over the boarding at *a c b d*, and marked round accordingly, it will produce the seat of the angle required; to obtain the opposite, just reverse the pattern. I have also given Fig. 7 to bend over Fig. 3, which is obtained by the same process, and likewise applied in the same manner. This, however, is more essential to cut the ends of the boards to joint on to the body range, than for any other purpose. To cut the boards, it will be observed, that the distances marked in Fig. 7, are equal to the boarding in Fig. 3; therefore, if they are cut according to the circles *c d* and *a d*, they will make a perfect joint to the boarding of the body range.

Fig. 6 is an elevation of one of the semi-circled centres and their jack ribs, (see the sections at Fig. 1.) *f* at Fig. 6, is an elevation of *f* in Fig. 1. *g* and *h* in Fig. 6 are also elevations of *g* 6 in Fig. 1. It will be understood that *f g h* in the plan, are the seats of the jack ribs *f g h* in Fig. 6 ; and likewise, that *f g h* will set on the circled sides of the body range, consequently they will require beveling.   The bevel may be obtained by applying to the sections *f g h* in Fig. 1, where the bevel may be seen at the seat of each section.

REFERENCES TO THE SMALL LETTERS.

l, in Fig. 1 represents an elevation on the elliptical centre.
o o o, in *l*, represents the boarding.
m n o p, &c. represents the plans of the centres, (see *l*, elevation of centre.)
o o o o o, long side of the piers C F I, represents the boarding.
a b c e f g h i j k, plans.   The same letters in Fig. 1, and also in 6.
1 2 3 4 5, &c. by the side of the piers B E H, represents the plates.
NOTE.—It may be understood that *a b c d*, at Fig. 5 will answer the same purpose as *a* 8 *d* in Fig. 5, for they precisely fit each other.

PL. 25.

Is a plastered groin arch designed for an oblong ceiling, and represented at its angles by the letters A B C and D.   The angle or groin ribs in this example, are all connected at the centre of the ceiling ; consequently it may be termed an entire groin ceiling—whereas if any part of the horizon or centre was horizontal or level, it might be termed a groin ceiling with a horizontal centre, which is often the case, and affords room for ornamental centre flowers, (by some called centre pieces.)
    This design may be executed of one, or one and one quarter inch boards.
    NOTE.—It would not be unsafe, to execute a ceiling of this kind, of 1 1-4 inch plank, over a span of from 30 to 40 feet, if care should be taken in the execution to avoid splits, by nailing in improper places.
    In this example I have represented a plan of the ribs, with the bevels applied at their places over the ground which they are to stand to the elevation with the square applied, to show the manner of cutting the common ribs to join the angle ribs—plan of the ribs laid horizontally over the elevation, with the bevel applied, to show the method of joining them to the angle rib, and also the angle rib, and the method of drawing it with three strips of wood, in place of the trammel moving through a groove, which produces the same curve as that of the trammel, and indeed is the same principle, and always convenient if the grooved trammel should not be at hand.

TO DRAW THE RIBS TO AN OBLONG PLAN.

First, determine the height of the ceiling in the centre.   In this design, the groin rib at Fig. 2, is a semi-circle; consequently it raises one half of the conjugate diameter, (that is one half of the smallest span,) and thus the given rib being a semi-circle, the transverse and angle rib required, will be a semi-ellipsis, which may be drawn by two methods.   In this example I have given both; one by transferring lines from the given rib Fig. 2, capital F, to the other two ribs, capital F, Fig. 1 and Fig. 4, which is both tedious and incorrect in practice; the other is drawn by a trammel and two strips of wood, and represented at Fig. 5.

The groin rib being got, at Fig. 2, proceed to draw Fig. 1, the angle rib. First, divide the semi-circumference into any number of equal parts, say seven; then drop lines from 1 2 3, &c. perpendicular to the base line B D, to intersect 1 2 3, &c.; then let the same lines extend to the figures 1 2 3, &c. on the base of the angle rib, Fig. 1; draw 1 1, 2 2, 3 3, &c. at right angles to the base line B D; take the distance 1 1, in Fig. 2, and transfer it to 1 1, in Fig. 1, and so also 2 2, 3 3, &c. to the same figures in Fig. 1; and by tracing round by 1 2 3 4 5 6 7, one half of the angle rib will be produced: and to obtain the other half, proceed the same way. The angle rib being drawn direct from one angle of the ceiling to the other, (that is, on the middle and thick line between B and C;) it will be observed that the outer edges of the rib will not be in range with the body range, and will not be so convenient to nail the ends of the lath: therefore in order to make the groin perfect, it will be necessary to make the angle ribs to accord in shape with Fig's. 6, 7, and 8. It will also be observed, that the angled recess in Fig's. 6, 7, and 8, are not the same distance in from the two extreme points, which is produced by the plan of the groin's being of an oblong figure; whereas if square, (that is, the same size on all four of its sides,) it would be the same. It will be further observed, that it requires more on the side C, than on the side B, which is likewise caused by C being on the side, and B on the end.

TO PRODUCE THE INNER CIRCLE THAT JOINS ON THE SIDE AT C, AND END AT B.

First, draw the lesser or inner circle, under Fig. 2, the given rib; then take the shorter distances 2 2, 3 3, &c. in Fig. 2, and transfer them to the same figures in Fig. 1; trace round as above described for the outer circle, and the circle required to correspond with the angle and body, will be produced.

TO SHOW THE METHOD OF CUTTING THE BODY RIBS, TO JOINT WITH THE ANGLE RIBS.

First, determine the location of the ribs, say at E F G and H; then raise two perpendiculars from the letters j i, in G, to cross the rib Fig. 4, which, when raised up, will range directly over G; then draw the lines y p, parallel to the base line C D; now take the square and apply it to the Fig's. 8 9 10; then scribe across from 8 to 9, and the plumb-cut required will be produced. To get the cut at the joint, just slide the square out to x y, which will give the cuts required. Proceed the same way down at the square 11 12 13, for the rib H.

TO CUT THE JOINT, JOINING ON THE SIDE OF THE ANGLE RIB.

Take the bevel 14 15 16, and apply it to H, the plan of the rib, and join the blade 14 16, to the plan of the angle rib A D; then take the bevel and apply it to H, directly over the rib Fig. 4, which is the same length of the shortest rib, (see the letters a, b, c, d, e, f, in H A, which shows that if the shortest rib in Fig. 4 is raised perpendicular and set over the plan H, would be in its practical position, and also joint to the angle rib.) It must be observed that the stock of the bevel must lay on the line 11 q, which is parallel to the base, and by applying the stock thus, the blade will not lay flat on the under side, but will only touch at the lower and opposite corner, but at the same time when thus applied and cut accordingly, the joints will be perfect.

REFERENCES TO THE FIGURES.

A, B, C, D, plan of the groin.

Fig. 1, Elevation of the angle rib.

Fig. 2, Elevation of the given rib across the smallest span.

Fig. 3, One half of the angle rib in the shape when cut out of the board.

Fig. 4, One half of the transverse rib, or rib over the greatest span.

Fig. 5, An Elevation of the angle rib drawn by a trammel.

Fig's. 6, 7, 8, plan of the angle rib at its butments.

t, u, v, w, x, y, represent an elevation of the rib, Fig. 2, when cut out of the board, and likewise are the same at Fig. 4, in the transverse rib.

E F G H, ground plan of the ribs. It will be noticed that E F G H are placed over the elevation of the ribs, which is done for the purpose of conveying a proper understanding of them.

a, b, c, d, e, f, in G H, over the elevation, will correspond with the same G, H, in the plan.

14, 15, 16, bevel applied.

8, 9, 10, Square applied to the horizontal y, p.

11, 12, 13, Square applied to cut the joint of the short rib, to the angle rib.

TO DRAW FIG. 5 WITH A TRAMMEL.

First, draw the line C B, the base line of the angle rib Fig. 1, in the plan; then get the centre of C B, and raise a perpendicular therefrom equal to 7 7, the height of the ceiling at the given rib, Fig. 2 ; then take the height 7 7, and apply it to the trammel at 1, on the circle of the ellipsis, and 2, on the base line ; then the distance 1 2, on the trammel, will be just equal to 1 2, in the perpendicular lines at the centre ; then take the semi-transverse diameter of the line C B, which is from C to 2, and apply it to the trammel from 1 to 4, which is also placed on the perpendicular line 1 4 ; now suppose the trammel first located perpendicular, and 1 4 of the trammel would be equal to, and on 1 4 on the perpendicular line. The trammel or strip being thus placed, fix brad-awls in 2 and 4 in the trammel ; the black dots represent the awl, and the outer circle the handle to the awl, to secure the strips z z ; if for a large span, they may be screwed on, and if for a smaller span, brads or small nails will answer. To describe the circle from 1 at the centre in the horizon, round to C, at the base of the rib, suppose the trammel x, to be placed perpendicular on 1 4—apply a lead pencil to the hole at 1 ; then move the trammel x round from 1 to 2, minding at the same time to keep the brad-awls at 2 4, snug to the strips z z, and one half of the rib will be complete. For the other half, if made in two pieces, take the half already obtained, and use it for a pattern thereto ; but if required in one entire rib or piece, the two strips *z z*, should be reversed ; then move the perpendicular piece on the opposite side of the centre line, and the horizontal piece directly under Fig. 5 ; for to describe the ellipsis, proceed as in the above already drawn, and the circle C 1 B, will be produced.

DESCRIPTION OF THE INNER CIRCLE.

First, it will be observed that the circle *b* 1 *d*, is a trifle to the right of the centre, which is caused by the plan of groins being of an oblong square ; (see the plan of the rib from C to B ; and the greater difference will be understood to proceed at C, from its sitting on the longest side ; and at the opposite angle at B, from its sitting on the shortest side of the plan.) To make the thing easily understood, I have given a plan of the butments at Fig's. 6 7 and 8, represented by the letters *a b c*—which will show that this difference will be right—the reverse on the opposite side. This inner circle is drawn the same way as that of the outer, with no other alterations than to take half the distance *b d*, which is at 3, on the opposite side of the line from 2, and set it on 5 on the trammel, just above 4. Now proceed the same way to describe the ellipsis as above directed ; for the outer line thus far, produces one side of the angle rib.* For the opposite side, the one obtained may answer for a pattern.

NOTE.—The transverse is drawn the same as that of the angle rib, and is generally represented first, which is, however, a matter of no difference, for they are of the same height in the centre of the ceiling. Further —if the ribs are drawn and cut as herein described, and executed accordingly, it will produce a perfect plastered groin ceiling in every respect.

PL. 26.

As a roof constitutes one of the principal parts of an edifice, I have given three examples in this plate, on which I shall make a few observations.

First, in order to make a roof uniformly strong and light, it is necessary for the architect or builder, in making preparations for the execution, to lay aside all suppositions, and apply mechanical principles ; which is the only true system by which any thing of the like nature can be made any where near perfect, or even to answer the purpose for which it was designed. For it is often the case, that a roof built on a continued tie beam, has a greater number of pieces than is actually necessary, and therefore contains too much material ; for, generally, a roof executed on a continued tie beam, there is no very considerable strength required of any piece, except the tie beam itself ; and the strength required of that is length-ways, in order to counteract the pressure of the rafters which are annexed to it ; that is when there are no ceiling

---

* This angle rib is made of two plank or boards, as occasion may require, and when cut and put together as here represented, will form a complete angle rib. (See the Fig's. 6 7 8.) At the centre it will be square.

joists. And further, the strength of a principal rafter required is quite inconsiderable, when on the construction of the design represented by the letter A, in this plate; for it has two prominent resting places at the junction of *c* and *d*, and that together with the exertion of the rafters against their butments renders them very strong, although they may be quite small. And it may, by examination, be ascertained, that the braces *c c*, and *d d d d*, have but little to do, but to counteract the falling or sagging of the two sides of the roof; for it is evident that the falling of one will tend to raise the other: therefore all the strength required of the braces, or trusses, is sufficient to resist the weight that will proceed therefrom, and retain their straight line. Consequently, by a mechanical examination, and with a judicious arrangement of the timbers in a roof, the contractor may save the expense which might be very imprudently applied; and that, many times the walls of buildings are made quite thin, and consequently not very strong, and are not well calculated to bear up unnecessary weight.

In making preparations for the erection of a roof to receive a pointed or Gothic arch above the base of its rafters, requires the utmost skill in the architect or builder, in order to avoid settling in its inclined sides, and extension of the rafters at their bases.

I have therefore thought proper to give three designs on roofs in this Plate, hoping they may be more or less useful to workmen, in their practical pursuits. I do not claim the examples here described as my own designs, although I have not seen any, either drawn or executed, like the one represented by the letter B. I do not claim any thing in A, unless the application of the truss running directly parallel, and under the principal rafter, should be mine. I feel satisfied, however, that either of the two upper designs are sufficient to span ninety, or even one hundred feet, without segment, or extension at the base of the rafter, that would be perceptible to the eye.

A is a design of a roof with a continued tie beam, showing two designs at the eave, one to show the projection required, if finished with a projecting eave-cornice, and on the opposite to show the method of executing a copper, lead, or stone water gutter behind the parapet wall, (see *n* the gutter.) This design is also calculated for a cove ceiling, consequently the tie beam is not required as large as otherwise.

REFERENCES TO A.

b king post, 7 by 18 inches below the trusses, and the head or joggle, 6 by 22; *c c* trusses, 7 by 6; *d d d d* trusses, 7 by 6; *e* tie beam, 7 by 16; *f f* iron rods, 1 by 1; *g g* walls, 22 by 6; *h* wall to show the method of framing for a parapet wall; *i i* wall plates, 8 by 12; *j* strengthening piece, 7 by 12, to the tie beam, when executed for a parapet wall, which will be seen necessary directly under the feet of the rafters; *k k k k* purline plates, 6 by 10, which should extend across three spaces, and will consequently join on the fourth rafter, whereby they will or can break joints, and give the strength necessarily required to bind the principal rafters sufficiently strong. In order to retain the strength of the purline plates and rafters, I shall advise the executor not to cut his gain entire across the rafter, but only about 1 inch in each side, and leave the middle uncut, which will tend not to weaken the rafters; and at the same time, the purline being thus cut to fit the gain, it has the whole plate for the support of the jack or common rafters. An introduction of braces in the inclined sides of a roof, in my opinion, will answer their desired purposes, if made of considerable length, and applied at or near the wall-plate, better than if applied in any other situation. The method here recommended is, to connect the lower end of the braces to the wall-plate, directly at and against the tie beam at the foot of the rafter, and the upper end to the rafters in the usual method of applying braces. It will be understood that the braces lie under the jack rafters. The braces, according to my views, should be locked together. If a dome, or any thing of a similar kind should be applied, the roof will require the more strength.

l l Principal rafters, 6 by 18.

m Jack or common rafters, 3 by 7, and placed two feet from centre to centre.

n Eave gutter behind the parapet wall, of lead, copper, or stone.

O Scale for each design.

This design raises one fourth of its whole span. The iron rods *f f* might be dispensed with, and remain sufficiently stiff and strong.

REFERENCES TO B.

B is a design of a roof to accommodate a gothic ceiling, and consequently requires a peculiar sort of construction and distribution of its timbers. This example is drawn to a 70 feet span, but would, I have no doubt, retain itself with the utmost perfection on 90 feet span; and if executing myself, I would not hesitate on 100 with a small addition to the size of the timber.

c c Principal rafters, 7 by 20 inches.

& King-post, below the joggle, 10 by 22 inches.

King-post, at the joggle, 10 by 31.

d d Hammer, or lock beams, 4 by 18.

The hammer or lock beams are coupled, (that is, one on both sides of the rafters and-king post.) These beams are halved together at the king-post, and likewise let into the king-post 1 1-2 on each side, or whatever the post is thicker than the rafter: (in this the rafter is 7 inches, and the post 10.)

e Collar beam, 8 by 15.

This beam is made equal to the thickness of the rafter and two hammer or lock beams, in order to make the iron work in the centre all in one mass or body. The beam may be made in two pieces, which would not render it so difficult to put together: it also receives a strap directly over it at the principal rafter.

f f King-posts to *d e* and *k*, 4 by 8.

g g Trusses, or rather a collar beam broken, and let down to meet the trusses *h h*, which, at their intersections form a resting point for the principal rafters, 7 by 8.

i i i Purline plates, which are disposed of as in the above Plate, 6 by 10.

j Sort of wooden butment for the rafters and truss *h*.   This butment is one inch thicker than the rafter.   The iron strap is let in a half inch on each side, 8 by 20.

k k Trusses running alongside the principal rafter, 4 by 8.

l l Wall plates, 9 by 12.

m m Walls.

n n at the dotted lines, are iron straps over the angle of the butment.

o o Water-gutters behind the parapet walls.

p p Common, or jack rafters, 3 by 7.

This roof is elevated at its ridge or summit, the sixth and one-half of its whole span, it gives room in its interior for a vaulted ceiling, sixteen feet nine inches above its butments.

Note.—The dotted lines are designed to represent the covering.

REFERENCES TO C.

C exhibits the design of a roof that will answer for from 40 to 55 feet span, without any king-post; but has an iron rod of 1 inch by 1 1-2, which would not cost any more, and at the same time be attended with much less trouble in putting together and raising.   This design may be executed with the purlines framed into the principal rafters, and the common rafters framed into the purlines; or otherwise, may be framed like the two preceding examples, which is much the best method.

REFERENCES TO THE NAMES AND SIZE OF TIMBERS.

a Iron rod, 1 by 1 1-2.

b b Trusses, 7 by 7.

c Tie beam, 7 by 11.

d d Principal rafters, 7 by 11.

The elevation and inclination of this design is equal to, and drawn by a pediment pitch, as follows.

TO DRAW A PEDIMENT PITCH.

First, set one point of the compasses in the centre *o*, and extend the other point out to *p*, either way; then let the point in *o* stand, and move the point *p* round down to *q*; then let the point *q* stand, and extend the other point diagonally up to *p*; then move *p* round to *r*, perpendicular to the point *q*, and the summit of the pediment is produced as required; then draw the rafter lines *r p p*, and the inclination of the pediment will be complete.

PL. 27.

This Plate exhibits an elevation of a trussed partition—a plan and elevation of a trussed beam, and likewise a plan and section of the common beams bridged, acting in concert with the trussed beam.

REFERENCES TO THE FIGURES AND LETTERS.

Fig. 1, Plan of the floor beams.
Fig. 2, A section of Fig. 1.
Fig. 3, An elevation of the trussed beam and partition.

LETTERS IN FIG. 1.

a a a Straining bolts (see *a a a* in C, Fig. 3.)
b b Bolts to gripe the trussed beam.
C Plan of the trussed beam.
d d d Plan of the common beams.
e e e Plan of bridging cap to connect the strength of the common beams with the trussed beam C,
f f, &c. Trusses, sometimes called bridging, (see *f f, &c.* in Fig. 2.)
g g, &c. Wedges to key up the bridging cap *e e e.*
NOTE.—This bridging cap is a piece of 1 1-4 inch oak or yellow pine plank about 5 inches wide. The wedges when sufficiently drove, secure them by driving a nail in the thin end. The bridging cap and wedges should be well seasoned, clear of knots, and straight grained.

LETTERS IN FIG. 2.

C Section of the trussed beam (see the plan C in Fig. 1.)
d d d Section of the common beams.
e e e Bridging cap (see *e e e* in Fig. 1.)

LETTERS IN FIG. 3.

a a a Straining bolts (see *a a a* in C at Fig. 1.)
b b Griping bolts, (see *b b* in C in Fig. 1.)
C An elevation of the trussed beam, showing the straining bolts, trusses *d d,* and straining beam *g ;* and likewise the griping bolts *b b.*
d d Iron or wooden trusses—most proper of iron,
E Floor beam.
f f Trusses to support E.
g Straining beam of iron.
h h Trusses to counteract the falling in of the beam E.
i i Brace to counteract the extension of the trusses *h h.*

Trussed beams are frequently necessary in great spans to accommodate the bearing of two lengths of beams or joists, but more frequently to support partitions that may be necessary to erect over the ceiling of a large room in the story below it, and to support gallery fronts, &c. without columns, or any thing of the kind between the outer butments, in order to secure the ceiling from falling in and destroying the elegance of the room—and further, this sort of partition and flooring will retain for ages their horizontal and vertical lines—if their butments are made secure—and will thereby experience no change in the internal part of the edifice, which is a highly important consideration, particularly in good buildings.

REMARKS ON THE GENERAL BEARING OF FIG. 3.

First, It will be seen that the partition is connected by two horizontal beams, and two perpendicular posts.

2d, That the two trusses $f f$ have their bearing on the butments.

3d, That the beam E has two prominent resting places on the trusses $f f$, hence it is evident that if E tends to fall, $h h$ will counteract every possible exertion of that kind—and it is likewise evident, that $h h$ cannot extend their span; for, in the attempt, they will meet $i i$ which is prepared to counteract it. Thus it is evident, that the partition will support itself, and leave but little for the beam to do but support its own weight, &c.

The general bearing of Fig. 2, will be seen to be very nearly the same as a straight or common piece of beam—for, as they are connected by the bridging cap $e e e$, they cannot separate; therefore, it is reasonable, if the bridging pieces $f f f$, &c. are properly placed and secured, that one beam cannot go down without the whole act in concert. The bridgings are generally thrown in of about 1 1-2 by 3 or 4 inches, and secured at the top and bottom with one or two nails as may be found necessary by the executor.

The bridgings or trusses $f f f$, &c. may be placed adjoining each other, or a small distance apart as in Fig. 1, at the letters $f f f$, &c.

NOTE.—This partition is calculated to accommodate three doors—whereas, if other locations of doors should be necessary, it might require a different set of trusses, and these very differently arranged.

PL. 28.

This Plate is a practical drawing for the carriages of a geometrical stair, raising over six winding steps, explained in two different ways: the first, by framing bearers of plank into plank risers; the latter, by cutting bearers out of plank to support three steps, rising from the centre and middle riser to the last riser of the winders, in an oblique direction, (that is, the front and middle bearers)—the one adjoining the wall, passes under only two steps.

REFERENCES TO THE FIGURES.

Fig. 1, Plan of the stairs, and framing to support the steps and risers over the circular or winders.

Fig. 2, Elevation of a part of the front string, in the straight part joining unto the winders: likewise the risers, brackets thrown in the angles of the bearers and risers, and the screw (a bedstead screw) to connect the straight string to the winders.

Fig. 3, An elevation of the middle carriage or horse, for three steps.

Fig. 4, Plan of the carriage or horse, for two steps.

Fig 5, Plan of the middle horse.

EXPLANATION TO THE LETTERS.

a a a a Carriages.

b b Front string.

e e e e e Bearers, framed into *c c, &c.* (see the dotted tenons on *c c,* &c. in Fig. 2.)

c c c Plank risers for the carriage way, (place *c c c* above *e e e*.)

d d d d d Common risers.

f f f f f f Staves for the front string, front worked to the circle, and finished with a rabbit or face of about 1 1-2 inch, with 1-2 inch worked in front, and returned on the under side. On the backside they are designed to fit against the brackets *p q r s*, and the risers *c c c*, and bearers *e e* in Fig. 2.

g Bracket line.

h h Bearers.

i i i i Studs or joists.

A B C D At the angles of the dotted lines round Fig. 5, represent the width and length of the plank required to cut a horse for three steps.

E F G H I J K L represent the steps and risers of Fig. 5, which the student will observe are drawn direct from the intersection of the risers and Fig. 5.

E F G H I J represent the steps and risers to Fig. 4.

a b c d in Fig. 4, represent the plan of the bearer.

NOTE.—The method of cutting the bearers after this method is, of at least one half less expense than to frame after the manner of Fig. 2, and in short steps, would answer equally as well.

LETTERS IN FIG. 2.

g h i j k l m Is a part of the front string, joining unto the winders.

c c c Plank risers.

d d d Common risers.

e e e Bearers tenoned into the plank risers, (see the dotted lines.)

f f f Ends of the steps.

m n o p An elevation of the bracket, fitted in the angle of *c* and *e*, directly behind the stave or front string *f f f, &c.* in Fig. 1. These staves are fitted all the way up, and screwed fast on the back side—and after thus fitted, they are taken down, and well glued, refitted and secured to their former places, which will render the front of the stairs very strong. The brackets under the middle and back bearers are of the same height at the joints as those of the front. Those brackets answer also for lathing joists under the stairway.

w A bedstead screw let through the riser into the string.

PL. 29.

In this Plate are two scrolls described by the same rules and centres, but have different proportions.

I have given these two examples with the same rule, in order to show that a scroll or spiral fret may be contracted by making the centres smaller, and extended by making them larger.

REFERENCES TO THE FIGS. 1 2 3 4 5 AND 6.

Fig. 1, A scroll of one revolution and three quarters, drawn by six centres got by dividing a geometrical square into 36 equal parts.

Fig. 2, An elevation of the wedges to strain the veneer round the block under the curtail step.

Fig. 3, A part of the riser and veneer, (see riser and veneer in Fig. 1.)

Fig. 4, Plan of a revolution, and a half scroll.

Fig. 5, Pitch board.

Fig. 6, Face Mould.

NOTE.—In Fig. 1, I have likewise described the block and curtail step, which will be explained.

TO DRAW THE SCROLL IN FIG. 1.

First, draw a circle (generally called the eye,) 3 1-4 or 3 1-2 inches, (in this it is 3 1-4 ;) then draw a geometrical square equal to one half of the eye—divide the geometrical square into 36 equal parts or squares, and at the same time extend one of those parts out to 6 ; now draw the spiral lines—set one point of the compass on 1, one square from the centre *o*, and extend the other point down to *o* on the edge of the eye—let 1 stand, move *o* round to 1 ; let the outer 1 stand, extend the inner 1 out two squares to 2 ; let 2 stand, move 1 round to 2 : let the outer 2 stand, move the inner 2 down to 3, move 2 round to 3 ; let the outer 3 stand, move the inner 3 out to 4 ; let 4 stand, move 3 round to 4 ; let the outer 4 stand, move 4 out to 5 ; let 5 stand, move 4 round to 5 ; let the outer 5 stand, move the inner 5 out to 6 ; let 6 stand, and move 5 round to 6, and the convex side of the scroll will be complete. To describe the inner or concave side, follow the same figures back—that is, after setting the width of the rail in at 6 6.

TO DRAW THE BLOCK AND VENEER FOR THE CURTAIL STEP.

First, set back from the front of the rail at *b*, Fig. 1, to I, one half of the projection of the nosing, which will be the front line of the bracket or front string; then draw the line I J M N P, by following the same centres of the rail, and the concave side of the block will be produced. For the veneer and convex side of the block, set one point of the compass in 5, and extend the other point out to K ; let 5 stand, move K round to L, and so round until the line or veneer meets the letter A—which is the end of the veneer let into the block from P to A, by running in the cut of a pannel saw.

TO FORM THE BLOCK, AND WORK IT OUT.

In order to secure the block from shrinking and breaking apart, it is necessary to glue it up into about five thicknesses, (see Fig. 2, the riser.*) These thicknesses must be equal in width to the line L 20, (that is, the ones that lay across the step,) and those that run lengthways the step, equal in width to the line C 21. To prepare the block for the reception of the front string and bracket, cut the gain I H D, noticing that the junction of the string and block is at I; the letter b is the bracket, and c d e H a part of the front string; from the bracket, it will be understood that the block is made sufficiently smooth round to P, not to require any veneer. To get the length of the veneer, take a small cord or twine, and apply one end at the end of the veneer at the letter A—then encircle the block from A round by L K to G, which will be the length of the veneer required; then calculate whatever thickness for the wedge may be thought proper; (in this it is one half of an inch)—from that to one inch is proper. It will be understood at the same time from Fig. 3, that the lower riser must be in the same piece with the veneer.

TO PREPARE THE RISER AND VENEER.

First, get the length as above described, then guage the veneer at B about 1-8th of an inch thick; then take a rip saw and cut the veneer from A to B, plane it up without the least variation that can be seen, crossways, giving it a gradual diminish from B to A, so that A may enter the cut of a pannel saw; then prepare a quantity of hot water and put the veneer into it, and there let it remain until it becomes as soft as a piece of leather. Prior to this, take a sizing of glue and size the block, and let it get dry before the application of the veneer—and at the application give it another good coat of well-prepared glue. Then take it and place the end perfectly square into the saw cut at A, and gradually bend it round the block, until it will admit of the riser's fitting in the block at E, minding to have it well glued at the same time; then take the wedges at Fig. 2, and drive one from the upper side and one from the under side, and the wedges being properly drove, will strain the riser smooth and snug to the block. Care must be taken to have the veneer lay snug to the block from K to B, which may be effected by placing the block in some proper place and applying a flat piece across it, and secure it by a weight or some other means, in which place it should remain until it becomes perfectly dry.

TO DRAW THE CURTAIL STEP.

In Fig. 1, the dotted lines represented by the letters k l h n, &c. is the outer line of the nosing of the curtail step, and is drawn by the same centres of the rail.

The dotted line g g at the right hand, is the width of the tread of the step from the

* And wedges to strain the veneer.

first rise to the second; 5 12 is likewise the width of the step; *h h*, nosing of the second step; *g i*, second riser; *j l k* is the return of the nosing round the bracket. In this plan, I have extended the nosing over the bracket, equal to the size of the bannister, which is not practised by all stair builders, though to me it appears most mechanical.

TO DRAW THE SCROLL FIG. 4.

Draw the eye or circle 3 1-4 or 3 1-2 inches, then draw a geometrical square in the centre, equal to one-third the diameter of the eye, and for the other parts, proceed precisely as in Fig. 1.

TO DRAW THE FACE MOULD FIG. 6.

Take the pitch-board Fig. 5, and apply the base line 5 12 to the convex side of the rail or scroll; then draw the ordinate lines 6, 5, 6, 6—7, 7, 8, 7—5, 9, 10, 5, &c. perpendicular to the base or under edge of the pitch-board 5 12, and extend them up to the hypothenuse or rake line 5 13, to intersect the figures 6, 7, 5, &c. then take the distance 6, 6, 6 from the line 5, 12 across the eye of the scroll in the point of the compass, and transfer them to 6, 6, 6, in Fig. 6, (noticing that the ordinates in 6 are drawn at right angles to the rake of the pitch-board.) Proceed the same way with 7, 5, 20, 21, &c. and then trace round from 6, 6, to 5, 5, and the size and shape of the face mould will be produced. Now to understand the practical position of the face mould, Fig. 6, suppose the pitch-board, Fig. 5 to stand on the line 5 12 across the eye—then it will be understood that the line 5 13 of the pitch-board is the rake of the stairs. Now, if the student observes with attention the pitch-board standing as above placed on the line 5 12 across the scroll, he will see that the face mould, Fig. 6, will range precisely over the corresponding one in the plan of the scroll, Fig. 4.

NOTE.—The letters *f f f*, *&c.* Fig. 1, represent the bannisters.

PL. 30.

Explains a practical method for obtaining the thickness of stuff* required to pass over the plan D, or one half of A, in Plate VI, and also the shank of the scroll, Fig. 4, in Plate XXIX.

METHOD FOR OBTAINING THE THICKNESS OF STUFF FOR HAND-RAILING.

REFERENCES TO THE FIGURES.

Fig. 1, Falling-mould, over the stretchout of Fig. 3, (see the letters *a b c* 1 2 3 4 5

* In this plate, I have given the twist, although it is not necessary; for when the extremities and backs are obtained, the thickness of the stuff will be produced for instance, see *a c* 1 5 7 6 are the extremities, and the two parallel lines contain the wood necessary, which is 2 and 3-4 thick. The rail is 1 3-4 by 2 1-4.

6 7 on the line A B,) under Fig. 1, which are the same as those on the convex of
Fig. 3, and also of the same length.

Fig. 2, The thickness of stuff required for the rail.

Fig. 3, Plan of the rail D or A in Plate VI.

Fig. 4, Shank of the scroll, Fig 4, Plate XXIX.

Fig. 5, Plan of the shank of Fig. 4, Plate XXIX, from 5 5, to 6 6.

Fig. 6, Stretchout of the falling-mould, Fig. 4, in Plate XXX.

TO DRAW OR OBTAIN THE THICKNESS OF STUFF.

Place tne stretchout of Fig. 3, on the line A B, from *a* to 7, then place the falling-
mould Fig. 1, in its practical position, meaning on the rake of the stairs ; divide *a* 7
into the same number and distances of the convex line of Fig. 3 from *a b c* round to 7,
then raise perpendiculars from *a b c* 1 2 3 4 5 6 7 to cross the falling-mould, Fig. 1,
draw lines parallel to A B from 1 1 2 2 3 3, &c. to cross Fig. 2, then raise lines from
the same figures on both sides of the plan Fig. 3 to cross Fig. 2, and where they cross,
the corresponding lines at 1 2 3 4, &c. will be the extremity and shape of the rail
when in its square shape, ready for moulding or rounding.

TO DRAW FIG. 4, THE SHANK OF THE SCROLL IN PLATE XXIX.

Lay the plan of Fig. 4, from the joint at 5 5 round to 6 6 in Plate XXIX, on Fig.
5, in this Plate, then divide the convex side of the rail into 5 1 2 3 4, &c. equal parts,
and then draw lines across the rail to the centre 6, which will also divide the concave
side into the same number of equal parts ; then take the falling-mould, Fig 6, the
same as that of Fig. 4, in Plate XXX, and take the stretchout of Fig. 5, from 5 round
by 1 2 3 4 5 6 7 6, (6 being the termination of the scroll,) 8 9 10 11, (11 is 5-8 below the second riser,) at which I have made the joint. This, however, may always
be discretionate with the executor. The falling-mould thus placed, and divided into
the same number of equal parts and distances from the two heavy lines 5 and 6, it
will be understood the same will apply and bind round the shank Fig. 4 when applied
over Fig. 5 in its practical position, (meaning the rake or inclination of the stairs.)
To draw the twist, and obtain the thickness of stuff for Fig. 4, raise perpendicular
lines through the line A B, from the figures 5 1 2 3 4 5 6 7 6, &c. in the convex and
concave sides of Fig. 5 up through the shank Fig. 4, to intersect the same and corresponding figures ; then take the distances 5 5 5 from Fig. 6, and transfer them to
5 5 5 on the outside of the plan Fig. 5, and the shanks Fig. 4, and so on* 1 1, 2 2,
3 3, 4 4, 5 5, 6 6, 7 7, 6 6, 8 8, 9 9, 10 10, and 0 0, and the upper edge of the convex side of the shank will be at the upper line of figures. To determine the upper
and under edge of the concave side of the rail, take the figures 1 1 1, 2 2 2, 3 3 3,
4 4 4, 5 5 5, 6 6 6, 7 7 7, 6 6 6, &c. and they will produce a perspective view of the

* The above distances are taken from the line A B, at Fig. 6, to the upper side of the same, which is the
falling-mould, and those that determine the other two lines will be taken from the line A B, and the under
and upper side of the falling-mould.

twist of the part of the rail contained in the shank of the scroll. C represents a section of the rail at the joint, with a screw nut and washer practically: D at the upper end and at the joint, represents the bolt which connects the shank and straight part of the rail. The two parallel lines in Fig. 4, represent the thickness of stuff requisite, with the most perfect workmanship; for it will be perceived that those dotted lines will produce a lack of wood on the upper edge of the convex side, and under of the concave; but as above observed, with precise workmanship it will make a perfect rail, and require only 2 1-2 inches thick of stuff; whereas, if made to work square all round, it would require 3 inches, which is not only an additional expense, but sometimes difficult to obtain a piece of that thickness, especially well seasoned.

NOTE.—All the above drawing is not necessary to obtain the thickness of stuff; for the lower angle at 5 in Fig. 4, and at 4 the highest extremity on the back will produce the thickness, and the four angles in Fig. 2, it may plainly be seen, will produce the same.

PL. 31.

As stairs of six to eight inch openings, are the most in use of any other kind, there are frequently instances of many being obliged to execute them, who are but little experienced in stair-building; consequently, I have thought proper to give the most difficult parts engaged therein, in the following practical manner.

REFERENCES TO THE FIGURES.

Fig. A, P an of the rail, front string and nosing: the outer dotted line represents the front line of the front string; (that is, the one farthest from the centre *o,* commencing at 1, and terminating at 2:) the inner dotted line represents the front line of the nosing on the platform.

Fig. B, Plan of the cylinder put up in staves, glued and screwed together.

Fig. C, The elevation and stretchout of the circular part of the front string passing over the dotted line 1 2, in Fig. A, with a part of the last step of the first flight, and part of the first of the short flight going off the platform, and landing on the floor.

Fig. D, Falling-mould for the concave side of the rail, passing over the line 5 7, in Fig. A.

Fig. E, Convex falling-mould, passing over the outer line 6 11, in the plan Fig. A.

EXPLANATIONS TO FIGURES A, B, C, D, AND E.

Fig. A, Is the plan of a rail corresponding precisely with the plan, letter A, in Plate VI, across the centre O, from 6 to 11; the tangent line 13 14, is the same as 13 14, in Plate VI, and is got by the same process. The dotted line 15 16, a tangent to the circular dotted line, (which is the front string,) is the stretchout of the circular part of the string; the line 17 18, is the stretchout of the concave side of the rail.

TO DRAW FIG: B, A PLAN OF THE STAIRS AND CYLINDER.

First, take the opening of the cylinder and draw it at any convenient place, say at Fig. B; then determine the location of the joint of the straight and circular part of the string,* say at *a h;* then take any number of staves, (in this design I have given only three, of which one is omitted for want of room,) and draw lines from the centre O, through the intersection of the two staves at *c f,* and *e d,* which will give the bevel for working the staves. For instance, take a bevel and apply the stock to the dotted line *c b,* of the stave that is connected with the straight string, and the blade, on the bevel line *c f;* then plane up the stave to fit that bevel, and so also *d c f,* and the two staves will stand precisely over the lines herein represented by the letters *b c, d e, f* and *g.* To work out the circle, together with the straight part annexed thereto, first take a thin piece of board, and make its shape precisely the same as the lines *b, a,* J, *c, f* and *g;* then take the pattern just described, and apply it to the end of the stave, and mark round, which will produce the scribes necessary for working the stave. Proceed the same way with the centre stave, which is described by the letters *c d e* and *f.*

TO GLUE UP THE STAVES IN THE BEST WAY TO AVOID A VARIATION BY SLIPPING OUT OF PLACE.

First, cut a place in the stave at *ı,* for the reception of a screw, then take the screw *k,* and screw the two staves together in order to make them permanent: two screws will be necessary. By thus proceeding, the cylinder may be nearly completed before glued up. The workman will also find a convenience in working the rabbit or faciæ, and bead; for he may work from both ways: whereas, if the whole was glued up, he would find difficulty, particularly in those small openings.

TO CUT THE JOINT, AND SCREW THE CYLINDER TO THE STRAIGHT STRING.

First, set a guage from the line J *b* across to the line *h i,* then guage the line *h i,* then saw the line *h i* through and through down to *h,* then cut the bevel joint from *a* into *h;* then the stave being cut, the same shape will fit at *a h* and *i;* the stave is thus fitted: now drive the screws *n n,* and they being inclined as described in the plan, will bring the joint *a h* to wood and wood. As seasoned stuff is important in cylinders, I have made the staves in this example only 2 1-4 thick, consequently, it causes a lack of wood between *f* and *i:* To remedy that, the triangular *f i* P might be left on the straight string: it is a matter of no great consequence whether on or omitted.

NOTE.—After the faciæ and bead are completed, then unscrew the joints, and put on a sufficient quantity of glue; then refit them, and drive the screws as before, and the joints will be permanent and regular. The letter *q* represents the back line of the bead—*r,* the front side of the bead and faciæ, and *s,* the front of the upper faciæ.

* I have located this 2 and 5-8ths of an inch from the circle, which renders it easier to make the intersections of the straight and circular parts perfect, or as near so as possible.

TO DRAW THE ELEVATION AND STRETCHOUT OF FIG. C.

First, take the dotted stretchout 15 16 at the plan Fig. A, and raise them perpendicular up to 15 16 on the under edge of the nosing of the platform ; then set up from 16 to 19 the height of a riser ; then set down from 15 to I the height of a riser. This produces the stretchout of the cylinder, and at the same time represents a part of two common steps. The figures 3 and 4, at the extremities of the nosing, are just equal to the stretchout of the dotted line 3 4 in the plan Fig. A, representing the nosing line.

TO GET THE LENGTH OF THE STAVES.

First, find the stretchout of the staves round from $b\,a\,$J$\,c$ and d, and apply them to the dotted lines on the under side of the falling-mould or under side of the elevation of the front string at 1 2 3 4 5 6 ; then commence at 1, and raise a perpedicular line from 1 up to 1, which will be the length ; the width will be from 1 to 2 on the horizontal dotted line : for the middle stave, take the perpendicular line 3 2 for the length, and the horizontal dotted line 3 4 for the width: $a\,a$ are the joints of the cylinder to the straight string,—$b\,b$ are the joints in the rabbit or faciæ, caused by cutting a bevel (see the joint in the plan of cylinder) at $a\,h$, and it will be seen at the bevel joint, by its passing from the letter h out to a, it makes the difference of the two dotted lines in crossing the projection of the rabbit of the faciæ, which is represented by the break in the two lines or joints of the cylinder marked $a\,b$, to the string in the elevation at the intersections of the straight and circular parts. The dotted lines 1 1 and 6 6, at the upper and lower ends, represent the line $b\,g$ in Fig. B.

NOTE.—Before I proceed any farther, it will be proper to mention the peculiarity of a winding or circular rail passing over any number of elevated steps.

First, It is known by practical demonstration, that a hand-rail raising and winding over any number of steps, terminating in a circular cylinder, that neither two of the front and back edges will be parallel to each other ; consequently it is evident that the cuts in the convex and concave falling-mould will not be parallel to each other ; if both are cut square to the rake of the falling-moulds, (see Fig's. D and E placed on their stretchouts) that they do not run parallel over the stretchout part, but at the same time run parallel down at $s\,s$ and up at $r\,r$, and is also the same distance apart at $s\,s$ that it is at $r\,r$, and so also is the underside of the falling-mould to the front string, Fig. C. It will likewise be observed that the four lines across the two falling-moulds at each end of Fig's. D and E, are square to the hypothenuse, or rake line of the pitch boards, and parallel to each other ; but at the same time, the cuts at the centre of the stretchouts are not parallel when cut square to the rake or hypothenuse line. Therefore, it is a duty that devolves on me, through the nature of my proposals for this work, to explain satisfactorily the mysterious parts connected with the various problems or examples that I include in this work. The above references and notices are inserted for the purpose of placing in view the proper object that will be most likely to lead the student to a more direct understanding of them : and at the same time it will be proper to direct the student to Plate XXXIV, for the application of the moulds and pitch boards or bevels,* more particularly than any succeeding Plate; for if I should explain the application of the moulds and pitch bevels to all the examples that will be included in this work, I should be obliged to omit examples of equal importance ; and as Plates VI and VII treat on the applications in the best practical manner, it would be taxing the patrons of the work with money and studies, which would be perfectly useless to them.

TO DRAW THE CUTS OF THE CONCAVE AND CONVEX SIDE OF THE RAIL PARALLEL, AND TO SHOW THE WOOD REQUIRED TO CUT THE JOINT IN VARIOUS POSITIONS.

First, As I have prepared this Plate to complete Plate XXXIV, it will be observed that the line 22 0 22 across the centre of Fig. E, which is the same as the letter C in Plate VI, is cut square to the rake or hypothenuse line of the stretchout. Next it will be seen that the concave† mould Fig. D, does not run parallel to Fig. E ; therefore 23 0 23, which is square to the mould, will not be parallel to the line 22 0 22 in Fig. E ; consequently, they will not make the joint required, although the moulds are both on their inclined planes : and to understand the thing perfectly, (see the two small portions of the common pitch boards at the upper and lower ends of the two moulds, Fig's. D and E, that they are raising equal distances at the letters *s s* and *r r* at the upper and lower ends of the moulds,) now to obtain a parallel cut to the outside of the rail, draw the line 22 0 22 across Fig. D, parallel to 22 0 22, which is square to Fig. E, and the parallel cut will be complete; but at the same time will not be a square joint in front, as in the back, or convex side of the rail.

TO GET THE JOINT SQUARE IN FRONT.

First, draw the line 23 *o* 23, square to the concave mould D ; then to make the convex side in Fig. E, parallel to it, draw 23 *o* 23, in E, parallel to 23 *o* 23, in Fig. D, and the joint will be complete—which is directly reversed to the above.

TO DIVIDE THE VARIATIONS, AND SHOW DIFFERENT QUANTITIES OF WOOD REQUIRED BY THE VARIATIONS OF THE DIFFERENT POSITIONS OF THE JOINT.

First, it is understood that the lines 22 *o* 22 and 23 *o* 23, are explained, and run parallel to each corresponding line in the two moulds ; then to divide the difference,

* Noticing that the pitch board of the front string in a stair with winding steps, will not answer for the rake and plumb cuts or lines, to neither side of the rail which may be seen by the variation of the two falling moulds and front string in this Plate, but a pitch board equal to the inside or outside of the rail will answer for the same.

† Meaning the inside of the rail in the circular part, for the same side of the rail in its straight parts might properly be termed the outside, for the well-hole is the outside of the stairs ; but any diminution towards the axis or centre of a cylinder or circle, will be coming into the centre ; consequently the concave mould will be the inside mould to the circular part.

divide the distance between the two lines 22 and 23, at the ends of the lines, and in the circles running through 22 23, into two equal parts; then draw the line *o o o*, through the moulds, which will produce the variation, and likewise will be square to the centre section of the rail; that is the same as to say, draw a falling-mould for the middle black line, running through the centre *o*, in the plan of the rail, at Fig. A, which is also the centre section of the elevation of the rail. Now to produce the wood required to cut the joint, when executed in either of the three positions represented by the lines 22 *o* 22, *o o o*, and 23 *o* 23, drop lines from each intersection of those lines, to the upper and under edge of the falling-mould Fig. D and E, down to the plan of the rail at Fig. A, and the over-wood for either will be produced at the three lines at the right and left of the line *o o o o*, round perpendicular through the axis of the cylinder or well-hole. The three lines each side are represented at the radiating lines 1 2 22 22 3 4, drawn from the convex side of the rail A. This, as above observed, must pass through the intersecting of the lines at the upper and under edge of the rail, or falling-moulds D and E.

NOTE.—In applying the falling-moulds D and E, care must be taken to have the plumb lines & &, placed perfectly parallel to the plumb cut on the piece to which they are applied, as in Plate XXXIV. where the falling mould C is applied over the plan, Fig. 2, (see the two letters *o c* in C.) Now if the convex and concave moulds are thus applied, and bent round in proper form, the joint will be perfect. The letters *o c*, *z z*, and *k f*, represent the plumb cuts at the centre joint and at the straight and circular parts.

PL. 32.

This Plate is designed to explain a falling-mould for starting off of the second floor, when in connection with the first-story rail; and also to bore for the ballusters without applying it to the stairs until it is finished.

REFERENCES TO FIGURES 1, 2, AND 3.

Fig. 1, Falling-mould or rail stretched out over the floor and stairs of the 2d story.
Fig. 2, Ground of the rail and well-hole.*
Fig. 3, Shows a practical position of the rail and twist passing over the platform, landing on the floor, and from thence ascending the second flight.

NOTE.—Generally the student in his practical pursuits of stair building, labours under some difficulties from not being aware of the method of drawing and applying the different falling moulds to their respective places—(for instance the falling-mould that connects the level rail on the floor with the rail that ascends the second flight,)—notwithstanding the similarity existing in this and all other falling-moulds. This is a matter of the first consideration that the student should inquire into, for by such

* This is a supposed well-hole in length, but the width is precisely the same as Plate XXXI, and is designed for the same stairs.

means he may execute the most intricate stairs with as much ease as he could the plainest branch connected with the building business.

Draw the floor line p O (which is the same as the floor line h O in Fig. 3,) then raise the first riser q u v of the second flight at the intersection of the straight rail ascending the circular part that passes round the well-hole, and connected with the straight part that lies horizontal until it intersects the casing over the last riser, and descends to the platform (as in Fig. 3)—then apply the falling mould to the steps and risers 1, 2, 3, 4—then raise u on the rise line q u v just half a rise (which will also be the same in the line A u A in Fig. 3,)—and from thus proceeding, the rail raises one half a riser on the floor, which is necessary—and then it raises only half a riser in passing round about two-thirds of the circular opening—which will not require as thick stuff as it would if the rail did not raise the half rise on the floor. Hence it will be understood that the line u s is raised half a rise from the floor, and is also the stretchout of Fig. 2. q r s, which is the same as in Plate XVI, only on a smaller scale. It will also be understood that the line p q r s t is the stretchout of Fig. 2, from P v r s t. To produce the rake of the falling-mould in the circular part of the rail, extend the under line of the rail from 6 down to 5 to intersect the lower line u 5 s t of the rail passing round the circle, then draw the intersecting lines as in all other examples, and then the ramp will be produced, as necessarily required.

To draw the joint in the centre at y, take any distance y z in the dividers, place one point in y, and mark by turning it from z to z on the upper edge of the mould—Then take the dividers and place one foot on z and extend the other to z—then let one point stand, and turn the other point out to &—then move the point & down to z, and turn the other point up to &—then draw a line from the intersection at & across the mould through the centre y, and the joint will be square to the rail.

In order to communicate the application of the falling-mould to the student more clear than it has been heretofore, I have given the elevation Fig. 3—to which the falling-mould Fig. 1 is applied as follows: First, take t t in the mould Fig. 1, which is the joint, and apply it to the same line or joint p p in Fig. 3, and bend it round Fig 3, so that the letters t t s s x v w w and y in the centre of Fig. 1 will commence with t t in Fig. 1, and apply to p p in Fig. 3, and so on, s s in Fig. 1 to u u in Fig. 3, y in the centre of Fig. 1 to y in Fig. 3, x v in Fig. 1 to A x in Fig. 3, w w in Fig. 1 to q q in Fig. 3, minding particularly to have all those plumb lines on the falling-mould Fig. 1 to apply precisely parallel to all the corresponding lines in Fig. 3—and the rail worked according to the application of the mould as described, must inevitably be perfect, or so nearly so, that it would require a more perfect executor than is often met with to point out the defects—w w in Fig. 1 is the same joint as that of q q in Fig. 3, and p in the plan Fig. 2; x v is the plumb line directly over the first riser, and at the junction of the straight and circular part of the rail—y is the centre of the rail, the same as r in

Fig. 2 and *y* in Fig. 3—1, 2, 3, 4, represent the steps and risers—*a b c d e f g h i, &c.* in Fig. 1 at the top of the dotted lines represent the centres of the bannisters.

EXPLANATION TO FIGURE 2.

Fig. 2 is a horizontal plan of the rail at the supposed well-hole in length which may be seen, but will explain the object in view just as well as if it included the whole extent of the long flights ; for it is only necessary to shew the joints, stretchout of the circle, plan of the bannisters, &c. which will very readily be seen by the dotted and full lines running from Fig's. 1 and 3—all corresponding, and intersecting their respective plans in the plan Fig. 2—from which the student will be enabled to see the position of all the risers and joints—*a b c d e f, &c.* are plans of the bannisters—*p p p p, t t t t* and *v v v v* plan of the joints, see *s s r r* in Fig. 3, and *w w* in Fig. 1, with the lines transferred from one to the other—*q r s* is the stretchout of the rail from *v* round by *r* to *o*, and is the same as the stretchout in Plate XVI, letter A from 13 to 14, and is the same as above mentioned, only on a reduced scale—the dotted line 2, 2, is the line of the nosing—and 3, 3, the front string.

EXPLANATION TO FIGURE 3.

Fig. 3 shows an elevation and twist of the rail,—line of the platform,—one step and riser of the lower long flight,—a piece of the rail over the same,—the line of the second floor with the rail passing over the same,—three risers and two steps of the second long flight,—and the rail passing over the same, twisting round the circular opening.—C, tread of the last step of the first long flight—E, last riser of the long flight —B, floor of the platform—D, first riser of the short flight starting off of the platform B, and ascending to the second floor—*h* O is the line of the second floor—A A is the first riser of the second long flight, which is the same as the riser *q v* in Fig. 1— *q q*, joint of the rail, the same as *w w* in Fig. 1—*p p*, joint corresponding with *t t* in Fig. 1—*y*, the centre of the rail at the joint, the same as *y* in Fig. 1—*r r* joint, see *u u u u* in Fig. 2—*s s s s* joints, see *v v v v* in Fig. 2.

The above application of the falling-mould, (for which this drawing is expressly designed,) is perhaps plainer than any extant at the present period—for it has heretofore been too much the case, that learned authors have explained this part of the work in such a manner that it has been difficult for a mechanic of common abilities to attain to this branch of his occupation.

TO BORE FOR THE BANNISTERS.

It will be seen that the dotted lines *a b c d e f g h i, &c.* are the centres of the bannisters ; therefore it will be understood that they are at equal distances, and may be stepped off with a divider, the same as on a horizontal plane, and then bored according to the hypothenuse or rake of the stairs by lines struck plumb across the rail by the pitchboard. This progress is before the rail is rounded or moulded. To set the bannisters in order on the platform or floor, just place the rail up in order to receive the bannisters, all in proper height ; then take a rod that will easily enter the bannister hole, and drive a point in the lower end ; then put the upper end in the rail, and make it precisely plumb ; then make an impression in the floor with the point, which will give the centre of the hole ; then let the bannister round the circles be the first set in the rail, as they cannot be entered at the bottom as in the steps.

RECIPROCAL SPIRALS, OR SCROLLS FOR STAIR-RAILING.

To join a scroll to an elliptical or even a circular stair-rail, in such a manner as to have them perfectly harmonize, is somewhat of a difficult task, and requires a workman of much taste and judgment. The reciprocal scroll is better adapted to a circular rail, than any other kind. It is easily drawn, may be expanded to a greater or less distance, and made to have more or less revolutions, as suits the pleasure of the operator. The four designs which follow, have, in the order of their numerical succession, one and a quarter, one and a half, one and three quarters, and two, revolutions.

PL. 33.

TO DRAW A RECIPROCAL SPIRAL, WHICH SHALL MAKE ONE REVOLUTION AND A QUARTER.

For the eye of the spiral, describe a circle (Plate XXXIII. Fig. 1,) having any diameter, say three and a half inches ; (see scale of inches at Fig. 5 ;) divide its circumference into eight equal parts, and from its centre draw radii to the points of division, and produce or continue those radii indefinitely ; in the line 5 1, thus produced, take any point, as for instance 1, as the extent or limit of the expansion of the scroll, and at 1, in the line 5 1, erect a perpendicular, 1 10, of any length, and divide it into ten equal parts ; on the line 5 1, set off the part o s, equal to the width of the rail, and from 1, in the perpendicular 1 10, count off as many divisions as are equal to the number of eighths of a circle that the scroll is to expand ; (as, in this instance, two divisions ;) from the point of division 2, in the perpendicular 1 10, draw the line 2 s, and from the point 10, the line 10 0, meeting the eye of the scroll at 0, and produce the lines 10 0, 2 s, till they meet ; the point where they meet, will be the point where the lines from all the other points of division in 1 10, will likewise meet ; which draw, accordingly.

TO DETERMINE THE LOCATION OF THE POINTS 2 3, &c. ON THE OUTSIDE OF THE SCROLL.

Take, in the compass, the distance from the centre of the eye to the point where the line 5 1 is intersected by the line from the first point of division 1, in the perpendicular 1 10, and with that distance as radius, keeping one point of the compass on the centre of the eye, describe an arc so as to cut the produced line 6 2: the point of intersection, 2, will be one point on the outside of the scroll. And to find other points, as 3, 4, &c. take, successively, the distance from the centre of the eye to the several points where the line 5 1 is intersected by the second, third, &c. lines from the perpendicular 1 10, and from the centre of the eye as a centre, with those distances successively as radii, describe arcs cutting the produced lines 7 3, 2 4, &c.; and the location of the points 3, 4, &c. on the outside of the scroll, will be ascertained.

TO FIND THE CENTRES FROM WHICH TO DESCRIBE THE CURVES 1 2, 2 3, &c. ON THE OUTSIDE OF THE SCROLL.

From the point 1, in the line 5 1, as a centre, and with the distance from that point to the centre of the eye as radius, describe any arc, as at 1; from the point 2, on the outside of the scroll, as a centre, and with the same radius, describe another arc, cutting the former in the point 1, and that point will be the centre for describing the curve 1 2; which describe, accordingly. In like manner, to find the centre for describing the curve 2 3, take the distance from the centre of the eye to the intersection of the first line from the perpendicular 1 10, with the line 5 1, and with that distance as radius, and from the points 2, 3, as centres, describe arcs so as to cut each other, and from the point of intersection, describe the curve 2 3. Proceed in the same way for the rest.

In the construction of Fig's. 2, 3, and 4, proceed as in drawing Fig. 1; bearing it in mind, that the number of parts into which the perpendicular is to be divided, must equal the number of eighths of a circle that the spiral is to revolve; that the number of divisions to be counted off on the perpendicular, (reckoning always from that extremity of it which meets the line 5 1,) in order to know from what point in it to draw a straight line to *s*, must equal the number of eighths that the spiral is to expand; that the outermost line from the perpendicular must pass through *o*, on the eye of the spiral; and that the point where, when produced, this outermost line and the one drawn to *s*, will meet, is the point to which all the other lines from the perpendicular must be drawn. The student will perceive, that one revolution and a quarter in the spiral, requires ten equal divisions in the perpendicular; one revolution and a half, twelve divisions; one and three quarters, fourteen; and so on.

Fig. 5 is a scale of inches for figures 1 and 2, and Fig. 6, a scale for figures 3 and 4.

PL. 34.

STAIR RAILING OVER A SMALL OPENING

To furnish such drawings and explanations of the several parts of stairs as can be comprehended by workmen, not versed in science, nor much experienced in the stair department, and as will enable them to execute with a considerable degree of accuracy, it is necessary to study simplicity, both in the drawings themselves, and in the terms used for their explanation. In what follows, I shall aim to do this, even if it be at the occasional sacrifice of that verbal polish, and that scientific arrangement and explanation, which a learned reader might desire.

THE PLAN OF THE SEMICIRCULAR PART OF A STAIR-RAIL BEING GIVEN, TO OBTAIN THE CONVEX FALLING MOULD.

Let A C E F H J (Fig. 1.) be the plan of the semicircular part of a stair-rail, having a portion of straight rail attached to it; with the diameter, G I, of the convex side of the plan for radius, and from the points G, I, as centres, describe arcs cutting each other at P, and join P I, P G; bisect the arc I H G in H, and through H draw a tangent, K H L, of any length, and produce the lines P I, P G, till they meet the tangent: the part K L, cut off by P I and P G produced, is the extension or stretch-out of the convex side, I H G, of the plan. Draw the line c e (Fig. 2.) equal to the tangent K L, and at e, in the base c e, erect a perpendicular, e f, equal to the height of a step, and join c, f; at each end of the hypothenuse c f, apply the pitch-board of a common step in the manner exhibited in Fig's. A and B, and make r b or q y in the pitch-board a b c, and f u in the pitch-board f g h, each equal in length, I J or D E, of the straight part of the rail: making allowance for the easings at c and f, the line a c f h, formed by the hypothenuse c f and the upper edges of the two pitch-boards, is the lower edge of the required convex falling-mould, of which the part q c f i is all that is required in this instance. On each side of the angles c, f, in the lower edge of said mould, set off any number of equal parts, say six or eight, and from that point of division which is nearest the angle on one side, draw a straight line to that point which is farthest from the angle on the other side; do the same from all the other points of division, and by the intersections of these lines, obtain the easings at c and f; parallel to the lower edge thus completed, and at whatever distance may be fixed upon for the width of the mould, draw a line for the upper edge, and the required convex falling-mould (Fig. C) will be completed.

The line l m n (Fig. C) represents a butt-joint, and C v, or H v, (Fig. 1.) shews the overwood necessary for cutting said joint, and are obtained thus: at the point H, (Fig. 1.) in the tangent K L, erect a perpendicular, and produce it so as to cross the convex mould C; bisect the part, z z, which crosses the mould, and through the point of bisection, m, draw l m n; at right angles to the hypothenuse c f, and from n, let fall a perpendicular, n v, upon the tangent K L: as already stated, the line l m n represents a butt-joint in the centre of the semi-circular part of the rail, and C v, or H v (Fig. 1) is the width of overwood required to cut it; for which overwood, allowance is made in Fig's. 4, 6, &c.

Figures 3 and D represent the stretch-out and falling-mould of the concave part of of the plan at Fig. 1, and are obtained in the same manner as Fig's. 2 and C; the base c e (Fig. 3) being equal to the tangent M N at Fig. 1; e f, equal to the height of a riser; q y and f u, equal to the same portions of straight rail as in Fig's. 2 and C; and so forth. It will be perceived, that the two falling-moulds (Fig's. C and D) have different angles of inclination; that the line l m n, in order to be parallel to l m n in Fig. C, (which it must be,) cannot be at right angles to the hypothenuse $c\ f$, as in Fig. C ; and lastly, that straight lines drawn across the mould C and D, at right angles to the base $c\ e$, will have unequal lengths, those crossing D, being necessarily the longest.   This fact must be particularly attended to by stair-builders if they would construct hand-rails in the best possible manner.   Even where attention is paid to it, some difficulty is experienced in the application of the moulds, and in the construction of the rail.   Mr. Coulter, of Philadelphia, recommends the method of dividing the difference in the width of the two falling-moulds into two equal parts, and lowering the concave side of the rail a distance equal to one of these parts, at the same time that the convex side is elevated a distance equal to the other.   This method, though liable to some trifling objections, is doubtless the best that has been devised. It will not, however, make an inelegant rail, if the convex side be elevated a distance equal to the whole difference in the width of the falling-moulds, without lowering the concave side at all.   I will just add that, further on, will be found drawings and explanations adapted expressly to this case ; and to these the student is referred for what further aid and information he may require.

THE PLAN BEING GIVEN, TO OBTAIN THE FACE MOULD OF A STAIR-RAIL, WHICH, WHEN PLACED OVER THE PLAN AT A PROPER ANGLE OF INCLINATION, WILL COINCIDE WITH THE SAID PLAN, PART WITH PART.

Let Fig. 1 be the given plan, as before, and draw A B $v\ v$ I J, (Fig. 4) equal to that part of Fig. 1 which is represented by the same letters ; join the ends of the dotted curve passing longitudinally through the centre of the semi-plan at Fig. 4, by the straight line $w\ w$; through the point A, and parallel to $w\ w$, draw a straight line, x A x, of any length, and parallel to it, draw another line, $y\ y$, of indefinite length, so as to touch the convex side of the semi-plan ; through the point J, draw a straight line at right angles to the tangent $y\ y$, and produce the said line through J and said tangent, till they meet in the point y ; through the middle point, w, of the end of the circular part of the semi-plan, and at right angles to the straight line $w\ w$, draw the line $n\ s\ n$, of any length, and make the part $s\ n$ (Fig. 5) equal to $s\ n$ in Fig. 2 ; through n, (Fig 5) draw the line $z\ n\ y$, (which line is the hypothenuse of the triangle $z\ y\ y$, and shews the rake or inclination the face mould is to have,) and through the points A, I, B, &c. in the semi-plan, and at right angles to the tangent $y\ y$, draw the lines A A, 9 9, &c. meeting the hypothenuse $z\ y$ in the points A, 9, &c. ; at the points where they meet said hypothenuse, erect the perpendiculars 9 I, 6 5, &c. (Fig. 6) making them equal to 9 I, 6 5, &c. in Fig 4, and the parts 6 B, 7 4, &c. in Fig. 6, equal to the similarly named parts in Fig. 4 ; through the points thus obtained, trace the curves J I v, A B v, and you will have the face mould required.

TO APPLY THE FACE MOULD TO A PLANK FOR GETTING OUT A RAIL PIECE.

Let the oblong 1, 2, 3, 4, (Fig. 7) represent the upper side of the plank , 2, 5, 6, 3, the thickness of the same ; and 5, 8, 7, 6, the under side.   Take the face mould (Fig.

6) and apply it, as at Fig. 7, keeping tne end *v v* as far from the edge of the plank as is indicated by Fig's. 4 and 6, and tracing out its shape A J *v v ;* take the pitch bevel A at Fig. 5, (which shows the angle of inclination that the rail is to have,) and apply it as at A and A ; (Fig. 8) make the plumb-cuts C C, A A, across the edge, and also the perpendicular *c v* on the under side of the plank, equal to *c v* on the upper side, and then, applying the face-mould again, as at Fig. 9, complete the out line for cutting the rail-piece.

TO APPLY THE CONVEX AND CONCAVE FALLING MOULDS TO A RAIL-PIECE.

When the rail-piece has been cut-out, as just described, take the convex mould Fig. C, (which is supposed to be made of pasteboard) and apply it to the convex edge of the rail-piece at Fig. 7, bending it round so that the points *p, o,* 3, in the upper edge of the mould, may coincide, each with each, with the points J, I, *v,* in the upper side of the convex edge of the rail-piece, and so that the lines *p q, o c,* 3 *n,* drawn across the mould C at right angles to its base, *c e,* may tally, each to each, with the plumb cuts A A, B B, C C, made on the concave edge of the rail-piece, and continued across the under side to meet the above mentioned lines. Having applied and bent round the mould in this manner, trace lines along its upper and lower edges, and you will have the outline for finishing the convex side of the rail.

In the same way, apply the concave mould D to the concave edge of the rail-piece, making the straight part, *p o,* in the upper edge of the mould, coincide with the straight part, A B, in the upper concave edge of the rail piece ; and thus far, the two falling moulds will have the same angle of inclination. To find what inclination to give to the circular part of the concave mould D, from the point *n,* in the lower edge of the convex mould C, (which is supposed to be bent round the convex edge of the rail-piece,) square across the under side of the rail-piece, and from the point 2, (Fig. D) where the line thus squared across, is supposed to meet the lower concave edge of the rail piece, draw the horizontal line 2 4 ; from 2, in the line 2 4, set off 2 *z,* equal to the overwood for a butt-joint, and *z* will be that point in the concave edge of the rail-piece, on which the middle point in the lower edge of the circular part of mould D, will rest. Now trace the outline for completing the concave side of the rail. Observe, that the difference in the length of *n* 2 in Fig. C, and *n* 2 in Fig. D, represents the difference the two falling moulds will have in their angle of inclination.

PL. 35.

For the method of finding the face and falling-moulds, exhibited in this and the following Plate, and for the drawings connected with the same, I am indebted to Mr. Joshua Coulter, of Philadelphia, of whom mention has already been made, in the preface to this work. The method exhibited in this plate, is well adapted to small openings of from seven to twelve inches in diameter. When the opening is enlarged it becomes necessary to throw the steps into the circle, in order to preserve, as nearly as possible, the same inclination in the circular, that belongs to the straight part of the rail. By pursuing this method, the usual droop in the middle of the circular part, will be almost wholly prevented ; and as any length of straight rail may be attached to the circular part, the disadvantage of having the grain of the wood run cross-wise, may be avoided.

TO OBTAIN THE FALLING-MOULD AT FIG. 4, FROM THE SEMI-PLAN AT FIG. 1.

Obtain the stretch-out, $e\,i$, of the curve $e\,d$, (Fig. 1) in the same way as in the last Plate, and draw the base C F, (Fig. 3) making each of its parts, C D, D F, equal to the stretch-out $e\,i$; at right angles C F, draw F H, equal to the height of a common step, and draw the hypothenuse H C ; place the pitch-boards A B C, H J K, in the position exhibited in the figure, and produce the side, B C, of the pitch-board A B C, any distance, C M, say about one third the length of B C ; through the point E, where a perpendicular from the middle of the base cuts the hypothenuse C H, draw M N, making E N equal to M E, and join N H ; from M towards N, in the line M N, set off a part equal to M C, and from N towards M, a part equal to N H, and divide the part thus set off, together with M C, N H, into any number of equal parts ; draw the intersecting lines for the easings at M and N, and complete the falling-mould, in the manner described in Plate XXXIV.

TO OBTAIN THE FACE MOULD AT FIG. 5, BY MEANS OF ORDINATES.

Perpendicularly over $h\,g$ in the semi-plan, form a section of the rail, (Fig. 7) so that its top shall be on a level with a line drawn from x (Fig. 4) parallel to the base F C, and so that the said line from x, and the line 2 3, in the upper edge of the falling-mould, may, when produced, meet in the middle point, 4, of the top of the section ; through any point, as a, in the straight part of the semi-plan, and at right angles to the sides of said straight part, draw a straight line, $a\,b$, across it, and produce $a\,b$ till it cuts the line $z\,h$ in q, and till it meets the upper edge of the falling mould at the point 2 ; divide the width of the rail, $a\,b$, into three equal parts, and at that point of division, r, nearest the point a, erect a perpendicular, $r\,s$, equal to $s\,z$ in Fig. 7 ; join q, s, (Fig. 1) and produce the line $q\,s$, till it meets the side of the rail at t ; produce the diameter d C, (Fig. 1) till it meets the upper edge of the falling mould, and at the points 3, 2, where the produced lines d 3, a 2, meet the upper edge of said mould erect the perpendiculars 3 a, 2 c, making the parts 3 w, 2 a, each equal to $t\,a$ in Fig. 1, and the parts $w\,a$, $a\,c$, each equal to $q\,t$ in Fig. 1 ; through the points $a\,w$, in the perpendiculars 2 c, 3 a, draw a straight line, $a\,h\,a$, of any length, and produce the line b 3, (Fig. 1) till it meets the line $a\,h\,a$ in the point 2 ; from said point, draw a straight line, 2 a, to the extremity, a, of the perpendicular 3 a, and the line 2 a will be the directing ordinate for the face-mould at Fig. 5. With this ordinate for radius, and from d (Fig. 1) as a centre, describe an arc cutting the line $z\,h$ at 2, and join d, 2 : the line d 2 will be the directing ordinate of the semi-plan. Parallel to d 2 draw other ordinates across the semi-plan, and from the points 5, 8, &c. where they meet the convex side of the semi-plan, draw straight lines at right angles to *z h*, and produce them till they meet the line *a h a* in Fig. 5; from the points where they meet *a h a*, draw the ordinates 3 5, 6 8, &c. parallel to the governing ordinate 2 *a*, and equal to 3 5, 6 8, &c. in the semi-plan, and complete the face-mould in the manner heretofore described.

Fig. 6 shews the bevel or spring of the plank, and is obtained by making *a f* and *c e* in Fig. 6 equal to *t a* in Fig. 1, and drawing the lines *e b*, *b c*, &c. as in the figure. The rhomboid *a b c d*, exhibits the shape and spring of the plank.

In the application of the face-mould, use the pitch-board in room of the pitch-bevel, and have the straight part of the mould parallel to the edge of the plank. Apply the falling-mould, and with the exception just mentioned, the face-mould also, precisely as directed in the preceding plate.

PL. 36.

This Plate exhibits a somewhat different and doubtless better method of drawing the face and falling-moulds of a stair rail, than that exhibited in the preceding Plate. As already stated, both were furnished me by Mr. Joshua Coulter. The face-mould, when drawn, as exhibited in this Plate, gives an equal proportion of width to the upper and lower ends; and the falling-mould is, by this method, drawn in the best manner, probably, of which it is susceptible. This mode of drawing it, has the effect to lower the concave side of the rail towards the nosings, and to elevate the convex side; as exhibited in the position of the two falling-moulds at Fig. A.

TO DRAW THE CONVEX AND CONCAVE FALLING-MOULDS AT FIG. A.

Let Fig. 1 be the plan of the semi-circular part of the rail, with a portion of straight rail attached, and let *j k* be the stretch-out of the convex side of the plan, and 5 7, that of the concave side; at the end, *k*, of the convex stretch-out *j k*, place the pitch-board 3 *k z*, so that its base, *k z*, shall form a continuation of the stretch-out line, and at the end, 7, of the concave stretch-out 5 7, place the pitch-board 5 7 &, in the same manner; at the other ends, *j*, 5, of the two stretch-outs, erect the perpendiculars *j* 3, 5 5, each equal in length to the height of the pitch-boards just mentioned and the stretchout of the winders put together, and at the upper ends of these perpendiculars, place the pitch-boards 3 6 &, 5 *y z*, in the position exhibited in the figure; connect the upper pitch-board, 3 6 &, with the lower one 3 *k z*, by the line 3 3, and allowing for the easings, *z* 3 3 & is the lower edge of the convex falling-mould; which mould is to be completed in the manner heretofore described. To obtain the butt-joint at *i j*, join the tops of the two lower pitch-boards by the line 3 5; bisect the distances, *j* 5, 7 *k*, intercepted between the ends of the two stretch-outs, and at the points of bisection, 2, 6, erect perpendiculars, and produce them till they meet the lines 3 5, 3 5; join the points where they meet those lines, by the line 2 2, bisecting the lower edge of the convex falling-mould ; bisect that part of the central perpendicular, *e f*, which crosses the falling-mould, and through the point of bisection, *g*, and at right angles to the line 2 2, draw the line *i j* for a butt joint.

To obtain the concave falling-mould, produce the side *k* 3, of the pitch-board 3 *k z*, till it meets the upper edge of the convex-mould in the point 4, and bisect the produced part, 3 4, in 1 ; at the point of bisection, erect a perpendicular, 1 1, producing said perpendicular and the side 7 5, of the pitch board 5 7 &, till they meet in the point 1 ; produce the perpendicular *j* 3, so that the part produced, 3 4, shall be equal to 3 4 at the lower end of the mould, and, bisecting 3 4 in 1, obtain the location of the point 1, in the line 5 5 1, in the same manner as at the lower end ; join the points 1, 1, thus obtained, by the line 1 1, (which line will pass longitudinally through the centre of the required concave mould,) and through the points, *i, j*, at the butt-joint, draw lines parallel to the centre line 1 1, and the concave falling-mould will be completed.

TO DRAW THE FACE MOULD AT FIG. 6.

Let Fig. 3 represent the semi-plan, or half of Fig 1, of which A is the centre, and A *g* a radius, cutting the semi-plan at the junction of the straight and circular parts of the rail ; join the ends of the curve passing lengthwise through the centre of the semi-plan, by the straight line *s t*, and through the inside corner (or corner nearest the centre A) of that end of the semi-plan which is straight, draw a straight line, *y h u*, of any length, and parallel to the line *s t* ; through the point *j*, in the butt-joint *i j*, (Fig. A) and parallel to the perpendicular *e f*, draw a straight line, meeting the base in the point 8, and the upper edge of the convex falling-mould in *s* ; set the length of the straight part of the rail in Fig. 1 from *k* to *m* on the base and at *m*, erect a perpendicular of sufficient length to meet the upper edge of the mould, as at *d* ; through the end *s*, of the line *s t*, (Fig. 3) and at right angles to *s t*, draw a straight line meeting the line *y h u* in *u*, and produce it in the opposite direction till the whole length, reckoning from *u*, is equal to the line 8 *s*, (making allowance for overwood,) intercepted between the base and the upper edge of the convex mould at Fig. A ; through the other end, *t*, of the line *s t*, (Fig. 3) and at right angles *s t*, draw the line *h t d*, meeting the line *y h u* in *h*, and produced in the other direction till the whole length *h d*, is equal to the perpendicular *m d* in Fig. A ; through the upper ends of the two lines thus formed, draw a straight line, *y u w*, (Fig. 6) of any length, and from the centre A, draw the line A 5.1 1, at right angles to *s t*, and meeting the rake-line *y u w* in the point 1 1 ; take, in the compass, the arc *g* 5, intercepted on the convex side of the semi-plan between the radii A *g*, A 5, and place it from *g* to *n* on the convex side of Fig. 1 ; from the point *p* in Fig. 1, (found when obtaining the convex stretch-out,) draw a straight line through *n* to the base, and at the point *g*, where it meets the base, erect the perpendicular *g* 10, meeting the upper edge of the falling-mould at 10 ; on the line A 5 11, (Fig. 3,) cut off the part *g* 10 equal to *g* 10 in Fig. A, and from the point 10, in the line A 5 11, let fall a perpendicular, 10 *w*, upon the rake line *y u w ;* with this perpendicular for radius, and from the point 10 as a centre, describe a circle, and parallel to A 5 11, draw the tangent 12 *w*, touching the circle (Fig. 6) at 12, and meeting the line *y h u* (Fig. 3) at *w ;* join the points *w*, 5, by the line *w* 5, and produce the perpendicular 10 *w* (Fig. 6) to *n*, making the part *w n* equal to the line *w* 5 in the semi-plan, and join *n*, 11 : the line *n* 11 will be the governing ordinate for the face-mould. With this ordinate as radius, and from the point 5 (Fig. 3) as a centre, describe an arc, cutting the line *y h u* in the point *v*, and join *v*, 5: the line *v* 5 will be the directing ordinate for the semi-plan. Parallel to *v* 5, draw other ordinates so as to meet the line *y h u*, and also the convex side of the semi-plan, and through the points where they meet the convex side, draw straight lines at right angles to *y h u*, producing them till they meet the rake-line *y u w ;* from the points where they meet said rake-line, draw the other ordinates of the face-mould, parallel to the governing one, *n* 11, and equal, each to each, to the corresponding ordinates in the semi-plan; and you will have the points through which to trace the outline of the face-mould, as required.

Fig. 5 is the face-mould for the upper rail piece, and is found in the same manner as the other, only that the base from which the heights are taken, is 2 *t* (Fig 2) instead of *j z*. *s s* and *t i* are the perpendiculars from the base 2 *t*, by which to obtain the proper rake or inclination of the upper face-mould, and 9 10, (Fig. 2.) is the one for finding the point for the centre of the circle in Fig. 5.

It will be observed, that the face-mould for the lower rail piece (Fig. 6) is considerably longer than the other, though the semi-plans for obtaining them are precisely alike. This difference is owing to the fact, that, at the junction of the straight with the circular part of the rail, the lower rail piece inclines upward with a steeper slope than before, while the upper one, at its junction with the straight part, has a gentler inclination than it had.

Fig. 7 represents the spring of the plank, and is obtained by making 9 *w* (Fig. 7) equal to 9 *w* in Fig. 3, drawing the perpendicular 9 *n* (Fig. 7) equal to 5 9 in Fig. 3 and joining *n*, *w :* the angle 9 *w n* (Fig. 7) is called the spring of the plank. Now when the rail pieces are cut out by the face-moulds at Fig's. 5 and 6, and bevelled according to Fig's. 8 and 9, if they are placed over the semi-plans at their proper angle of inclination, and so that the points *o*, *o*, in the centre of their extremities, shall be perpendicularly over the lines *s t*, *s t*, in the semi-plans, the several points and lines in the rail pieces will be vertically over their corresponding points and lines in the semi-plans.

In the application of the falling-moulds, place that part of the convex one which extends from *s* (Fig. A) downward, upon the convex edge of Fig. 6, (supposing the rail piece cut out, and plumb cuts made on it according to the pitch-bevels,) so that the points *j*, *c*, *z*, in the convex falling-mould may, each to each, coincide with the points *y*, *g*, *y*, on the convex edge of Fig. 6, and the lines *j s*, *c x*, *z d*, on the falling-mould, with the plumb cuts supposed to be made across the convex edge of Fig. 6 from the points *y*, *g*, *y ;* trace lines around the edges of the mould thus applied, and the outline for the convex side of the rail will be obtained. In applying the concave falling-mould, proceed in the same way ; observing in both cases, the directions given in Plate XXXIV.

PL. 37.

This Plate is precisely like the last, except that the face-moulds are omitted, and the falling-moulds, besides being located as in that Plate, are laid down separately, that their shape and their different inclinations may be more distinctly perceived. An explanation, therefore, of the method of drawing the falling-mould, would be a needless repetition.

PL. 38.

THE PLAN OF THE EMI-CIRCULAR PART OF A RAIL THAT SHALL HAVE EIGHT WINDERS AROUND THAT PART, BEING GIVEN, TO FIND THE FALLING-MOULD FOR THE CONVEX SIDE OF THE RAIL.

Let Fig. 1 represent the given plan, having portions of straight rail attached, and divide the arc $c\,e\,g$, and also the stretch-out of that arc, when obtained, into eight equal parts; obtain the stretch-out, $j\,k$, of the convex side of the plan, by the method heretofore described, and set it from j to k, on the base in Fig. 2 ; at the point k, in the said base, place the pitch-board of a common flyer in the manner described in Plate XXXVI, and at the point j in the same base, erect a perpedicular, $j\,o$, equal to the whole height of the risers in the eight winding steps and that of the pitch-board at the base, put together ; at the end o, of the perpendicular $j\,o$, place a pitch-board in the position exhibited in the figure, and join the two pitch-boards by the line $o\,o$; obtain the easings at the angles o, o, and the lower edge of the falling-mould at A, will be completed. Parallel to it, at any distance determined upon, draw the upper edge, and you will have the required convex falling-mould.

TO OBTAIN THE BUTT-JOINTS IN THE RAMPS OR EASINGS.

Let the length, $a\,c$, or $b\,d$, of the straight part of the rail in Fig. 1, from k to m, on the base, and at m, erect the perpendicular $m\,d$, meeting the upper edge of the falling-mould at d ; on the upper edge of said mould, set off, on each side of d, any equal distances, as $d\,a$, $d\,t$, and from the points t, a, as centres, with the chord length of $t\,a$ as radius, describe arcs cutting each other at c ; join the points c, d, by the line $c\,d$, and produce said line across the falling mould: the part which crosses the mould, will give the position of the butt-joint in the lower ramp. Find the upper butt-joint by the same process ; and to obtain the central one, $i\,j$, bisect $h\,f$ in g, and through g, draw $i\,j$, at right angles to the edges of the mould.

To show the overwood necessary to cut the central butt-joint, $i\,j$, draw straight lines through the points i, j, parallel to the central line f A, and cutting the plan (Fig. 1) in the points 8, 8: the width intercepted on the plan between the central line f A and either of the lines $j\,8$, $i\,8$, is the width of overwood necessary for cutting the butt-joint $i\,j$.

TO FIND THE FACE-MOULD AT FIG. 7.

With the exception of making the height lines start from the line *s t*, (Fig. 3) instead of the outer one, 2 *h n*, proceed exactly as in drawing Fig. 6, Plate XXXVI. till you have found the point *m*, in the line A *m* 2 ; instead of describing a circle with *m* for the centre, as in Plate XXXVI, draw *m o*, at right angles to A 2, and meeting the rake line 2 *s* in the point *o ;* through *o*, and parallel to A 2, draw *o w*, meeting the line *s t* (Fig. 3) in the point *w*, and from *w*, draw a straight line to the point *v*, where the line A 2 cuts the dotted curve that passes longitudinally through the centre of the semi-plan ; produce the said straight line both ways, so as to meet the line 2 *h n*, (Fig. 3) and also the convex side of the semi-plan, and parallel to it as the directing ordinate for the semi-plan, draw other ordinates, and erect perpendiculars to meet the rake line, as directed in Plate XXXVI. From the point *m*, in the line A 2, let fall a perpendicular, *m r*, upon the rake line 2 *s*, and produce it indefinitely on the other side of said rake line ; take the distance *w v*, intercepted on the directing ordinate (Fig. 3) between the line *s t* and the dotted curve, and from the point *o*, (Fig. 7) as a centre, with said intercepted distance as a radius, describe an arc cutting the produced perpendicular, *m v*, in *v* ; join *o*, *v*, and the line *o v* will be the directing ordinate for the face-mould, and its extremity *v*, one of the points through which to trace the concave edge of said mould. Complete Fig. 7 by transferring to it the ordinates in Fig. 3, as directed in the last Plate but one.

By the same process, the face-mould for the upper rail piece (Fig. 8) is obtained ; the line 4 *x* (Fig. 2) being taken as a base, and the lines *t i, s s*, being the heights by which to find the proper inclination of the rake line.

Fig. 6 shews the spring or bevel of the plank, at an acute angle, adapted to the lower rail piece, and is obtained thus : draw any straight line, *n m*, (Fig. 6) and from it cut off a part, *m r*, equal to *m r* in Fig. 7 ; at *r*, (Fig. 6) erect a perpendicular *r v*, equal to the part, *u v*, of the line A 2, (Fig. 3) intercepted between the line *s t* and the dotted curve ; join *v, m*, (Fig. 6) and the acute angle *v m r*, shows the proper spring of the plank for the lower rail piece. In a similar manner, obtain, from Fig's. 4 and 8, the bevel of the plank at an obtuse angle, as shown by the angle *v r y*, in Fig. 5.

In the application of the falling-mould A, proceed as directed in Plate XXXIV ; making *d x*, in the upper edge of the mould, coincide with 2 2, at the lower end of the convex side of Fig. 7, and *s*, in the mould, with 8, on the convex side of Fig. 7 ; and bending the mould round the convex edge of the rail piece, as heretofore described.

In applying the pitch-bevels to the plank, when getting out rail pieces, let the stocks of the bevels coincide with that edge of the plank represented by the rake line 2 *s*, in Fig's. 7 and 8, and let their blades fall across the thickness of the plank, so as to have the plumb cuts parallel to the perpendiculars raised from the semi-plan.

PL. 39.

In this Plate, the falling-moulds are adapted to a stair having ten winders around the semi-circular part of the rail, and instead of running parallel to the nosing line, as they ordinarily do, they are drawn so as to have, at the perpendicular height of one riser above the centre g, (see Fig. 2) a horizontal distance from the nosing line equal to the width of one tread or step, as at h; while, at the second nosing below the centre, they cut the nosing line, as at w. It is thought by some, that the hand can glide more easily up or down a rail of this shape, than over those which are parallel to the nosing line. The mode of drawing the convex mould at Fig. 2, is as follows. Having, in the same manner as in preceding plates, obtained the convex stretch-out $j\,k$, erected the perpendicular $j\,o$, (equal to the combined height of the lower pitch-board and ten risers,) placed the upper and lower pitch-boards, and joined them by the hypothenuse $o\,o$, erect the central perpendicular $e\,f$, and set the height of a riser from g to h, on the said perpendicular; through the point h, thus found, and the point w, at the second nosing below g, draw a straight line, and produce said line, as also the sides $t\,o$, $t\,o$, of the upper and lower pitch-boards, till they meet in the points r, r; obtain the easings at the angles r, r, and parallel to the lower edge, $t\,w\,h\,t$, thus completed, draw the upper one, $d\,s\,s$, and you will have the required convex falling-mould.

Proceed in the same way, in drawing the falling-mould for the concave side of the rail.

Fig's. 5 and 6, represent the face-moulds for the upper and lower rail pieces, and Fig's. 4 and 3, the semi-plans from which they are obtained. The several steps of the process by which they are obtained, correspond exactly with those detailed in Plate XXXVI, and render a formal explanation quite unnecessary. As in Plate XXXVI, the lines $m\,d$, $8\,s$, $t\,i$, $5\,s$, (Plate XXXIX. Fig. 2,) are those by which the respective inclinations of the rake-lines are determined; and the lines $9\,10$, $9\,10$, at the upper and lower parts of the elevation, are those by which the centres of the circles in Fig's. 5 and 6 are ascertained. To obtain the last named lines, make the arcs $g\,n$, $g\,n$, on the convex side of Fig. 1, each equal to the arc $g\,n$ on the convex side of Fig. 3, and from the point p, (Fig. 1) draw straight lines through the points n, n, to the stretch-out $j\,k$; at the points m, m, where the said straight lines meet $j\,k$, erect perpendiculars, and produce them till they meet the upper edge of the convex falling-mould: the parts $9\,10$, $9\,10$, intercepted between the upper edge of said mould and the respective bases $j\,t$, $5\,t$, are the lines required.

The lines $5\,n$, $5\,n$, (Fig's. 3 and 6) are, respectively, the governing ordinates semi-plan and the face mould, and are obtained precisely as in Plate XXXVI.

The spring of the plank is represented by the angle $9\,w\,n$, in the semi-plan at Fig. 3.

PL. 40.

This plate exhibits the plan, and the face and falling moulds of an elliptical stair. The plan (Fig. 1.) is, by means of chords, divided into as many parts as there are to be pieces in the rail, and upon these chords, height lines (taken from the elevation) and perpendiculars are erected, the rake lines and ordinates are drawn, and the face moulds (Fig's. 3, 4, and 5) completed, just as in the foregoing plates, except that the ordinates are at right angles to the rake lines. (Fig. 6 is a face mould, with its ordinates drawn so as to form an oblique angle with the rake line, and be adapted to the spring of the plank; and Fig. 7 represents the said spring or bevel.

The triangle $b\ a\ c$, (Fig. 12) represents a square step or flyer, and the line $c\ d\ f$, represents a portion of floor at the top of the first flight of steps. The line $d\ e$, intercepted between said floor line and the under edge of the convex falling mould, is equal the half of $a\ c$, that is, half the height of a riser; and the rail, after reaching that elevation above the floor, will pass on horizontally till it reaches the foot of the second flight.

PL. 41.

In this plate, Fig. 1 is the plan of an elliptical stair, and Fig. 4, a section or semi-elevation of the same. Fig. 3 represents a bearer for supporting the winders; of which bearer, Fig. 2 is the plan. Fig. 3 is obtained in the following manner:—at the point c, where the lower side of the plan (Fig. 2) meets the elliptical wall, erect a perpendicular, $c\ 9$, equal to the height or stretch-out of the risers in as many winding steps as the bearer is intended to support; divide said perpendicular into as many equal parts as there are risers in said steps, and at the points of division, 1, 2, &c., erect perpendiculars of any length; at the point c, c, &c., where the lines representing the division of the steps cut the lower side of Fig. 2, erect perpendiculars, and produce them till they meet, each with each, their corresponding perpendiculars erected on $c\ a$; from the points a, a, &c., where they meet, set off, on the perpendiculars from Fig. 2, the parts $a\ a$, $a\ a$, &c. each equal to $a\ a$ in the semi-elevation at Fig. 4, and through the lower points a, a, &c. thus obtained, trace the curve for the under edge of the bearer. The parallel straight lines on either side of this curve, shew the width of stuff requisite for getting out the bearer.

It will be perceived, that, in its ultimate position, that is, when raised up at right angles to its plan, the several parts of Fig. 3 will be in a vertical range with the several parts of Fig. 2. The method of placing bearers exhibited in this Plate, possesses decided advantages over the old and common mode, as it regards both time and expense, and is recommended to the notice of such stair-builders as have not already put it in practice.

PL. 42.

This Plate exhibits the plans and elevations of the front and back strings of a circular stair. The arc A (Fig. 1) represents the plan of the front string, or string adjacent to the opening, and C, the plan of the string contiguous to the wall. B and D are the stretch-outs of said arcs, and the several divisions in them correspond, in location, with the several divisions made in A and C by the dotted radii, which, from the centre O, pass through the front of each step to the plan of the back string. In the plans A and C, *a*, *b*, *c*, &c. represent the wedges supposed to be inserted on the convex side of the two stair-strings, and made to penetrate to a greater or less depth, and to be a greater or less distance apart, according to the greater or less extent of the circles in which the strings are spirally to wind. In this example, the wedges in the front string are made to reach to within about an eighth of an inch (see the scale at bottom) of the concave side, and to be about seven-eighths of an inch apart ; while those in the back string, only come within about a quarter of an inch of the concave side and are about an inch and a quarter apart. The wedges may be shorter and further apart in the back string than in the other, for the reason that the back string winds in a larger circle than the front one, and of course has a less prominent curvature. The depth to which the wedges penetrate and their distance apart, must be left to the discretion of the workman. Care must be taken that they be not too far apart, for if they are, the concave sides of the stair-strings will present a succession of plane surfaces and angles, instead of that regular curvature which they are intended to exhibit.

Fig's. 2 and 3 represent the elevations of the front and back strings, and are obtained by a process so very similar to that by which the falling moulds in the preceding plates are found, that no explanation will be necessary.

In Fig. 2, *c* represents a separate piece, intended for insertion, at its upper edge, into a groove to be made in the under edge of the front string, after it has bent to its true shape and has become entirely dry. In the same way a separate piece may be inserted into a groove in the upper edge of the back string at Fig. 3. The line *a* (Fig. 3) shews the width of the skirting when got out separately, and the line *b* is the width of the back string and skirting, when they are got out in one piece. When got out in one piece, channels or mortises are made in it, for admitting the ends of the treads and risers. Whether the string be mortised for inserting the ends of the steps, or whether it be notched, a pitch-board must be applied to it, and lines traced for the treads and risers ; but the places for the ends of the steps must not be cut out until the string is bent, wedged, and dried.

To give the strings of a circular stair their proper curvature and spiral twist, make, for each string, a cylindrical block, that is, make two frames with battens or narrow strips of board nailed on longitudinally and rounded off at the outer edges, so that each frame shall, following the outline of the battens, be cylindrical, and have the respective curvatures of the circular wall and well-hole. Around these cylindrical frames bend your stair strings, gluing in the wedges as you proceed, and, if you please, gluing a piece of coarse canvass over the wedges.

NOTE.—In making the apertures for the wedges on the convex side of the strings at Fig's. 2 and 3, care must be taken to cut them at right angles to the stretch-out D, (or any other horizontal line,) instead of cutting them at right angles to the edges of the elevations.

PL. 43.

OF THE CHORAGIC MONUMENT OF THRASSYLLUS.

(From Stewart's Antiquities.)

Just above the place on which I have supposed the Odeum of Pericles to have been built, there is, in the rock of the Acropolis, a cavern or grotto, the entrance into which is fronted, and completely closed up, by the building here treated of. The cavern is now a christian church, called the Panagia Speliottissa, or the Blessed Lady of the Grotto. On the front of the building are three inscriptions, recording victories obtained either in the Odeum or in the theatre, which prove it to have been a Choragic monument; not indeed so highly ornamented as the monument of Lysicrates, but wrought nevertheless with great accuracy, and deserving our notice both for the singularity of its composition and the form of its mouldings. Besides which I must observe, that the mutilated statue yet remaining on it is the work of an excellent sculptor. There were inscriptions cut on the middle of the architrave.

This is the most ancient of the three inscriptions above-mentioned, as Wheler and Spon have already observed, and was doubtless made when the monument was first erected. By it we learn, that " Thrasyllus, the son of Thrasyllus of Deceleia (a demos or township of the tribe of Hippothoon,) dedicates this building, having been at the expense of exhibiting the games, in which, with the men of his own tribe, he obtained the victory; that Evius of Chalcis was the musician; and Karchidamus the son of Sotis composed the piece, Neaechmus being Archon." This was in the first year of the 115th Olympiad, or about 318 years before the Christian era; so that this building was erected above two thousand years ago.

The other two inscriptions record victories of the same kind with the former, obtained about fifty years afterwards, when Pytharatus was Archon. The following is on the left hand, or towards the west:

The people gave the games, Pytharatus was Archon,
Thrasycles the son of Thrasyllus, a Decelian, was Agonothetes,
The boys of the tribe of Hippothoon got the victory,
Theon the Theban performed on the flute,
Pronomus the Theban composed the piece.

Pronomus was a celebrated musician of Thebes, remarkable for having a great beard. He was contemporary with Aristophanes, who took occasion to scoff at Agyrrhius, an Athenian magistrate, ludicrously supposing he had borrowed his beard from Pronomus. As the piece which gained the prize in these games was composed by a musician, it seems to prove that the inscription relates rather to a musical than a dramatic performance; and that the victory it records was obtained in the Odeum, not in the theatre. It is also to be remarked that these games were given more than a hundred years after the time when Aristophanes made free with our musician's beard: may we not therefore conclude, that on this occasion, long after his decease, some favourite composition of his was performed with great applause? Nor shall we find this to have been without a precedent; for by what Pausanias relates to have happened at the rebuilding of the walls of Messene, in the third year of the 102d Olympiad, it appears there were at the time two parties among the frequenters of musical entertainments, some deciding in favour of Pronomus, while others continued to prefer the more ancient compositions of Sacadas, a musician of Argos, then doubtless many years dead, for he had gained a prize at the Pythian games in the 48th Olympiad: and although the works of his antagonist had long enjoyed great reputation, Pronomus appears to have had the suffrages of a majority in his favour.

PL. 44.

OF THE TEMPLE OF THESEUS.

(From Stewart's Antiquities.)

The travellers who have visited the city of Athens, and the authors who have described its antiquities, all agree, that this Doric Temple, one of the noblest remains of its ancient magnificence, and at present the most entire, was built in honour of Theseus. This opinion is abundantly justified by the sculptures in some of the metopes, for, mutilated as they are, it is evident that several of the exploits of the hero are there represented.

Nor can it be doubted, that this is the temple which both Plutarch and Pausanias place near the Gymnasium of Ptolemy; great remains of that Gymnasium are yet standing, and their situation in regard to this temple agrees exactly with the information those authors have left us.

On what occasion Theseus was thus honoured, we are taught by the above-mentioned authors. Plutarch particularly, after recounting his heroic deeds, and the ingratitude of the factious Athenians towards him, with his banishment and death, says, " In after-times, several motives concurring, the Athenians honoured him as a hero. Many of those who fought against the Medes at Marathon, imagined they saw his apparition in complete armour, rushing before them on the enemy. After the conclusion of the Median war, Phædon being archon, the Athenians consulting the oracle, the Pythian priestess answered, that they should bring back the bones of Theseus, deposit them honourably in their city, and with a religious observance keep them there."

This was accomplished when Cimon, the son of Miltiades, had conquered Scyros; there, after a diligent search, he discovered the venerable remains of the hero, of superior stature, with the brazen point of a spear, and a sword lying by him (these weapons in the heroic age were of brass;) and having embarked them on board his ship, he carried them to Athens, where they were received by the citizens with splendid processions and sacrifices, as if the hero himself had returned to visit them. His remains were deposited in the middle of the city, near the present Gymnasium.

Nor was this all; festivals were instituted, and games celebrated, in honour of the event; and on this occasion, as it has been generally supposed, happened that famous contest between Æschylus and Sophocles, two competitors for dramatic glory, who, since that time, if we except Euripides, have hardly, either of them, had a rival: the victory was adjudged to Sophocles, and his high-spirited antagonist, unable to support the disgrace, or submit to the decision of his judges, left his country, and passed into Sicily a voluntary exile. This was transacted, we are told by Plutarch, in the year that Aphepsiôn was archon, which the best authorities place in the fourth year of the seventy-seventh Olympiad, 467 before Christ; that is, exactly forty years before the death of Pericles, or precisely at the time when he began to acquire popularity and power in Athens: so that this temple may well be accounted a work of the age of Pericles.

It is built of Pentelic marble, and in the language of Vitruvius, is a Peripteros. The principal front faces the east; and the pediment of that front appears to have been adorned, like those of the Parthenon, with figures of entire relief, fixed in their places by cramps of metal; for on the face of this pediment remain several holes, in which the ends of those cramps have been inserted, though the figures they supported are all of them destroyed.

On the metopes in this eastern front, are represented ten of the labours of Hercules; and on the four metopes next that front, both on the northern and southern sides, are eight of the achievements of Theseus. It will appear the less extraordinary, that the labours of Hercules should make so considerable a part of the ornaments of this temple, when we recollect the respect and gratitude which Theseus professed to that hero, who was his kinsman, had delivered him from a tedious captivity, and had restored him to his country; on his return to which, he consecrated to Hercules all the places that the gratitude of his citizens had formerly dedicated to himself, four only excepted; and changed their names from Theséa to Heracleia. Nor could it be esteemed a slight compliment to Theseus, when on building this temple to his honour, their labours were thus placed together. The remainder of the metopes, and the pediment of the Posticum, or western front, have never been adorned with sculptures.

It is now a church dedicated to St. George, for whom the present Athenians have as high a veneration as their ancestors had for Theseus ; and to this we probably owe that it is not in a more ruinous condition. It seems scarcely worth mentioning, that Mr. Vernon, who visited Athens in the year 1675, and Dr. Spon, with Sir George Wheler, who came there early in the following year, have written their names on the wall within the temple ; their example has been followed by several other travellers of distinction.

PLATES 45, 52, AND 53.

THE DORIC ORDER OF THE TEMPLE OF MINERVA, CALLED THE PARTHENON AND HECATOMPEDON.

(From Stewart's Antiquities of Athens.)

This temple was built during the administration of Pericles, who employed Callicrates and Ictinus as architects, under Phidias, to whom he committed the direction of all works of elegance and magnificence.

It has been celebrated by some of the most eminent writers of antiquity, whose accounts are confirmed and illustrated in the descriptions given us by those travellers, who saw it almost entire in the last century. Even in its present state, the spectator on approaching it, will find himself not a little affected by so solemn an appearance of ruined grandeur. Accustomed as we were to the ancient and modern magnificence of Rome, and by what we had heard and read, impressed with an advantageous opinion of what we were come to see, we found the image, our fancy had pre-conceived, greatly inferior to the real object.

When Sir George Wheler and Dr. Spon visited Athens in the year 1676, this temple was entire ; and the former has given the following description of it :

" It is situated about the middle of the citadel, and consists altogether of admirable white marble. The plane of it is above twice as long as it is broad ; being 217 feet 9 inches long, and 98 feet 6 inches broad. It hath an ascent every way of five degrees. or steps ; which seem to be so contrived, to serve as a basis to the portico, which is supported by channelled pillars of the Doric order, erected round upon them, without any other basis. These pillars are 46 in number, being eight to the front, and as many behind, and 17 on each side, counting the four corner ones twice over to be deducted. They are 42 feet high and $17\frac{1}{2}$ feet about. The distance from pillar to pillar is 7 feet 4 inches. This portico beareth up a front, and frieze round about the temple, charged with historical figures of admirable beauty and work. The figures of the front, which the ancients called the eagle, appear, though from that height, of the natural bigness ; being in entire relievo, and wonderfully well carved. Pausanias saith no more of them, than that they concern the birth of the goddess Minerva. What I observed and remembered of them, is this :

" There is a figure that stands in the middle of it, having its right arm broken, which probably held the thunder. Its legs straddle at some distance from each other, where without doubt was placed the eagle; for its beard and the majesty which the sculptor hath expressed in his countenance, although those other usual characters be wanting here, do sufficiently shew it to have been made for Jupiter. He stands naked, for so he was usually represented, especially by the Greeks. At his right hand is another figure, with its hands and arms broken off, covered down half way the legs, in a posture as coming towards Jupiter; which, perhaps was a Victory, leading the horses of the triumphant chariot of Minerva which follows it. The horses are made with such great art, that the sculptor seems to have out-done himself, by giving them a more than seeming life, such a vigour is expressed in each posture of their prancing and stamping, natural to generous horses. Minerva is next represented in the chariot, rather as the goddess of learning than of war, without helmet, buckler, or a Medusa's Head on her breast. Next behind her is another figure of a woman sitting with her head broken off; who it was is not certain. But my companion made me observe the next two figures, sitting in the corner, to be of the Emperor Adrian and his Empress Sabina, whom I easily knew to be so, by the many medals and statues I have seen of them. At the left hand of Jupiter are five or six other figures; my companion taketh them to be an assembly of the gods, where Jupiter introduceth Minerva, and owneth her for his daughter. The postick, or hind-front, was adorned with figures, expressing Minerva's contest with Neptune about naming the city of Athens; but now all of them are fallen down, only part of a sea-horse excepted. The architrave is also charged with a basso-relievo at several distances, divided into squares of about two or three feet broad, and three or four feet high. Within the portico on high, and on the outside of the cella of the temple itself, is another border of basso-relievo round about it, or at least on the north and south sides, which, without doubt, is as ancient as the temple, and of admirable work; but not so high a relievo as the other. Thereon are represented sacrifices, processions, and other ceremonies of the heathens' worship. Most of them were designed by the Marquis De Nointel; who employed a painter to do it two months together, and shewed them to us, when we waited on him at Constantinople. The cella of the temple without is 158 feet long, and broad 67 feet. Before you enter into the body of the temple from the front, is the Pronaos, whose roof is sustained by six channelled pillars of the same order and bigness with those of the portico, and contains near the third part of the cella; to wit, 44 feet of the length. We observed in place of one of the pillars, a great pile of stone and lime, of most rude work; which they told us the Kislar-Haga had ordered to be so done to help to support the roof; because he could never find a stone big enough to supply the place of the old pillar broken down, although he had spent two thousand crowns to do it.—From the Pronaos we entered into the temple by a long door in the middle of the front. But my companion and I were not so much surprised with the obscurity of it, as Monsieur Guiliter; because the observations we had made on other heathen temples did make it no new thing to us. When the Christians consecrated it to serve God in, they let in the light at the east end, which is all that it yet hath; and not only that, but made a semi-circle for the Holy-place, according to their rites; which the Turks have not yet much altered. This was separated from the rest by jasper pillars, two of which on each side yet remain. Within this chancel is a canopy sustained by four porphyry pillars, with beautiful white marble chapters of the Corinthian order: but the holy table under it is removed. Beyond the canopy are two or three degrees one above another in a semi-circle, where the bishop and presbyters used to sit in time of communion, upon certain solemn days. The bishop sat in a marble chair above the rest; which yet remaineth above the degrees, against the window. On both sides and towards the door, is a kind of gallery, made with two ranks of pillars, twenty-two below, and twenty-three above; the odd pillar is over the arch of the entrance, which was left for the passage. They shewed us the place where two orange-trees of marble had stood, which being taken thence to be carried to Constantinople, the vessel miscarried with them. The roof over the altar and choir, added to the temple by the Greeks, hath the picture of the Holy Virgin on it, of Mosaic work, left yet by the Turks. This temple was covered outwardly with great planks of stone, of which some are fallen down, and are to be seen in the Mosque."

Thus far Sir George Wheler, who has copied this account from Dr. Spon, and added to it some mistakes of his own, which I have omitted. Dr. Spon tells us the measures were taken in French feet; therefore reckoning the diameters of the columns $5\frac{57}{100}$ such feet, the extent of the front between the outer surfaces of the angular columns, reduced to English measure, will be found nearly 102 feet two inches, that of the side 225 feet $10\frac{1}{2}$ inches. But measures obtained by girting the circumferences of columns are little to be depended on.

In the year 1687 Athens was besieged by the Venetians, under the command of the Proveditore Morosini and Count Koningsmark; when an unlucky bomb, falling on this admirable structure, reduced it to the state in which we saw it.

In our way to it from the city, we passed by the theatre of Bacchus, and came to the propylæa, which are miserably ruined, and thence through a street of scattered houses to the western front of the temple, the majestic appearance of which cannot easily be described.

On this front the walls with their antæ, and all the columns of the portico, with their entablature and pediment, are standing; and the architecture has suffered little; but the sculptures in the metopes, and the figures in the pediment, are defaced and ruined.

The columns of the portico stand on a pavement, raised three steps above the ground; and there are two more from the portico to the pronaos (or rather posticum, for the pronaos was in reality at the opposite front;) from this there is another step, little more than an inch in height, into the temple; so inconsiderable a rise has occasioned this step to remain hitherto unnoticed.

The inside of the temple was divided by a cross wall; and the lesser division, the pavement of which is level with the top of the little step last mentioned, is the part into which you first enter ; Wheler and Spon have called it improperly the pronaos.

This was undoubtedly the opisthodomus, where the public treasure was kept. Here the columns, mentioned by those travellers, are no longer remaining ; but part of the rude mass, said to have been erected by a Kislár-Agá, is still to be seen. Hence you pass into the greater division ; at the western end of which, and on both the sides, the pavement of the opisthodomus is continued on the same level, to about 15 feet from the walls, enclosing an area sunk a little more than an inch below it. Near the edge of the little step down into this area are still to be seen, distinctly traced, certain circles ; on these doubtless the columns of the peristyle were placed, which supported the galleries mentioned by Wheler ; at present not only those galleries are entirely destroyed, but the walls of this part, with fourteen of the columns of the peripteros, are no longer standing ; and the pavement is strewed with pieces of sculpture, some of which are very large, and all of them of excellent workmanship.

In this division stood the famous statue of Minerva, of ivory and gold, the work of Phidias. Pausanias says, it was standing erect, her garment reaching to her feet ; she had a helmet on, and a Medusa's Head on her breast ; in one hand she held a spear, and on the other stood a victory of about four cubits high. Pliny tells us the statue was twenty-six cubits high, in which he perhaps included the pedestal ; whereon they both say, the birth of Pandora was represented. We are not told whether the ivory was painted ; but by what Strabo says, that Panænus, the brother or nephew of Phidias, assisted him in colouring the statue of Jupiter at Elis, which was likewise of ivory and gold, it probably was. The reason why ivory was used in statues of of this kind, rather than wood, seems not to have been on account of its colour, but because wood is apt to crack, and to be destroyed by worms : for ivory is not of a uniform colour, being yellow near the outside of the tooth, and white in the middle ; it therefore would require painting on that account, and likewise to hide the joinings of the pieces.

Thucydides says, the gold about it weighed 40 talents, which, according to the value of gold at that time, was worth above 120,000l. sterling. Lachares stript it off about 130 years after the death of Pericles, and we do not read that it was ever replaced.

The eastern front of this temple hath suffered more than the western ; all the walls and five of the columns of the pronaos are down ; but the eight columns in front with their entablature, remain pretty entire in their original situation, though much the greater part of the pediment is wanting.

The metopes on the south side were adorned with sculptures in alto-relievo of Centaurs and Lapithæ, several of which are not yet entirely defaced.

The outside of the cell was surrounded at the top with a continued frieze of about three feet four inches deep, representing the Panathenaïc pomp or procession, in basso-relievo ; part of which was copied by a young French painter, employed by the Marquis de Nointel in the year 1674 ; two or three of whose drawings are represented in Montfauçon's Antiquities.

Pausanias gives but a transient account of this temple ; nor does he say whether Adrian repaired it ; though his statue, and that of his empress Sabina in the western pediment, have occasioned a doubt whether the sculptures in both were not put up by him.   Wheler and Spon were of this opinion, and say they were whiter than the rest of the building ; the statue of Antoninus, now remaining at Rome, may be thought a proof, that there were artists in his time capable of executing them ; but this white-ness is no proof that they were more modern than the temple, for they might be made of a whiter marble ; and the heads of Hadrian and Sabina might be put on two of the ancient figures, which was no uncommon practice among the Romans.   And if we may give credit to Plutarch, the buildings of Pericles were not in the least impaired by age in his time, therefore this temple could not want any material repairs in the reign of Hadrian ; unless the damage the Opisthodomus once suffered by fire, for which, Demosthenes tells us, not only the treasurers of the goddess, but likewise those of the other gods, were imprisoned, had remained so long unrepaired, which is not probable.

I have said that the lesser division of the temple was called the Opisthodomus, where the public treasure was kept.   Thucydides tells us it was kept in the Acropo-lis ; and having reckoned up what it amounted to, he says, " the riches out of the other temples may likewise be used ;" which implies, that the treasure he had been speaking of was kept in a temple.   Aristophanes places Plutus, the god of riches, in the opisthodomus of the Temple of Minerva.   His scholiast, indeed, says, that this was the Temple of Minerva Polias ; which is a mistake, for that temple had only a single cell, as will appear hereafter ; nor could it be the temple meant by Thucydi-des, since it was not finished till after the death of Pericles, as appears by the in-scription brought from Athens at the expense of the Society of Dilettanti.   Demos-thenes calls the treasury opisthodomus, which properly signified the back of a tem-ple ; and Hesychius, Harpocration, Suidas, and the Etymologicum, agree that the Athenian treasury was in the opisthodomus of the Temple of Minerva, which could be no other than this.

The third, fourth, and fifth marbles, in the second part of Dr. Chandler's Inscrip-tions, are registers of the delivery of donations in this temple, by the treasurers to their successors in office.   The third and fourth were found among its ruins.   It is called hecatompedon in both, and its opisthodomus is expressly mentioned in the lat-ter.   The fifth calls it Parthenon.

There is a passage in Vitruvius, which, if it relates to this temple, as I am persuad-ed it does, would prove it to have been an hypæthros ; that author says, " The hy-pæthros has ten columns in the pronaos and posticum, in all other respects it is like the Dipteros : within, it has two rows of columns, one above the other, at a distance from the wall, so that you may pass round it, as in the portico of peristyles ; but in the middle it is open to the sky, without a roof ; the entrance is at each end, by doors in the pronaos and the posticum. There is no example of this at Rome, but at Athens an octastyle, and in the Olympian Temple."

I shall now remark the particulars in which the Parthenon agrees with what Vitruvius hath here delivered.

The description I have quoted from Wheler, shews that this temple, when he saw it, had within the cell on each side, two rows of columns one above the other, standing at a distance from the wall. The decorations on the eastern front, prove the principal entrance to have been originally placed there; though it was most probably closed by the Greek Christians, because otherwise they could not have placed their Communion Table at the east end of the temple, a custom they always religiously observe. It is likewise evident, that the door we now see in the western front was originally there, for the threshold or step into it still remains; and thus far the construction of this temple agrees with what Vitruvius has delivered and favours my opinion. It is true the roof with which it was completely covered when Wheler and Spon, and other travellers examined it, may seem to furnish a plausible objection to what I have here advanced; but as great additions and alterations have certainly been made, to adapt it to the performance of the numerous ceremonies of the Greek ritual, and the pompous functions of the archbishop and his attendant clergy, it is extremely probable that the roof was completed at the same time; and this supposition will acquire additional support, when we consider that the space between the columns did not much exceed thirty feet, and must have been covered in, before it was fit for the reception of a Christian congregation; and that this work would not have been of a more expensive kind, nor have required greater skill in the execution, than the alterations which Wheler and Spon inform us were made in the eastern end.

Another objection may be deduced from what Vitruvius himself has said (Book IV. Chap. VII.) where, enumerating several deviations from the usual form of temples, he tells us, "Temples are also built of other kinds, ordered with the same proportions, but differently disposed, as that of Castor, in the Circus Flaminius, and that of Vejovis, between the two groves; also, but more ingeniously, that of Diana Nemorensis, with columns added to the right and left on the shoulders of the pronäos; but this kind of temple, like that of Castor, in the Circus, was first erected in the Fortress of Athens to Minerva," &c.

Vitruvius having already told us, that there was no Hypæthros at Rome, seems, by remarking the similarity between those Temples he has here enumerated, and that of Minerva in the Acropolis, to furnish a proof that the latter was not an Hypæthros; but it must be observed, that in this place he is treating of the disposition of the external columns only.

It appears extraordinary, that in the account Virtuvius has given of the Hypæthros, the examples he produces are exceptions to his doctrine; but we may be the less surprised at it, as the same unusual proceeding occurs in his account of the Peripteros; and it is obvious, that an hypæthros, having eight columns in front, differs from one having ten, only in this particular, that the exterior columns form a peripteros instead of a dipteros, round the cell of the temple ; as the Marquis Galiani hath well observed in his comment on this place.

Hitherto my remarks on what Vitruvius has said concerning this form or aspect of temple, regard only that part of it which, I suppose, relates to the Parthenon ; but I find myself obliged to add some farther remarks on that passage, on account of an error I have committed in the fifth chapter of our first volume, which treats of a ruin supposed by me to have been the Poikilè. Wheler and Spon have called it the Temple of Jupiter Olympius ; and Monsieur Le Roy has followed them in this, as well as in many other mistakes. I have there shewn, that neither the situation nor the dimensions of this ruin answer to what the ancients have delivered concerning the Temple of Jupiter at Athens, which I have inadvertently said was an octastyle, when it certainly was a decastyle. I was led into this error by Philander, and those Editors of Vitruvius, who since his time have, as before observed, followed his conjectural emendation ; and who, instead of, " But an octastyle at Athens, and in the Olympian Temple," read " But an octastyle at Athens in the Temple of Jupiter Olympius."

The plan of the Athenian Temple of Jupiter Olympius, which I shall give at the end of this chapter, will shew that it was a decastyle, and therefore could not possibly be that meant by Vitruvius, but some other ; how then are we to understand him ? I shall venture to suppose, that it is the Olympian Temple, in the territory of Elis, he has here mentioned ; it was of great magnificence, the Olympic games were celebrated there, and a prodigious concourse of people from every part of Greece attended their solemnization. It seems to have been erected immediately after the Parthenon, at a time when the study of architecture was highly cultivated, and therefore, might well deserve to be cited as an example by Vitruvius.

Pausanias has given a more particular description of this temple, than of any other he had seen ; he says, it was a Doric structure, that it was 68 feet from the pavement to the top of the pediment, and that the breadth was 95 feet ; whence it is evident, there could not have been more than eight columns in its front ; for if we suppose the entablature and pediment occupied two-fifths of its height, as in the Parthenon they nearly do, the columns being of Doric proportion, must have been more than six feet in diameter, and eight such columns would not have left more than seven feet for each intercolumniation.

The same author continuing his account, describes the two doors, one in the pronaos, and the other in the posticum ; and tells us that there were, within the cell, columns which supported lofty porticos through which you passed on to the image of the god ; this, like that of Minerva in the Parthenon, was of a colossal size, and made of ivory and gold by the same great artist. These circumstances answer to the description Vitruvius hath given of the hypæthros ; there is however one particular mentioned by Strabo, which may appear to contradict this opinion ; he says this statue of Jupiter was of so great a magnitude, that though he was represented sitting, he almost touched the roof, and it seemed, if he were to rise, he would uncover the temple, which he adds, was of the amplest dimensions.

Hence, indeed, it is plain, that the statue was under cover; nor can it be supposed that so magnificent and costly a work, composed of ivory and gold, and delicately painted, was exposed in the open air to all the varieties of weather. Yet those who would contend, that the Temple of Jupiter Olympius at Athens, and not that at Elis, is the hypæthros which Vitruvius meant to exemplify, will be under the same difficulty; for Pausanias informs us, a colossal statue of the god, formed likewise of ivory and gold, was placed in it. We must therefore allow, that in temples of this kind, some effectual covering was contrived to shelter such statues from dust, sun and rain; though we are no where told, nor is it easy to ascertain, the precise manner in which this was effected.

It must be observed, however, that the peristyle or internal colonnade, supported a roof which sheltered great part of the area of the cell, and seems to have projected over the statue; this perhaps was the roof, which Strabo thought would have been in danger, if Jupiter had risen from his seat. And may we not conjecture, that the Peplus of Minerva, in the Parthenon, and the Parapetasma of Jupiter Olympius in Elis, mentioned by Pausanias in his description of that temple, were each of them suspended in their respective situations, so as to afford the requisite shade or shelter to those most celebrated statues?

Thus I have said what has occurred to me on the subject of temples without continued roofs, and with only eight columns in front; of which kind both the Parthenon at Athens, and the Olympiëum at Elis, two of the most celebrated temples in Greece, seem to have been. And if I am right in my conjectures concerning them, might not Virtuvius think himself obliged to acquaint his reader with these exceptions to his general doctrine?

The name of this Temple (Hecatompedon) implying that it extended 100 feet, led me to inquire into the measure of the attic foot. For which purpose I compared the length of the lower step in front, with its length on the side, and found them incommensurable; neither were the front and side lengths of the step above it commensurable with each other. But the third step, on which the columns of the portico stand measured 101 feet $1\frac{7}{10}$ inch English in front, and 227 feet $7\frac{1}{20}$ inch on each side, which are so nearly in the proportion of 100 to 225, that, had the greater measure been $\frac{1}{4}$ of an inch less, it would have been deficient of it.

These measures were taken from a brass scale of three feet, divided by that eminent artist Mr. John Bird, whose works are known all over Europe.

The front measure gives an attic foot of 12,137 London inches and decimals; the side measure one of 12,138.

Hence the Roman foot, which, according to Pliny, was to the attic in the proportion of 600 to 625, or of 24 to 25, will be found to be 11,651 London inches and decimals or 971 such parts, as the London foot contains 1000, which does not sensibly differ from what has been determined by other methods.

I cannot conclude this chapter without mentioning, that while I measured the steps of this portico, I observed the blocks of marble, of which they are composed, appeared to be united and grown together, on their contiguous edges, the whole height of the step ; and this apparent junction continued to some distance within the portico. To satisfy myself in this particular, I traced the joint till no doubt remained of the separation ; then returning to the edge of the step, I broke off a piece across the joint with a hammer, which verified my conjecture ; for in the piece thus broken off, one half of which was part of one block, and the other, part of the block next to it, the two parts adhered together as firmly as if they had never been separate.

Other instances of this coalition we met with, which were always as here in the perpendicular joint, never in the horizontal.

PLATES 46 and 47.

Plate XLVII is the volute on a large scale.

OF THE IONIC TEMPLE ON THE ILISSUS.

(From Stewart's Antiquities of Athens.)

On the Southern bank of the Ilissus, not far from the Fountain Enneacrunos, which at present has recovered its more ancient name, and is called Callirrhoë, stands a little Ionic Temple, the mouldings of which differ much from all the examples of that order, hitherto published ; their forms are extremely simple, but withal so elegant, and the whole is so well executed, that it may doubtless be reckoned among those works of antiquity which best deserve our attention.

It should be observed, that most of the ancient structures in Athens, of which there are any remains, were entirely built of an excellent white marble, on which the weather has very little effect ; whatever part therefore of these antiquities, has not been impaired by violence, is by no means in that mouldering state of decay, to which the dissolvent quality of the air reduces the ordinary buildings of common stone : from which cause it is, that, notwithstanding great part of this temple has long since been thrown down, and destroyed, whatever remains of it is still in good preservation. The Athenians, probably several centuries ago, repaired this building ; and with some barbarous additions, transformed it into a church, dedicated to the mother of Christ ; and called from its situation, St. Mary's on the Rock : which name it still retains, although the repairs which were then bestowed on it, are now also gone to decay, and the church is at present totally deserted. Spon supposes, that it was anciently dedicated to Ceres, and appropriated to the celebration of the Lesser Mysteries. It were to be wished that he had produced the authorities on which his opinion is founded ; it had then perhaps never been controverted, or at least he would have enabled his readers to determine with more ease and greater accuracy, how far they could concur with him in his sentiments on this subject.

The spot on which it is built, commands a very beautiful and extensive prospect; and in the neighbourhood are still visible the ruins and foundations of many edifices which formerly improved this pleasing situation, and adorned the banks of the Ilissus. Among these were the Lyceum, the Stadium, the Altar of the Muses Ilissiades, the Monument of Nisus, and the Temple of Diana Agrotera; all which Pausanias has enumerated; and of this number likewise was the Temple of Boreas, mentioned by Herodotus. But it is evident from many circumstances, that none of them can be the temple here described: these circumstances however do not effect the conjecture of Monsieur Spon, which so far deserves credit, as it is certain, that the temple dedicated to Ceres Agrotera, was near the city, and on the South side of the Ilissus.

It should not however be omitted, that there was a temple, a statue, and a fountain, which were dedicated to an Athenian hero, named Panops, and they were all of them, probably, near this place; since by a passage in Plato the fountain appears to have been just without that gate of Athens which was nearest the Lyceum and the Ilissus. So small a temple as this we have treated of, seems not to correspond with the high veneration in which the Goddess Ceres was held at Athens; and it could by no means be sufficient for the reception of that train and pomp, which doubtless accompanied the celebration even of the lesser mysteries. It may therefore rather be imagined, that the hero Panops was honoured in this temple.

PLATES 48, 49, AND 50.

OF THE TEMPLES OF ERECHTHEUS, MINERVA POLIAS, AND PANDROSUS.

(From Stewart's Antiquities of Athens.)

To the north of the Parthenon, at the distance of about one hundred and fifty feet, are the remains of three contiguous temples. That towards the east was called the Erechtheum; to the westward of this, but under the same roof, was the Temple of Minerva, with the title Polias, as protectress of the city; adjoining to which, on the south side, is the Pandrosium, so named because it was dedicated to the nymph Pandrosus, one of the daughters of Cecrops.

Pausanius has not given a more particular description of this building than he has of the Parthenon. He tells us it was a double temple, and that in the Erechtheum was the spring of sea-water produced by the stroke of Neptune's trident, when he contended with Minerva for the patronage of the city. Before the entrance was an altar of Jupiter the Supreme, and within the temple an altar of Neptune, on which, by command of an oracle, they sacrificed likewise to Erechtheus; whence we may conclude, it was not originally dedicated to him, but to Neptune. Here was likewise an altar of the hero Butes, the brother of Erechtheus; and another on which they sacrificed to Vulcan. On the walls were paintings (inscriptions) relating to the family of Butes, in which the priesthood of these temples was hereditary.

In the Temple of Minerva Polias was the ancient statue of the goddess; it was of wood, and said to have fallen from heaven; this I suppose to have been one of those ancient statues, which Pausanias tells us were entire but black, and so scorched with the flames when Xerxes burnt the temple, that they would not bear a blow. Here was likewise a Hermes, or statue of Mercury, dedicated by Cecrops; it was almost hid from the sight by branches of myrtle, on account, it should seem of the indecency and absurdity of such an image in the temple of a virgin; superstition alone could have prevented the Athenians from removing it, for a Hermes appears to have been as obscene a figure as a Priapus. Here also was the golden lamp made by Callimachus, who invented the Corinthian capital: it was said to burn all the year without fresh supplies of oil: this lamp was placed under a brazen palm-tree, the branches of which extended up the roof, and conveyed away the smoke.

The Padrosium is the only ancient example we know of, in which the entablature and roof is supported by Caryatides. Pausanius has not mentioned them, though they are certainly more ancient than the time in which he wrote. Vitruvius probably alludes to this building, when he tells us, that after the defeat of the Persians, and the destruction of the city of Carya, the architects of those times placed female figures of this kind in public buildings, to perpetuate the ignominy of those who deserted the cause of liberty and their country.

Within the Pandrosium was the olive-tree, said to have been produced by Minerva in her contest with Neptune above-mentioned, it was called Pankyphos (incurvated) from its branches being bent downwards after it had grown up to the roof. Under this tree stood the altar of Jupiter Herceus. Some have imagined that an olive-tree grew in the temple of Minerva Polias; but it is quite improbable that any tree should grow in a place so unfavourable to vegetation; for it appears to have been a close room, illuminated only by a lamp; whereas, in this of Pandrosus a free admission was given to light and air, the spaces between the caryatides being left entirely open.

The olive and the spring of sea-water prove this to be the fabulous scene of contention between the two divinities; they also prove that these Temples were rebuilt on the same spot where those stood that were burnt by Xerxes, which doubtless were of great antiquity, probably the most ancient in Athens. Homer mentions that of Minerva, under which name he seems to include them all, as Herodotus afterwards does under that of Erechtheus.

An inscription brought from Athens at the expense of the Society of Dilettanti, and published by Dr. Chandler, contains a survey of such parts of these temples as were at that time unfinished, with what seems to be an estimate in Attic minas of the expense of completing them, amounting to between three and four hundred pounds sterling.

This survey was taken by order of the people of Athens when Diocles was archon which was in the twenty-third year of the Peloponnesian war; hence it is not improbable, that this building was begun during the administration of Pericles, and a stop put to it either by his death or the calamities and expenses of that war.

By the grammatical inaccuracies in this inscription, it seems to have been drawn up by the mason employed in the survey. And the terms of architecture not to be found in any writer now remaining, together with our ignorance in what manner the survey was taken, whether by going regularly round the building, or by classing similar deficiencies together, render it very obscure, and in a great measure unintelligible.

The situation of some of the most unfinished parts, is described as being near the Cecropium; of others near the Pandrosium, some on the south wall, others on the east. By the Cecropium I understand the Temple of Minerva Polias, which might be so called, from the opinion that Cecrops was buried there, as the contiguous Temple of Neptune, probably for a like reason, was called the Erechtheum.

We read of no other building called Cecropium; the Acropolis, which was the ancient city, and said to have been built by Cecrops, was called Cecropia.

In this survey no part of the Cecropium, or of the Pandrosium, is said to be unfinished. In the forty-fourth line it mentions columns on the wall next the Pandrosium; and in the sixty-second, pilasters next to the Cecropium; some other particulars occur in it, which seem to belong to the present building, but the measures assigned to them prove the contrary. This circumstance is a confirmation of a passage in Xenophon, where this temple is said to have been burnt about three years after this survey was taken, though the names of the archon and ephorus are generally believed to be interpolated.

These temples are now in a very ruinous condition. Those of Erechtheus and Minerva have at present no roof or covering of any kind. The wall which separated them, and that by which the Pronaos, or passage to the Pandrosium, was parted off from the Temple of Minerva, are so demolished, that hardly any traces of them remain, except where they joined the side walls. The pavements are so encumbered with large blocks of marble and variety of rubbish, as to render the inside almost impassable, and a more particular disquisition there, fruitless. The Pandrosium, though it has suffered least, is filled up to a great height in the same manner, and one of the Caryatides is wanting. We found the portico of Minerva Polias walled up, and being a magazine of military stores, all entrance into it was denied us

In the time of Wheler and Spon this building was more entire, for it was then inhabited, a Turkish officer having made it his seraglio; but that circumstance was an insurmountable obstacle to the curiosity of those gentlemen, who, had they viewed the inside, might possibly have given us some information which we now want.

Although these three temples compose one body, they are not on the same level; for the pavement of the Temple of Erechtheus, is about eight feet higher than that of the rest of the building. Neither has the architect attempted to form them into one regular whole, but seems purposely to have kept them, as we now see them, in three distinct forms.

PL. 51.

OF THE CHORAGIC MONUMENT OF LYSICRATES, COMMONLY CALLED THE LANTHORN OF DEMOSTHENES.

(From Stewart's Antiquities of Athens)

The modern Athenians call this edifice to Phanária tou Demosthéneos, or the lanthorn of Demosthenes, and the vulgar story which says, it was built by that great orator for a place of retirement and study, is still as current at Athens as it was in the time of Wheler and Spon; but like many other popular traditions, it is too absurd to deserve a serious refutation.

Wheler and Spon have described this building. They are the first authors who have taken notice of the inscription upon it, from the tenour of which they conclude, that this building was erected in honour of the several persons mentioned in the inscription; and that it was the monument of a victory they had obtained in one of the public shows or games.

Their opinion will be confirmed in the course of the present chapter, and the purpose which this monument was designed to answer, will be farther explained; for it appears upon a diligent examination, that besides recording the names of the victors it likewise supported a tripod which they had contended for, and had won in these games. It appears also that neither the building itself, nor the sculpture which adorns the frieze, have any relation to Hercules; though all the writers who have hitherto described them, imagine they had: neither do they relate to athletic combats of any species. This sculpture represents one of the adventures of Bacchus; and the victory which this monument celebrates, was not obtained in the stadium, but in the theatre.

This monument of antiquity, which is exquisitely wrought, stands near the eastern end of the Acropolis and is partly enclosed in the hospitium of the Capuchins. It is composed of three distinct parts. First, a quadrangular basement: secondly, a circular colonnade, the intercolumniations of which were entirely closed up; and thirdly, a Tholus or cupola with the ornament which is placed on it.

There is no kind of entrance of aperture in the quadrangular basement; it is entirely closed on every side. On breaking through one of the sides, it was found however not to be quite solid. But the void space is so small and so irregular, that a man can hardly stand upright in it.

This basement supports the circular colonnade, which was constructed in the following manner, six equal pannels of white marble placed contiguous to each other, on a circular plan, formed a continued cylindrical wall; which of course was divided from top to bottom, into six equal parts, by the junctures of the pannels. On the whole length of each juncture was cut a semi-circular groove, in which a Corinthian column was fitted with great exactness, and effectually concealed the junctures of the pannels. These columns projected somewhat more than half their diameters from the surface of the cylindrical wall, and the wall entirely closed up the intercolumniation. Over this was placed the entablature, and the cupola, in neither of which any aperture was made, so that there was no admission to the inside of this monument, and it was quite dark. It is besides, only 5 feet 11 inches and a half in the clear, and therefore was never intended for a habitation, or even a repository of any kind.

An entrance however has been since forced into it, by breaking through one of the pannels; probably in expectation of finding treasures here; for in these countries, such barbarism reigns at present, every ancient building which is beautiful or great, beyond the conception of the present inhabitants, is always supposed by them to be the work of magic, and the repository of hidden treasures. At present three of the marble pannels are destroyed; their places are supplied by a door, and two brick-walls, and it is converted into a closet.

It should be observed that two tripods with handles to them, are wrought in basso-relievo on each of the three pannels which still remain. They are perhaps of the species which Homer and Hesiod describe by the name of eared tripods.

The architrave and frieze of this circular colonnade are both formed of only one block of marble. On the architrave there were inscriptions, from which we may conclude that on some solemn festival which was celebrated with games and plays, Lysicrates of Kikyna, a demos or borough town of the tribe of Akamantis, did on behalf of his tribe, but at his own expense, exhibit a musical or theatrical entertainment; in which the boys of the tribe of Akamantis obtained the victory; that in memory of their victory, this monument was erected; and the name of the person at whose expense the entertainment was exhibited, of the tribe that gained the prize, of the musician who accompanied the performers, and of the composer of the piece, are all recorded on it; to these the name of the annual Archon is likewise added, in whose year of magistracy all this was transacted. From which last circumstance it appears that this building was erected above three hundred and thirty years before the Christian era; in the time of Demosthenes, Apelles, Lysippus, and Alexander the Great.

Round the frieze is represented the story of Bacchus and the Tyrrhenian pirates. The figure of Bacchus himself, the fauns and satyrs who attend him on the manifestation of his divinity, the chastisement of the pirates, their terror and their transformation into dolphins, are expressed in this basso-relievo, with the greatest spirit and elegance.

The cornice which is otherwise very simple, is crowned with a sort of Vitruvian scroll, instead of a syma. It is remarkable that no cornice of an ancient building actually existing, and decorated in this manner, has hitherto been published; yet temples crowned with this ornament, are frequently represented on medals; and there is an example much resembling it among those ancient paintings which adorn a celebrated manuscript of Virgil, preserved in the Vatican library. This cornice is composed of several pieces of marble; they are bound together by the cupola, which is of one entire piece.

The outside of the cupola is wrought with much delicacy ; it imitates a thatch, or covering of laurel leaves ; this is likewise edged with a Vitruvian scroll, and enriched with other ornaments. The flower on the top of the cupola, is a very graceful composition of foliage. This ornament appears to have been a tripod.

It was the form of the upper surface of the flower, and principally indeed, the disposition of four remarkable cavities in it, which first led to this discovery. Three of them are cut on the three principal projections of the upper surface, their disposition is that of the angles of an equilateral triangle ; in these the tripod were probably fixed. In the fourth cavity, which is much the largest, and is in the centre of this upper surface, a ballister was in all likelihood inserted ; its use was to support the tripod, and to give it that stability which its situation required.

Every body knows that the games and plays which the ancient Grecians exhibited at the celebration of their greater festivals were chiefly athletic exercises and theatric or musical performances ; and that these made a very considerable, essential, and splendid part of the solemnity. In order, therefore, to engage a greater number of competitors, and to excite their emulation more effectually, prizes were allotted to the victors ; and these prizes were generally exhibited to public view during the time in which these games were celebrated.

> " In view amid the spacious circle lay
> The splendid gifts, the prizes of the day,
> Arms on the ground, and sacred tripods glow,
> With wreaths and palms to bind the victor's brow."
>
> PITT'S TRANSLATION OF VIRGIL.   ÆNEID V. VERSE 140.

None of these prizes seem to have been in higher estimation than tripods, or more frequently the reward of superior force, address, and genius.

Homer, when he describes the games which were celebrated at the funeral of Patroclus, introduces Achilles proclaiming tripods as the principal prizes to be contended for, both by the charioteers and by those who engaged in wrestling. Pindar celebrates Castor and Iolaus for their excellence in the chariot race, the naked and the armed course, throwing the javelin, and tossing the discus ; and he represents them adorning their houses with tripods, and other prizes, which they had won in these games. But Hesiod celebrates his own victory : he obtained it in the games which were solemnized at Chalcis. On this occasion, he describes himself bearing off the prize tripod from his competitors in poetry, and consecrating it to the Muses.

It was the usual custom, and a very ancient one, for the victors to dedicate these tripods to some divinity, and to place them, either in temples already built, or upon the top of some consecrated edifice erected for that purpose ; thus they participated of the sanctity of the place, and were secure from injury and violence : to have destroyed or defaced them, had doubtless been esteemed an act of sacrilege. A tripod thus dedicated, was always accompanied with an inscription ; so that it became a permanent, authentic, and public monument of the victory, and of the person who had obtained it.

The tripod seems to have been the peculiar reward bestowed by the people of Athens on that Choragus who had exhibited the best musical or theatrical entertainment: for we find these kind of tripods had obtained a particular name from this custom, and were called Choragic tripods. The gaining of this prize was attended with considerable expense: each Choragus disbursed the money for the entertainment he exhibited, but the victor was moreover at the charge of consecrating the tripod he had won; and sometimes, also, of building the temple on which it was placed.

There were formerly many edifices or temples of this sort in Athens: one of them as Plutarch informs us, was built by Nicias within the place consecrated to Bacchus: and Pausanius says, that there was a street leading from the Prytaneum, which took its name from the number of tripods in it. He tells us, they were placed on temples, that they were of brass indeed, but, on account of the workmanship, they merited our attention.

That the building usually called the lanthorn of Demosthenes was of this sort, the particulars already recited seem to evince. The three principal projections, which give a triangular form to the upper surface of the flower, and the number and disposition of the cavities in it, which seem so aptly suited to receive the feet of the tripod, must immediately suggest this opinion to any one who recollects that tripods were sometimes placed on temples. The tripods represented on all the pannels which are not destroyed; and the inscription, so exactly like those which were inscribed on Choragic tripods, do greatly confirm this opinion: besides all which, we may add, that as this building was entirely closed all round, it seems that no other use can with any show of probability be assigned to it.

We may therefore conclude, that this building supported the choragic tripod of Lysicrates; and we may suppose that the sculpture on it, represents the subject of the theatric or musical entertainment, which was exhibited at his expense by the chorus of boys. If we further suppose, that these games were celebrated during the Dionysia, or festivals in honour of Bacchus, both the subject of the sculpture, and the custom of giving tripods particularly to the victors in those games, will concur to support the conjecture.

PL. 56.

Exhibits a plan of a box frame sitting in a brick wall, with the stone sill, wooden sill, sash, shutters closed over the window, shutters folded in the box, and inside pilaster annexed thereto, and likewise a section of the stone sill, wooden sill, inside back and brick wall, with an elevation of one side of the frame at Fig. 2.

As this sort of work falls into almost every carpenter's hand, it may sometimes be found a difficult job by some; consequently I shall be more particular in my explanations than otherwise.

REFERENCES TO FIGURES 1, 2, 3, AND 4.

Fig. 1, is a plan of the box frame, shutter box, inside shutters in the box, inside shutters closed over the window, inside pilaster, stud or joist, stone sill, wooden sill, sash, and the path of the shutters when closing or unclosing.

a, Stone sill, made with a drip or wash from *y y*, which is the same as *y y*, in Fig. 2.

b, Wood sill.

c, Sash.

d d d d, Inside shutter.

e, Upright sash bar.

f, Inside bead or stop.

g, Parting bead.

h, Outside lining.

i, Outside casing, or hanging style to blinds or shutters.

j, Pulley style.

k, Inside lining.

l, Back lining.

m m, Weights.

n, Brick wall, one foot thick.

o, Back lining to the shutter box.

p, Inside grounds.

q, Inside pilaster.

r, The line of the plinth of the pilaster.

s, Stud or joist.

t, The circle or path of the middle shutter when folding or unfolding.

u, The path of the shutter hung to the box when folding or unfolding.

v w x, To show the method of calculating the proportion of the shutter and box.

3, The thickness of the lath.

4, Thickness of brown wall.

5,   Do.   of hard finish

TO GET THE PROPORTION OF THE SHUTTERS AND SHUTTER BOXES.

First, obtain the centre of the window at *x*, then allow about 1-8th or 1-4th of an inch at *w ;* then take the remaining distance from *w* to *x*, noticing that *x* includes the whole rabbit, and divide it into two equal parts : make *x* the centre of the hinge, then make the rabbit all clear of the hinge, and the proportion or width of the shutters will be complete, as may be seen by the two circles *t* and *u*.   In order to make it perfectly plain, I have given the shutters folded and unfolded.

Fig. 2 is a section of the stone sill.   Wood sill, inside back, and brick wall ; and likewise an elevation of a part of the brick wall and sash frame.

a, Stone sill.

b, Wood sill.

c, Section of sash sill.

d, Inside bead or stop.

e, Bead on the back, and passes over the elbows.

f, Inside back.

g, Pannel to back.

h, Section of brick wall under stone sill.

i, Elevation of the brick wall up the side of the window.

j, Parting bead.

k, Groove or channel for the upper sash.

l, Outside bead.

m, Outside casing or nanging style—(see *i*, in Fig. 1.)

n, Wash to stone sill—(see 3 4 5, at the dotted line in Fig. 1.)

y y, Represents the part of the stone sill in front of the wood sill—(see *y y*, in Fig. 1.)

z z, The part in front of the hanging style *j*, in Fig. 1.

2 2, The part projecting past the brick wall.

THE METHOD OF TAKING OUT AND RE-FITTING THE POCKET PIECE.

Fig. 3, is a side of the pulley style, and Fig. 4, an edge.

d I, In Fig. 3, is a face of the pocket piece; when in the style *a*, in Fig. 4, it is a sectional view of the pocket piece.

PL. 84.

TO DESCRIBE THE ANGLE BARS FOR SHOP FRONTS.

In Fig. 1, B is a common bar, and A is the angle bar of the same thickness; take the raking projection 1, 1, in A, and set the foot of your compass in 1 at B, and cross the middle of the base at the other 1; then draw the lines 2 2; 3 3, &c. parallel to 1 1; then prick your bar at A from the ordinates so drawn at B, which being traced will give the angle bar.

HOW TO FIND THE RAKING MOULDINGS OF A PEDIMENT.

In Fig. 2, let the simarecta on the under side be the given moulding at A, and let lines be drawn upon the rake at discretion; but if you please, let them be equally divided upon the simarecta, and drawn parallel to the rake; then the mould at the middle being pricked off from these level lines at the bottom, will give the form of the face. The return moulding at the top must be pricked upon the rake, according to the letters.

N. B. If the middle moulding, Fig. 2, be given, perpendiculars must be drawn to the top of it; then horizontal lines must be drawn over the mouldings at each end, with the same divisions as are over the mouldings; and lines being drawn perpendicularly down, as above, will show how to trace the end mouldings.

AN EXPLANATION OF TERMS USED IN CARPENTRY AND JOINERY.

(From Nicholson's New Practical Builder.)

ABUTMENT.—The junction or meeting of two pieces of timber, of which the fibres of the one extend perpendicular to the joint, and those of the other parallel to it.

ARRIS.—The line of concourse or meeting of two surfaces.

BACK OF A HAND-RAIL.—The upper side of it.

BACK OF A HIP.—The upper edge of a rafter, between the two sides of a hipped roof, formed to an angle, so as to range with the rafters on each side of it.

BACK-SHUTTERS OR BACK-FLAPS.—Additional breadths hinged to the front shutters for covering the aperture completely, when required to be shut.

BACK OF A WINDOW.—The board, or wainscoting between the sash-frame and the floor, uniting with the two elbows, and forming part of the finish of a room. When framed, it has commonly a single pannel, with mouldings on the framing, corresponding with the doors, shutters, &c., in the apartment in which it is fixed.

BASIL.—The sloping edge of a chisel, or of the iron of a plane.

BATTEN.—A scantling of stuff from two inches to seven inches in breadth, and from half an inch to one inch and a half in thickness.

BAULK.—A piece of fir or deal, from four to ten inches square, being the trunk of a tree of that species of wood, generally brought to a square, for the use of building.

BEAD.—A round moulding commonly made upon the edge of a piece of stuff. Of beads they are two kinds ; one flush with the surface, called a *quirk-bead*, and the other raised, called a *cock-bead*.

BEAM.—A horizontal timber, used to resist a force or weight ; as a *tie-beam*, where it acts as a string or chain, by its tension ; as a *collar-beam*, where it acts by compression ; as a *bressummer*, where it resists a transverse insisting weight.

BEARER.—Any thing used by way of support to another.

BEARING.—The distance in which a beam or rafter is suspended in the clear: thus, if a piece of timber rests upon two opposite walls, the span of the void is called the *bearing*, and not the whole length of the timber.

BENCH.—A platform supported on four legs, and used for planing upon, &c.

BEVEL.—One side is said to be *bevelled* with respect to another, when the angle formed by these two sides is greater or less than a right angle.

BIRD'S MOUTH.—An interior angle, formed on the end of a piece of timber, so that it may rest firmly upon the exterior angle of another piece.

BLADE.—Any part of a tool that is broad and thin ; as the blade of an axe, of an adze, of a chisel, &c.: but the blade of a saw is generally called the plate.

BLOCKINGS.—Small pieces of wood, fitted in, or glued, or fixed, to the interior angle of two boards or other pieces, in order to give strength to the joint.

BOARD.—A substance of wood contained between two parallel planes: as when the baulk is divided into several pieces by the pit-saw, the pieces are called *boards*. The section of boards is sometimes, however, of a triangular, or rather trapezoidal form; that is, with one edge very thin; these are called *feather-edged boards*.

BOND-TIMBERS.—Horizontal pieces, built in stone or brick walls, for strengthening them, and securing the battening, lath, and plaster, &c.

BOTTOM RAIL.—The lowest rail of a door.

BOXINGS OF A WINDOW.—The two cases, one on each side of a window, into which the shutters are folded.

BRACE.—A piece of slanting timber, used in truss-partitions, or in framed roofs, in order to form a triangle, and thereby rendering the frame immoveable; when a brace is used by way of support to a rafter, it is called a *strut*. Braces, in partitions and span-roofs, are always, or should be, disposed in pairs, and placed in opposite directions.

BRACE AND BITS,—The same as *stock and bits*, as explained hereafter.

BRAD.—A small nail, having no head except on one edge. The intention is to drive it within the surface of the wood, by means of a hammer and punch, and to fill the cavity flush to the surface with putty.

BREAKING DOWN, in sawing, is dividing the baulk into boards or planks; but, if planks are sawed longitudinally, through their thickness, the saw-way is called a *ripping-cut*, and the former a *breaking-cut*.

TO BREAK-IN.—To cut or break a hole in brick-work, with the ripping-chisel, for inserting timber, &c.

BREAKING-JOINT is the joint formed by the meeting of several heading joints in one continued line, which is sometimes the case in folded floors.

BRESSUMMER OR BREASTSUMMER.—A beam supporting a superincumbent part of an exterior wall, and running longitudinally below that part.—See SUMMER.

BRIDGED GUTTERS.—Gutters made with boards, supported below with bearers, and covered over with lead.

BRIDGING FLOORS.—Floors in which *bridging-joists* are used.

BRIDGING-JOISTS.—The smallest beams in naked flooring, for supporting the boarding for walking upon.

BUTTING-JOINT.—The junction formed by the surfaces of two pieces of wood, of which one surface is perpendicular to the fibres, and the other in their direction, or making with them an oblique angle.

CAMBER.—The convexity of a beam upon the upper edge, in order to prevent its becoming straight or concave by its own weight, or by the burden it may have to sustain, in course of time.

CAMBER-BEAMS.—Those beams used in the flats of truncated roofs, and raised in the middle with an obtuse angle, for discharging the rain-water towards both sides of the roof.

CANTALIVERS.—Horizontal rows of timber, projecting at right angles from the naked part of a wall, for sustaining the eaves or other mouldings. Sometimes they are planed on the horizontal and vertical sides, and sometimes the carpentry is rough and cased with joinery.

CARRIAGE OF A STAIR.—The timber-work which supports the steps.

CARCASE OF A BUILDING.—The naked walls, and the rough timber-work of the flooring and quarter partitions, before the building is plastered or the floors laid.

CARRY-UP.—A term used among builders or workmen, denoting that the walls, or other parts, are intended to be built to a certain given height; thus, the carpenter will say to the bricklayer, *Carry-up that wall; carry-up that stack of chimneys;* which means, build up that wall or stack of chimneys.

CASTING OR WARPING.—The bending of the surfaces of a piece of wood from their original position, either by the weight of the wood, or by an unequal exposure to the weather, or by unequal texture of the wood.

CHAMFERING.—Cutting the edge of any thing, originally right-angled, aslope or bevel.

CLAMP.—A piece of wood fixed to the end of a thin board, by mortise and tenon, or by groove and tongue; so that the fibres of the one piece, thus fixed, traverse those of the board, and by this mean prevent it from casting: the piece at the end is called a *clamp* and the board is said to be *clamped.*

CLEAR STORY WINDOWS, are those that have no transom.

CROSS-GRAINED STUFF, is that which has its fibres running in contrary positions to the surfaces; and, consequently, cannot be made perfectly smooth, when planed in one direction, without turning it, or turning the plane.

CROWN-POST.—The middle post of a trussed roof.—See KING-POST.

CURLING STUFF.—That which is occasioned by the winding or coiling of the fibres round the boughs of the tree, when they begin to shoot from the trunk.

DEAL TIMBER.—The timber of the fir-tree, as cut into boards, planks, &c. for the use of building.

DISCHARGE.—A post trimmed up under a beam, or part of a building which is weak or overcharged by weight.

DOOR-FRAME.—The surrounding case of a door, into which, and out of which, the door shuts and opens.

DORMER OR DORMER-WINDOW.—A projecting window, in the roof of a house; the glass-frame, or casements, being set vertically, and not in the inclined sides of the roofs: thus *dormers* are distinguished from *skylights,* which have their sides inclined to the horizon.

DRAG.—A door is said to *drag* when it rubs on the floor. This arises from the loosening of the hinges, or the settling of the building.

DRAGON-BEAM.—The piece of timber which supports the hip-rafter, and bisects the angle formed by the wall-plates.

DRAGON-PIECE.—A beam bisecting the wall-plate, for receiving the heel or foot of the hip-rafters.

EDGING.—Reducing the edges of ribs or rafters, externally or internally, so as to range in a plane, or in any curved surface required.

ENTER.—When the end of a tenon is put into a mortise, it is said to *enter* the mortise.

FACE-MOULD.—A mould for drawing the proper figure of a hand-rail on both sides of the plank ; so that, when cut by a saw, held at a required inclination, the two surfaces of the rail-piece, when laid in the right position, will be every where perpendicular to the plan.

FANG.—The narrow part of the iron of any instrument which passes into the stock.

FEATHER-EDGED BOARDS.—Boards, thicker at one edge than the other, and commonly used in the facing of wooden walls, and for the covering of inclined roofs, &c.

FENCE OF A PLANE.—A guard, which obliges it to work to a certain horizontal breadth from the arris.

FILLING-IN PIECES.—Short timbers, less than the full length, as the jack-rafters of of a roof, the puncheons, or short quarters, in partitions, between braces and sills, or head-pieces.

FINE-SET.—A plane is said to be fine-set, when the sole of the plane so projects as to take a very thin broad shaving.

FIR POLES.—Small trunks of fir-trees, from ten to sixteen feet in length, used in rustic buildings and out-houses.

FREE STUFF.—That timber or stuff which is quite clean, or without knots, and works easily, without tearing.

FROWY STUFF.—The same as free stuff.

FURRINGS.—Slips of timber nailed to joists or rafters, in order to bring them to a a level, and to range them into a straight surface, when the timbers are sagged, either by casting, or by a set which they have obtained by their weight, in length of time.

GIRDER.—The principal beam in a floor for supporting the binding-joists.

GLUE.—A tenacious viscid matter, which is used as a cement, by carpenters, joiners, &c.

Glues are found to differ very much from each other, in their consistence, colour, taste, smell, and solubility. Some will dissolve in cold water, by agitation ; while others are soluble only at the point of ebullition. The best glue is generally admitted to be transparent, and of a brown yellow colour, without either taste or smell. It is perfectly soluble in water, forming a viscous fluid, which, when dry, preserves its tenacity and transparency in every part ; and has solidity, colour, and viscidity, in proportion to the age and strength of the animal from which it is produced. To distinguish good glue from bad, it is necessary to hold it between the eye and the light ; and if it appears of a strong dark brown colour, and free from cloudy or black spots, it may be pronounced to be good. The best glue may likewise be known by immersing it in cold water for three or four days, and if it swells considerably without melting, and afterwards regains its former dimensions and properties by being dried, the article is of the best quality.

In preparing glue for use, it should be softened and swelled by steeping it in cold water for a number of hours. It should then be dissolved, by gently boiling it till it is of a proper consistence to be easily brushed over any surface. A portion of water is added to glue, to make it of a proper consistency, which proportion may be taken at about a quart of water to half a pound of glue. In order to hinder the glue from being burned, during the process of boiling, the vessel containing the glue is generally suspended in another vessel, which is made of copper, and resembles in form a tea-kettle without a spout. This latter vessel contains only water, and alone receives the direct influence of the fire.

A little attention to the following circumstances will tend, in no small degree, to give glue its full effect in uniting perfectly two pieces of wood : first, that the glue be thoroughly melted, and used while boiling hot ; secondly, that the wood be perfectly dry and warm ; and, lastly, that the surfaces to be united should be covered only with a thin coat of glue, and after having been strongly pressed together, left in a moderately warm situation, till the glue is completely dry. When it so happens that the face of surfaces to be glued cannot be conveniently compressed together in any great degree, they should, as soon as besmeared with the glue, be rubbed lengthwise, one on the other, several times, in order thereby to settle them close. When all the above circumstances cannot be combined in the same operation, the hotness of the glue and the dryness of the wood should, at all events, be attended to.

The qualities of glue are often impaired by frequent meltings. This may be known to be the case when it becomes of a dark and almost black colour ; its proper colour being a light ruddy brown : yet, even then, it may be restored, by boiling it over again, refining it, and adding a sufficient quantity of fresh ; but the fresh is seldom put into the kettle till what is in it has been purged by a second boiling.

If common glue be melted with the smallest possible quantity of water, and well mixed by degrees with linseed oil, rendered dry by boiling it with litharge, a glue may be obtained that will not dissolve in water. By boiling common glue in skimmed milk the same effect may be produced.

A small portion of finely levigated chalk is sometimes added to the common solution of glue in water, to strengthen it and fit it for standing the weather.

A glue that will resist both fire and water may be prepared by mixing a handful of quick lime with four ounces of linseed oil, thoroughly levigated, and then boiled to a good thickness, and kept in the shade, on tin-plates, to dry. It may be rendered fit for use by boiling it over a fire like common glue.

GRIND STONE.—A cylindrical stone, by which on its being turned round its axis, edge-tools are sharpened, by applying the basil to the convex surface.

GROUND-PLATE OR SILL.—The lowest plate of a wooden building for supporting the principal and other posts.

GROUNDS.—Pieces of wood concealed in a wall, to which the facings or finishings are attached, and having their surfaces flush with the plaster.

HANDSPIKE.—A lever for carrying a beam, or other body, the weight being placed in the middle, and supported at each end by a man.

HANGING STILE.—The stile of a door or shutter to which the hinge is fastened: also, a narrow stile fixed to the jamb on which a door or shutter is frequently hung.

HIP-ROOF.—A roof the ends of which rise immediately from the wall-plate, with the same inclination to the horizon, as its other two sides. The *Backing of a Hip* is the angle made on its upper edge to range with the two sides or planes of the roof between which it is placed.

HOARDING.—An enclosure of wood about a building, while erecting or repairing.

JACK RAFTERS.—All those short rafters which meet the hips.

JACK RIBS.—Those short ribs which meet the angle ribs, as in groins, domes, &c.

JACK TIMBER.—A timber shorter than the whole length of other pieces in the same range.

INTERTIE.—A horizontal piece of timber, framed between two posts, in order to tie them together.

JOGGLE-PIECE.—A truss-post, with shoulders and sockets for abutting and fixing the lower ends of the struts.

JOISTS.—Those beams in a floor which support, or are necessary in the supporting, of the boarding or ceiling; as the *binding, bridging,* and *ceiling joists:* girders are, however, to be excepted, as not being joists.

JUFFERS.—Stuff of about four or five inches square, and of several lengths. This term is out of use, though frequently found in old books.

KERF.—The way which a saw makes in dividing a piece of wood into two parts.

KING-POST.—The middle post of a trussed roof, for supporting the tie-beam at the middle and the lower ends of the struts.

KNEE.—A piece of timber cut at an angle, or having grooves to an angle. In hand-railing a *knee* is part of the back, with a convex curvature, and therefore the reverse of a *ramp,* which is hollow on the back.

KNOT.—That part of a piece of timber where a branch had issued out of the trunk.

LINING OF A WALL.—A timber boarding, of which the edges are either rebated or grooved and tongued.

LINTELS.—Short beams over the heads of doors and windows, for supporting the inside of an exterior wall; and the super-incumbent part over doors, in brick or stone partitions.

LOWER RAIL.—The rail at the foot of a door next to the floor.

LYING PANEL.—A panel with the fibres of the wood disposed horizontally.

MARGINS OR MARGENTS.—The flat part of the stiles and rails of framed work.

MIDDLE RAIL.—The rail of a door which is upon a level with the hand when hanging freely and bending the joint of the wrist.   The back of the door is generally fixed in this rail.

MITRE.—If two pieces of wood be formed to equal angles, or if the two sides of each piece form equal inclinations, and two sides, one of each piece, be joined together at their common vertex, so as to make an angle, or an inclination, double to that of either piece, they are said to be *mitred* together, and the joint is called the *mitre*.

MORTISE AND TENON.—The tenon, in general, may be taken at about one-third of the thickness of the stuff.

When the mortise and tenon are to lie horizontally, as the juncture will thus be unsupported, the tenon should not be more than one-fifth of the thickness of the stuff; in order that the strain on the upper surface of the tenoned piece may not split off the under cheek of the mortise.

When the piece that is tenoned is not to pass the end of the mortised piece, the tenon should be reduced one-third or one-fourth of its breadth, to prevent the necessity of opening one side of the tenon.   As there is always some danger of splitting the end of the piece in which the mortise is made, the end beyond the mortise should, as often as possible, be made considerably longer than it is intended to remain; so that the tenon may be driven tightly in, and the superfluous wood cut off afterwards.

But the above regulations may be varied, according as the tenoned or mortised piece is weaker or stronger.

The labour of making deep mortises, in hard wood, may be lessened, by first boring a number of holes with the auger, in the part to be mortised, as the compartments between may then more easily be cut away by the chisel.

Before employing the saw to cut the shoulder of a tenon, in neat work, if the line of its entrance be correctly determined by nicking the place with a paring chisel, there will be no danger of the wood being torn at the edges by the saw.

As the neatness and durability of a juncture depend entirely on the sides of the mortise coming exactly in contact with the sides of the tenon; and, as this is not easily performed when a mortise is to pass entirely through a piece of stuff, the space allotted for it should be first of all correctly guaged on both sides.   One-half is then to be cut from one side, and the other half from the opposite side; and as any irregularities which may arise from an error in the direction of the chisel, will thus be confined to the middle of the mortise, they will be of very little hindrance to the exact fitting of the sides of the mortise and tenon.   Moreover, as the tenon is expanded by wedges after it is driven in, the sides of the mortise may, in a small degree, be inclined towards each other, near the shoulders of the tenon.

MULLION OR MUNNION.—A large vertical bar of a window-frame, separating two casements, or glass-frames, from each other.

Vertical *mullions* are called *munnions;* and those which extend horizontally are *transoms*.

MUNTINS OR MONTANTS.—The vertical pieces of the frame of a door between the stiles.

NAKED FLOORING.—The timber-work of a floor for supporting the boarding, or ceiling, or both.

NEWEL.—The post, in dog-legged stairs, where the winders terminate, and to which the adjacent string-boards are fixed.

OGEE.—A moulding, the transverse section of which consists of two curves of contrary flexure.

PANEL.—A thin board, having all its edges inserted in the groove of a surrounding frame.

PITCH OF A ROOF.—The inclination which the sloping sides make with the plane, or level of the wall-plate; or it is the proportion which arises by dividing the span by the height. Thus, if it be asked, What is the pitch of such a roof? the answer is, one-quarter, one-third, or half. When the pitch is half, the roof is a square, which is the highest that is now in use, or that is necessary in practice.

PLANK.—All boards above one inch thick are called *planks*.

PLATE.—A horizontal piece of timber in a wall, generally flush with the inside, for resting the ends of beams, joists, or rafters, upon; and, therefore, denominated floor or roof plates.

POSTS.—All upright or vertical pieces of timber whatever; as *truss-posts, door-posts, quarters* in partitions, &c.

PRICK POSTS.—Intermediate posts in a wooden building, framed between principal posts.

PRINCIPAL POSTS.—The corner posts of a wooden building.

PUDLAIES.—Pieces of timber to serve the purpose of handspikes.

PUNCHIONS.—Any short post of timber. The small quarterings in a stud partition above the head of a door, are also called *punchions*.

PURLINS.—The horizontal timbers in the sides of a roof, for supporting the spars or small rafters.

QUARTERING.—The stud work of a partition.

QUARTERS.—The timbers to be used in stud partitions, bond in walls, &c.

RAFTERS.—All the inclined timbers in the sides of a roof; as *principal rafters, hip rafters*, and *common rafters;* the latter are called in most countries, *spars*.

RAILS.—The horizontal pieces which contain the tenons in a piece of framing; in which the upper and lower edges of the panels are inserted.

RAISING PLATES OR TOP PLATES.—The plates on which the roof is raised.

RANK-SET.—The edge of the iron of a plane is said to be *rank-set* when it projects considerably below the sole.

RETURN.—In any body with two surfaces, joining each other at an angle, one of the surfaces is said to *return* in respect of the other; or, if standing before one surface, so that the eye may be in a straight line with the other, or nearly so: this last is said to *return*.

RIDGE.—The meeting of the rafters on the vertical angle, or highest part of a roof.

RISERS.—The vertical sides of the steps of stairs.

ROOF.—The covering of a house ; but the word is used in carpentry for the wood-work which supports the slating, or other covering.

SCANTLING.—The transverse dimensions of a piece of timber ; sometimes, also the small timbers in roofing and flooring are called *scantlings*.

SCARFING.—A mode of joining two pieces of timber, by bolting or nailing them transversely together, so that the two appear but as one.   The joint is called a *scarf*, and timbers are said to be *scarfed*.

SHAKEN STUFF.—Such timber as is rent or split by the heat of the sun, or by the fall of the tree, is said to be *shaken*.

SHINGLES.—Thin pieces of wood used for covering, instead of tiles, &c.

SHREADINGS.—A term not much used at present.

SKIRTINGS OR SKIRTING BOARDS.—The narrow boards round the margin of a floor, forming a plinth for the base of the *dado*, or simply a plinth for the room itself, when there is no dado.

SKIRTS OF A ROOF.—The projecture of the eaves.

SLEEPERS.—Pieces of timber for resting the ground-joists of a floor upon, or for fixing the planking to, in a bad foundation.   The term was formerly applied to the *valley-rafters* of a roof.

SPARS.—A term by which the common rafters of a roof are best known in almost every provincial town in Great Britain ; though, generally, called in London *common rafters*, in order to distinguish them from the principal rafters.

STAFF.—A piece of wood fixed to the external angle of the two upright sides of a wall, for floating the plaster to, and for defending the angle against accidents.

STILES OF A DOOR, are the vertical parts of the framing at the edges of the door.

STRUTS.—Pieces of timber which support the rafters, and which are supported by the truss-posts.

SUMMER.—A large beam in a building, either disposed in an outside wall, or in the middle of an apartment, parallel to such wall.   When a *summer* is placed under a superincumbent part of an outside wall, it is called a *bressummer*, as it comes in abreast with the front of the building.

SURBASE.—The upper base of a room, or rather the cornice of the pedestal of the room, which serves to finish the dado, and to secure the plaster against accidents from the backs of chairs, and other furniture on the same level.

TAPER.—The form of a piece of wood which arises from one end of a piece being narrower than the other.

TENON.—See MORTISE.

TIE.—A piece of timber, placed in any position, and acting as a string or tie, to keep two things together which have a tendency to a more remote distance from each other.

TRANSOM WINDOWS.—Those windows which have horizontal mullions.

TRIMMERS.—Joists into which other joists are framed.

Trimming Joists.—The two joists into which a trimmer is framed.

Truncated Roof.—A roof with a flat on the top.

Truss.—A frame constructed of several pieces of timber, and divided into two or more triangles by oblique pieces, in order to prevent the possibility of its revolving round any of the angles of the frame.

Trussed Roof.—A roof so constructed within the exterior triangular frame, as to support the principal rafters and the tie-beam at certain given points.

Truss-Post.—Any of the posts of a trussed roof, as a *king-post, queen-post,* or *side-post,* or posts into which the braces are formed in a trussed partition.

Trussels.—Four-legged stools for ripping and cross-cutting timber upon.

Tusk.—The bevelled upper shoulder of a tenon, made in order to give strength to the tenon.

Valley Rafter.—That rafter which is disposed in the internal angle of a roof.

Uphers.—Fir-poles, from twenty to forty feet long, and from four to seven inches in diameter, commonly hewn on the sides, so as not to reduce the wane entirely. When slit they are frequently employed in slight roofs : but mostly used whole for scaffolding and ladders.

Wall Plates.—The joist-plates and raising plates.

Web of an Iron.—The broad part of it which comes to the sole of the plane.

ORNAMENTAL MASONRY.

COLUMNS.—These comprise, generally, a conoidal shaft, with a small diminution towards their upper diameter, amounting, generally, to about one-sixth less than the lower diameter. The proportion of columns, from the Egyptians, varied but little ; the columns of this people, in their larger temples, amounting only to about four and a half diameters in height. Those of Greece, as in the *Parthenon,* at Athens, are little more than five. In the best Roman examples, the proportion was increased to upwards of seven diameters. The columns of *all* the Grecian remains are fluted though in different manners. The Doric shafts have their flutes in very flat segments, finished to an arris : sometimes flutings of the semi-ellipsis shape, with fillets, were adopted.

The genius of an architect is generally displayed in the application of columns. The Greeks surrounded their public walks with them ; their porticoes carried this kind of splendour to its highest pitch ; as in them may be found the whole syntax of architecture and masonry. To construct a temple, in the Greek manner, required the greatest taste and judgment, combined with a perfect knowledge of architecture. The Parthenon, at Athens, exhibits, or rather did exhibit, the most elaborate display of masonry in the world.

The comparatively perfect state in which the monuments of Greece remain, is a proof of the great judgment with which they were constructed. The famous Temple of Minerva would have been entire to this day, if it had not been destroyed by a bomb. The *Propylea*, which was used as a magazine for powder, was struck by lightning and blown up.   The Temple of Thesus, having escaped accidental destruction, is almost as entire as when first erected.   The little choragic monument of Thrasybulus, as well as that of Lysicrates, are also entire.   These instances should impress on modern architects the utility of employing large blocks, and of uniting them with the greatest accuracy ; without which, masonry is not superior to bricklaying.   The core of the rubble-work of the Grecian walls is impenetrable to a tool ; which is an additional proof of the care which was taken in cementing their masonry.

The joining of columns in free-stone, has been found more difficult than in marble ; and the practise used by the French masons, to avoid the failure of the two arrisses of the joint, might be borrowed with success for constructing columns of some of our softer kinds of free-stone.   It consists in taking away the edge of the joints, by which means a groove is formed at every one throughout the whole column.   This method is employed only in plain shafts.   It appears to have been occasionally used by the ancients, though for a different purpose : *viz.* to admit the shaft to be adorned with flowers, and other insignia, on the occasion of their shows and games.   In the French capital, they affix rows of lamps on their columns, making use of these grooves to adjust them regularly, which produces a very good effect.

The shafts of columns, in large works, intended to be adorned by flutes, are erected plain, and the flutings chisseled out afterwards.   The ancients commonly formed the two extreme ends of the fluting previously, as may be seen in the remaining columns of the Temple of Apollo, in the Island of Delos ; a practice admitting great accuracy and neatness.   The finishing the detail of both sculpture and masonry on the building itself, was an universal practice among the ancients : they raised their columns first in rough blocks, on them they placed the architraves and friezes, and surmounted the whole by the cornice ; finishing down only such parts as could not be got at in the building ; hence, perhaps, in some measure, arose that striking proportion of parts, together with the beautiful curvature and finish given to all the profiles in Grecian buildings.

PILASTERS, in modern design, are frequently very capriciously applied.   They are vertical shafts of square-edged stone, having but a small projection, with capitals and bases like columns ; they are often placed by us on the face of the wall, and with a cornice over them.   In Greek architecture, they are to be met with commonly on the ends of the walls, behind the columns, in which application their face was made double the width of their sides ; their capitals differing materially from those of the accompanying columns, and somewhat larger at bottom than at top, but without any *entasis* or swell.

PARAPETS.—Parapets are very ornamental to the upper part of an edifice. They were used by the Greeks and Romans, and are composed of three parts ; viz. the *plinth*, which is the blocking course to the cornice ; the *shaft* or *die*, which is the part immediately above the plinth ; and a cornice, which is on its top, and projects in its moulding, sufficiently to carry off the rain water from the shaft and plinth. In buildings of the Corinthian style, the shaft of the parapet is perforated in the parts immediately over the apertures in the elevation, and balustrade-enclosures are inserted in the perforations. The architects have devised the parapet with reference to the roof of the building which it is intended to obscure.

ASHLARING is a term used by masons to designate the plain stone work of the front of a building, in which all that is regarded is getting the stone to a smooth face, called its *plain work*. The courses should not be too high, and the joints should be crossed regularly, which will improve its appearance, and add to its solidity.

CILLS.—These belong to the apertures of the doors and windows, at the bottom of which they are fixed; their thickness varies, but is commonly about one inch and a half; they are also fluted on their under edges, and sunk on their upper sides, projecting about two inches, in general, beyond the ashlaring.

CORNICE.—This forms the crown to the ashlaring, at the summit of a building; it is frequently the part which is marked particularly by the architect, to designate the particular order of his work; hence *Doric, Ionic*, and *Corinthian*, cornices are employed, when, perhaps, no column of either is used in the work; so that the cornice alone designates the particular style of the building. In working the cornice, the top or upper side should be splayed away towards its front edge, that it may more readily carry off the water. At the joint of each of the stones of the cornice throughout the whole length of the building, that part of each stone which comes nearest at the joints, should be left projecting upwards a small way; a process by workmen called *saddling* the joints; this is done to keep the rain-water from entering them, and washing out the cement. These joints should be chased or indented, and such chases filled with lead, and even when dowels of iron are employed, they should be fixed by melted lead also.

RUSTICATING, in architecture and masonry, consists in forming horizontal sinkings, or grooves, in the stone ashlaring of an elevation, intersected by vertical or cross ones; perhaps invented to break the plainness of the wall, and denote more obviously the bond of the stones. It is often formed by splaying away the edge of the stone only; in this style, the groove forms the elbow of a geometrical square. Many architects omit the vertical grooves in rustics, so that their walls present a uniform series of horizontal sinkings. There are many examples, both ancient and modern, of each kind.

ARCHITRAVES adorn the apertures of a building, projecting somewhat from the face of the ashlaring; they have their faces sunk with mouldings, and also their outside edges. When they traverse the curve of an arch, they are called *archivolts*. They give beauty to the exterior of a building, and the best examples are among the Greek and Roman buildings.

BLOCKING COURSE.—This is a course of stone, traversing the top of the cornice to which it is fixed; it is commonly, in its height, equal to the projection of the cornice. It is of great utility in giving support to the latter by its weight, and to which it adds grace.   At the same time, it admits of gutters behind it to convey the superfluous water from the covering of the building.   The joints should always cross those of the cornice, and should be plugged with lead, or cramped on their upper edges with iron.   The Romans often dove-tailed such courses of stone.

FASCIA is a plain course of stone, generally about one foot in height, projecting about an inch before the face of the ashlaring, or in a line with the plinth of the building: it is fluted or *throated* on its upper edge, to prevent the water from running over the ashlaring; its upper edge is sloped downwards for the same purpose.   It is commonly inserted above the windows of the ground-stories; *viz.* between them and those of the principal story.

A PLINTH, in masonry, is the first stone inserted above the ground; it is in one or more pieces, according to its situation, projecting beyond the walls above it about an inch, with its projecting edge sloped downwards, or moulded, to carry off the water that may fall on it.

IMPOSTS.—These are insertions of stone, with their front faces generally moulded: when left plain, they are prepared in a similar manner to the facias.   They form the spring-stones to the arches in the apertures of a building, and are of the greatest utility.

AN EXPLANATION OF TERMS, AND DESCRIPTION OF TOOLS, USED IN MASONRY; INCLUDING THE COMPOSITION OF CEMENTS, OR MORTAR, &c.

ABUTMENT.—A term used both in carpentry and masonry.   In masonry, the *abutments* of a bridge mean the walls adjoining to the land, which support the ends of the extreme arches or roadway.

APERTURE.—An opening through a wall, &c. which has, generally, three straight sides; of these, two are perpendicular to the horizon, and the other parallel to it, connecting the lower ends of the vertical stones or *jambs*.   The lower side is called the the *cill*, and the upper side the *head*.   The last is either an arch or a single stone.   If it be an arch, the aperture is called an *arcade*.   Apertures may be circular or cylindrical; but these are not very frequent.

ARCH.-—Part of a building suspended over a hollow, and concave towards the area of the same.

ARCHIVOLT *of the Arch of a Bridge.*—The curved line formed by the upper sides of the arch stones in the face of the work; by the *archivolt* is also understood the whole set of arch-stones that appear in the face of the work.

ASHLAR.—A term applied to common or free-stones, as they come out of the quarry.   By *ashlar* is also meant the facing of squared stones on the front of a building.   If the work be so smoothed as to take out the marks of the tools by which the stones were first cut, it is called *plane-ashlar*: if figured, it may be *tooled ashlar*, or *random tooled*, or *chiselled*, or *boasted*, or *pointed*. If the stones project from the joints, it is said to be *rusticated*.

BANKER.—The stone bench on which work is cut and squared.

BANQUET.—The raised footway adjoining to the parapet on the sides of a bridge

BATTER.—The leaning part of the upper part of the face of a wall, which so inclines as to make the plumb-line fall within the base.

BEDS *of a Stone.*—The parallel surfaces which intersect the face of the work in lines parallel to the horizon.

In arching, the beds are, by some, called *summerings ;* by others, with more propriety, *radiations* or *radiated joints.*

BOND.—That regular connection, in lapping the stones upon one another, when carrying up the work, which forms an inseperable mass of building.

CAISSON.—A chest of strong timber in which the piers of a bridge are built, by sinking it, as the work advances, till it comes in contact with the bed of the river, and then the sides are disengaged, being constructed for that purpose.

CEMENT AND MORTAR *Composition of.*—It is almost superfluous to say, that cement or mortar, is a preparation of lime and sand, mixed with water, which serves to unite the stones, in the building of walls, &c.

On the proper or improper manner in which the cement or mortar is prepared and used, depends the durability and security of every building : we shall, therefore, here introduce many particulars on this head, discovered by *Dr. Higgins,* but which, not being generally known, have never been reduced into general practice.

For the preparation of every kind of mortar, or cement, the subsequent remarks should always be known. Of *Sand,* the following kinds are to be preferred ; first, *drift-sand,* or *quarry sand,* which consists chiefly of hard quartose flat-faced grains, with sharp angles ; secondly, that which is the freest, or may be most easily freed by washing, from clay, salts, and calcareous, gypseous, or other grains less hard and durable than quartz ; thirdly, that which contains the smallest quantity of pyrites or heavy metallic-matter, inseparable by washing ; and, fourthly, that which suffers the smallest diminution of its bulk in washing. Where a coarse and fine sand of this kind, and corresponding in the size of their grains with the coarse and fine sands hereafter described, cannot be easily procured, let such sand of the foregoing quality be chosen as may be sorted and cleansed in the following manner :—

Let the sand be sifted in streaming clear water, through a sieve which shall give passage to all such grains as do not exceed one-sixteenth of an inch in diameter ; and let the stream of water, and the sifting, be regulated so that all the sand which is much finer than the Lynn-sand, commonly used in the London glass-houses, together with clay, and every other matter specifically lighter than sand, may be washed away with the stream ; whilst the purer and coarser sand, which passes through the sieve, subsides in a convenient receptacle, and the coarse rubbish and rubble remain on the sieve to be rejected.

Let the sand, which thus subsides in the receptacle, be washed in clean streaming water, through a finer sieve, so as to be further cleansed, and sorted into two parcels ; a coarser, which will remain in the sieve, which is to give passage to such grains of sand only as are less than one-thirtieth of an inch in diameter, and which is to be saved apart under the name of *coarse sand ;* and a finer, which will pass through the sieve and subside in the water, and which is to be saved apart under the name of *fine sand.* Let the coarse and the fine sand be dried separately, either in the sun, or on a clean iron-plate, set on a convenient surface, in the manner of a sand-heat.

Let *stone-lime* be chosen, which heats the most in slaking, and slakes the quickest when duly watered ; that which is the freshest made and closest kept ; that which dissolves in distilled vinegar with the least effervescence, and leaves the smallest residue insoluble, and in the residue the smallest quantity of clay, gypsum, or martial matter. Let the lime, chosen according to these rules, be put in a brass-wired sieve to the quantity of fourteen pounds. Let the sieve be finer than either of the foregoing ; the finer the better it will be : let the lime be slaked, by plunging it into a butt filled with soft-water, and raising it out quickly, and suffering it to heat and fume ; and by repeating this plunging and raising alternately, and agitating the lime until it be made to pass through the sieve into the water ; and let the part of the lime which does not easily pass through the sieve be rejected : and let fresh portions of the lime be thus used, until as many ounces of lime have passed through the sieve as there are quarts of water in the butt.

Let the water, thus impregnated, stand in the butt closely covered until it becomes clear, and through wooden cocks, placed at different heights in the butt, let the clear liquor be drawn off, as fast and as low as the lime subsides, for use. This clear liquor is called *lime-water.* The freer the water is from saline matter, the better will be the cementing liquor made with it.

Let fifty-six pounds of the aforesaid chosen lime be slaked, by gradually sprinkling the lime-water on it, and especially on the unslaked pieces, in a close clean place. Let the slaked part be immediately sifted through the last mentioned fine brass-wired sieve : let the lime which passes be used instantly, or kept in air-tight vessels ; and let the part of the lime which does not pass through the sieve be rejected. This finer and richer part of the lime, which passes through the sieve, may be called *purified-lime.*

Let bone-ash be prepared in the usual manner, by grinding the whitest burnt bones ; but let it be sifted, so as to be much finer than the bone-ash commonly sold for making cupels.

The best materials for making the cement being thus prepared, take fifty-six pounds of the coarse sand, and forty-two pounds of the fine sand ; mix them on a large plank of hard wood placed horizontally ; then spread the sand so that it may stand to the height of six inches, with a flat surface on the plank, wet it with the lime-water, and let any superfluous quantity of the liquor, which the sand in the condition described cannot retain, flow away off the plank. To the wettest sand add fourteen pounds of the purified lime, in several successive portions ; mixing and beating them up together in the mean time, with the instruments generally used in making fine mortar : then add fourteen pounds of the bone-ash, in successive portions, mixing and beating all together.

The quicker and the more perfectly these materials are mixed and beaten together and the sooner the cement thus formed is used, the better it will be. This may be called *coarse-grained water cement,* which is to be applied in building, pointing, plastering, stuccoing, or other work, as mortar and stucco generally are; with this difference chiefly, that, as this cement is shorter than mortar, or common stucco, and dries sooner, it ought to be worked expeditiously in all cases ; and, in stuccoing, it ought to be laid on by sliding the trowel upwards on it. The materials used along with this cement in building, or the ground on which it is to be laid in stuccoing, ought to be well wetted with the lime-water in the instant of laying on the cement. The lime-water is also to be used when it is necessary to moisten the cement, or when a liquid is required to facilitate the floating of the cement.

When such cement is required to be of a still finer texture, take ninety-eight pounds of the fine sand, wet it with the lime-water, and mix it with the purified lime and the bone-ash, in the quantities and in the manner above described ; with this difference only, that fifteen pounds of lime, or thereabouts, are to be used instead of fourteen pounds, if the greater part of the sand be as fine as Lynn sand. This may be called *fine-grained water-cement.* It is used in giving the last coating, or the finish, to any work intended to imitate the finer-grained stones or stucco. But it may be applied to all the uses of the *coarse-grained water-cement,* and in the same manner.

When, for any of the foregoing purposes of pointing, building, &c., a cement is required much cheaper and coarser-grained than either of the foregoing, then much coarser clean sand than the foregoing coarse sand, or well-washed fine rubble, is to be provided. Of this coarse sand, or rubble, take fifty-six pounds, of the foregoing coarse sand twenty-eight pounds, and of the fine sand fourteen pounds ; and after mixing these, and wetting them with the cementing-liquor, in the foregoing manner, add fourteen pounds, or somewhat less, of the purified lime, and then fourteen pounds, or somewhat less, of the bone-ash, mixing them together in the manner already described. When the cement is required to be white, white sand, white lime, and the whitest bone-ash, are to be chosen. Grey sand, and grey bone-ash formed of half-burnt bones, are to be chosen to make cement grey; and any other colour of the cement is obtained, either by choosing coloured sand, or by the admixture of the necessary quantity of coloured talc in powder, or of coloured, vitreous, or metallic, powders, or other durable colouring ingredients, commonly used in paint.

This water-cement, whether the coarse or fine-grained, is applicable in forming artificial stone, by making alternate layers of the cement and of flint, hard stone, or bricks, in moulds of the figure of the intended stone, and by exposing the masses so formed to the open air, to harden.

When such cement is required for water fences, two-thirds of the prescribed quantity of bone-ashes are to be omitted ; and, in the place thereof, an equal measure of powdered terras is to be used ; and, if the sand employed be not of the coarsest sort, more terras must be added, so that the terras shall be one-sixth part of the weight of the sand.

When such a cement is required of the finest grain, or in a fluid form, so that it may be applied with a brush, flint-powder, or the powder of any quartose or hard earthy substance, may be used in the place of sand ; but in a quantity smaller, in proportion as the flint or other powder is finer ; so that the flint-powder or other such powder, shall not be more than six times the weight of the lime, nor less than four times its weight.   The greater the quantity of lime within these limits, the more will the cement be liable to crack by quick drying, and, *vice versa.*

Where the above described sand cannot be conveniently procured, or where the sand cannot be conveniently washed and sorted, that sand which most resembles the mixture of coarse and fine sand above prescribed, may be used as directed, provided due attention be paid to the quantity of the lime, which is to be greater as the quality is finer, and, *vice versa.*

Where sand cannot be easily procured, any durable stony body, or baked earth, grossly powdered, and sorted nearly to the sizes above prescribed for sand, may be used in the place of sand, measure for measure, but not weight for weight, unless such gross powder be specifically as heavy as sand

Sand may be cleansed from every softer, lighter, and less durable, matter, and from that part of the sand which is too fine, by various methods preferable in certain circumstances, to that which has been already described.

Water may be found naturally free from fixable gas, selenite, or clay ; such water may, without any great inconvenience, be used in the place of the lime-water ; and water approaching this state will not require so much lime as above prescribed to make the lime-water ; and a lime-water sufficiently useful may be made by various methods of mixing lime and water in the described proportions, or nearly so.

When stone-lime cannot be procured, chalk-lime, or shell-lime, which best resembles stone-lime, in the foregoing characters of lime, may be used in the manner described, excepting that fourteen pounds and a half of chalk-lime will be required in the place of fourteen pounds of stone-lime.   The proportion of lime, as prescribed above, may be increased without inconvenience, when the cement of stucco is to be applied where it is not liable to dry quickly ; and, in the contrary case, this proportion may be diminished.   The defect of lime, in quantity or quality, may be very advantageously supplied, by causing a considerable quantity of lime-water to soak into the work, in successive portions, and at distant intervals of time ; so that the calcareous matter of the lime-water, and the matter attracted from the open air, may fill and strengthen the work.

The powder of almost every well-dried or burnt animal substance may be used instead of bone-ash ; and several earthy powders, especially the micaceous and the metallic ; and the elixated ashes of divers vegetables, whose earth will not burn to lime, as well as the ashes of mineral fuel, which are of the calcareous kind, but will not burn to lime, will answer the ends of bone-ash in some degree.

The quantity of bone-ash described may be lessened without injuring the cement; in those circumstances especially which admit the quantity of lime to be lessened, and in those wherein the cement is not liable to dry quickly. The art of remedying the defects of lime may be advantageously practised to supply the deficiency of bone-ash, especially in building, and in making artificial stone with this cement.

As the preceding method of making mortar differs, in many particulars, from the common process, it may be useful to inquire into the causes on which this difference is founded.

When the sand contains much clay, the workmen find that the best mortar they can make must contain about one-half lime; and hence they lay it down as certain, that the best mortar is made by the composition of half sand and half lime.

But with sand requiring so great a proportion of lime as this, it will be impossible to make good cement; for it is universally allowed that the hardness of mortar depends on the crystallization of the lime round the other materials which are mixed with it; and thus uniting the whole mass into one solid substance. But, if a portion of the materials used be clay or any other friable substance, it must be evident that, as these friable substances are not changed in one single particular, by the process of being mixed up with lime and water, the mortar, of which they form a proportion, will consequently be, more or less, of a friable nature, in proportion to the quantity of friable substances used in the composition of the mortar. On the other hand, if mortar be composed of lime and good sand only, as the sand is a stony substance, and not in the least friable, and as the lime, by perfect crystallization, becomes likewise of a stony nature, it must follow, that a mass of mortar, composed of these two stony substances, will itself be a hard, solid, unfriable, substance. This may account for one of the essential variations in the preceding method from that in common use, and point out the necessity of never using, in the place of sand, which is a durable stony body, the scrapings of roads, old mortar, and other rubbish, from ancient buildings, which are frequently made use of, as all of them consist, more or less, of muddy, soft, and minutely divided particles.

Another essential point is the nature and quality of the lime. Now, experience proves that, when lime has been long kept in heaps, or untight casks, it is reduced to the state of chalk, and becomes every day less capable of being made into good mortar; because, as the goodness or durability of the mortar depends on the crystallization of the lime, and, as experiments have proved, that lime, when reduced to this chalk-like state, is always incapable of perfect crystallization, it must follow that, as lime in this state never becomes crystallized, the mortar of which it forms the most indispensable part, will necessarily be very imperfect; that is to say, it will never become a solid stony substance; a circumstance absolutely required in the formation of good durable mortar. These are the two principal ingredients in the formation of mortar; but, as water is also necessary, it may be useful to point out that which is the fittest for this purpose ; the best is rain-water, river-water the second, land-water next, and spring-water last.

The ruins of the ancient Roman buildings are found to cohere so strongly, as to have caused an opinion that their constructors were acquainted with some kind of mortar, which, in comparison with ours, might justly be called *cement ;* and that, to our want of knowledge of the materials they used, is owing the great inferiority of modern buildings in their durability. But a proper attention to the above particulars would soon show that the durability of the ancient edifices depended on the manner of preparing their mortar more than on the nature of the materials used. The following observations will, we think, prove this beyond a possibility of doubt :

Lime, which has been slaked and mixed with sand, becomes hard and consistent when dry, by a process similar to that which produces natural *stalactites* in caverns. These are always formed by water dropping from the roof. By some unknown and inexplicable process of nature, this water has had dissolved in it a small portion of calcareous matter, in a caustic state. So long as the water continues covered from the air, it keeps the earth dissolved in it; it being the natural property of calcareous earths, when deprived of their fixed air, to dissolve in water. But, when the small drop of water comes to be exposed to the air, the calcareous matter contained in it begins to attract the fixable part of the atmosphere. In proportion as it does so, it also begins to separate from the water, and to re-assume its native form of lime-stone or marble. When the calcareous matter is perfectly crystallized in this manner, it is to all intents and purposes lime-stone or marble of the same consistence as before. If lime, in a caustic state, is mixed with water, part of the lime will be dissolved, and will also begin to crystallize. The water which parted with the crystallized lime will then begin to act upon the remainder, which it could not dissolve before ; and thus the process will continue, either till the lime be all reduced to an *effete,* or crystalline state, or something hinders the action of the water upon it. It is this crystallization which is observed by the workmen when a heap of lime is mixed with water, and left for some time to macerate. A hard crust is formed upon the surface, which is ignorantly called *frostling,* though it takes place in summer as well as in winter. If, therefore, the hardness of the lime, or its becoming a cement, depends entirely on the formation of its crystals, it is evident that the perfection of the cement must depend on the perfection of the crystals, and the hardness of the matters which are entangled among them. The additional substances used in making of mortar, such as sand, brick-dust, or the like, serve only for a purpose similar to what is answered by sticks put into a vessel full of any saline solution ; namely, to afford the crystals an opportunity of fastening themselves upon it. If, therefore, the matter interposed between the crystals of the lime is of a friable brittle nature, such as brick-dust or chalk, the mortar will be of a weak and imperfect kind; but, when the particles are hard, angular, and very difficult to be broken, such as those of river or pit-sand, the mortar turns out exceedingly good and strong. That the crystallization may be the more perfect, a large quantity of water should be used, the ingredients be perfectly mixed together, and the drying be as slow as possible. An attention to these particulars would make the buildings of the moderns equally durable with those of the ancients. In the old Roman works, the great thickness of the walls necessarily required a vast length of time to dry. The middle of them was composed of pebbles thrown in at random, and which, evidently, had thin mortar poured in among them. Thus a great quantity of the lime would be dissolved, and the crystallization performed in the most perfect manner. The indefatigable pains and perserverance, for which the Romans were so remarkable in all their undertakings, leave no room to doubt that they would take care to have the ingredients mixed together as well as possible. The consequence of all this is, that the buildings formed in this manner are all as firm as if cut out of a solid rock ; the mortar being equally hard, if not more so, than the stones themselves.

CENTRES.—The frame of timber-work for supporting arches during their erection.

COFFER-DAM, or BATTARDEAU.—A case of piling, without a bottom, constructed for enclosing and building the piers of a bridge. A coffer-dam may be either single or double, the space between being filled with clay or chalk, closely rammed.

DRAG.—A thin plate of steel indented on the edge, like the teeth of a saw, and used in working soft stone, which has no grit for finishing the surface.

DRIFT.—The horizontal force of an arch, by which it tends to overset the piers.

EXTRADOS OF AN ARCH.—The exterior or convex curve, or the top of the archstones. This term is opposed to the *Intrados*, or concave side.

EXTRADOS OF A BRIDGE.—The curve of the road-way.

FENCE-WALL.—A wall used to prevent the encroachment of men or animals.

FOOTINGS.—Projecting courses of stone, without the naked superincumbent part, and which are laid in order to rest the wall firmly on its base.

HEADERS.—Stones disposed with their length horizontally, in the thickness of the wall.

JETTEE.—The border made around the stilts under a pier.

IMPOST OR SPRINGING.—The upper part or parts of a wall employed for springing an arch.

JOGGLED JOINTS.—The method of indenting the stones, so as to prevent the one from being pushed away from the other by lateral force.

KEY-STONES.—A term frequently used for *bond-stones*.

KEY-STONE.—The middle voussoir of an arch over the centre.

KEY-STONE OF AN ARCH.—The stone at the summit of the arch, put in last for wedging and closing the arch.

LEVEL.—Horizontal, or parallel to the horizon.

NAKED, OF A WALL.—The vertical or battering surface, whence all projectures arise.

OFF-SET.—The upper surface of a lower part of a wall, left by reducing the thickness of the superincumbent part upon one side or the other, or both.

PARAPETS.—The breast-walls erected on the sides of the extrados of the bridge, for preventing passengers from falling over.

PAVING.—A floor, or surface of stone, for walking upon.

PIERS IN HOUSES.—The walls between apertures, or between an aperture and the corner.

PIERS OF A BRIDGE.—The insulated parts between the apertures or arches, for supporting the arches and road-way.

PILES.—Timbers driven into the bed of a river, or the foundation of a building for supporting a structure.

PITCH OF AN ARCH.—The height from the springing to the summit of the arch.

QUARRY.—The place whence stones are raised.

RANDOM COURSES, IN PAVING.—Unequal courses, without any regard to equi-distant joints.

SPAN.—The span of an arch is its greatest horizontal width.

STERLINGS.—A case made about a pier of stilts in order to secure it. See the following article.

STILTS.—A set of piles driven into the bed of a river, at small distances, with a surrounding case of piling driven closely together, and the interstices filled with stones, in order to form a foundation for building the pier upon.

STRETCHERS.—Those stones, which have their length disposed horizontally in the length of the wall.

THROUGH STONES.—A term employed in some countries for bond-stones.

TOOLS USED BY MASONS.—The masons' *Level, Plumb-Rule, Square, Bevel, Trowel, Hod, and Compasses*, are similar in every respect to those tools which bear the same name among bricklayers ; and which are described hereafter. Those tools, which differ from such as are used by the bricklayer, are as follow :—

The *Saw* used by masons is without teeth, and stretched in a frame nearly resembling the joiner's saw-frame. It is made from four to six feet or more, in length, according to the size of the slabs, which are intended to be cut by it. To facilitate the process of cutting slabs into slips and scantlings, a portion of sharp silicious sand is placed upon an inclined plane, with a small barrel of water at the top, furnished with a spiggot, which is left sufficiently loose to allow the water to exude drop by drop ; and thus, by running over the sand, carries with it a portion of sand into the kerf of the stone. The workman sits at one side of the stone, and draws the saw to and fro, horizontally, taking a range of about twelve inches each time before he returns. By this means, calcareous stones of the hardest kinds may be cut into slabs of any thickness with scarcely any loss of substance. But, as this method of sawing stone is slow and expensive, mills have been erected in various parts of Great Britain, by which the same process is performed at a much cheaper rate, and in some of these mills every species of moulding upon stone is produced.

Masons make use of many *chisels*, of different sizes, but all resembling, or nearly resembling, each other in form. They are usually made of iron and steel welded together; but, when made entirely of steel, which is more elastic than iron, they will naturally produce a greater effect with any given impulse. The form of masons' chisels is that of a wedge, the cutting-edge being the vertical angle. They are made about eight or nine inches long. When the cutting-edge is broader than the portion held in the hand, the lower part is expanded in the form of a dove-tail. When the cutting-edge is smaller than the handle, the lower end is sloped down in the form of a pyramid. In finishing off stone, smooth and neat, great care should be taken that the arris is not splintered, which would certainly occur, if the edge of the chisel were directed outwards in making the blow: but if it be directed inwards, so as to overhang a little, and form an angle of about forty-five degrees, there is little danger of splintering the arris in chipping.

Of the two kinds of chisels, which are the most frequently made use of, *the tool* is the largest; that is to say, in the breadth of its cutting-edge; it is used for working the surface of stone into narrow furrows, or channels, at regular distances; this operation is called *tooling*, and the surface is said to be *tooled*.

The *Point* is the smallest kind of chisel used by masons, being never more than a quarter of an inch broad on its cutting-edge. It is used for reducing the irregularity of the surface of any rough stone.

The *Straight-Edge* is similar to the instrument among carpenters, of the same name; it being a thin, broad, planed true, to point out cross-windings and other inequalities of surface, and thus direct the workmen in the use of the chisel.

The *Mallet* used by the mason differ from that of any other artizan. It is similar to a bell in contour, excepting a portion of the broadest part, which is rather cylindrical. The handle is rather short, being only just long enough to be firmly grasped in the hand. It is employed for giving percussive force to chisels, by striking them with any part of the cylindrical surface of the mallet.

The Hammer used by masons is generally furnished with a point or an edge like a chisel. Both kinds are used for dividing stones, and likewise for producing those narrow marks or furrows left upon hewn-stone work which is not ground on the face.

VAULT.—A mass of stones so combined as to support each other over a hollow.

UNDER BED OF A STONE —The lower surface generally placed horizontally.

UPPER BED OF A STONE.—The upper surface, generally placed horizontally.

VOUSSOIRS.—The arch-stones in the face or faces of an arch; the middle one is called the *key-stone*.

WALL.—An erection of stone, generally perpendicular to the horizon; but sometimes *battering*, in order to give stability.

WALLS, EMPLECTION.—Those which are built in regular courses, with the stones smoothed in the face of the work. They are of two kinds, Roman and Grecian, as already noticed. The difference is, that the core of the Roman emplection is rubble; whereas, in the Grecian emplection, it is built in the same manner as the face, and every alternate stone goes through the entire thickness of the wall.

WALLS, ISODOMUM; those wherein the courses are of equal thickness, compact, and regularly built; but the stones are not smoothed on the face.

WALLS, PSEUDO-ISODOMUM; those which have unequal courses.

PLASTERING.

(From Nicholson's New Practical Builder.)

IN modern practice, PLASTERING, by its recent improvements occurs in every department of architecture, both internally and externally. It is more particularly applied to the sides of the walls and the ceilings of the interior parts of buildings, and, also, for stuccoing the external parts of many edifices.

In treating on this subject, we shall divide Plastering under its several heads: as *plastering on laths*, in its several ways; *rendering* on brick and stone; and, finally, the finishing to all the several kinds of work of this description; as well as modelling, and casting the several mouldings, both ornamental and plain; stuccoing, and other outside compositions, which are applied upon the exterior of buildings; and, the making and polishing the *scagliola*, now so much used for columns, and their antæ, or pilasters, &c.

LIME form an essential ingredient in all the operations of this trade. This useful article is vended at the wharfs about London in bags, and varies in its price from thirteen shillings to fifteen shillings per hundred pecks. Most of the lime made use of in London is prepared from chalk, and the greater portion comes from Purfleet in Kent; but, for stuccoing, and other work, in which strength and durability is required, the lime made at Dorking, in Surry, is preferred.

The composition, known as PLASTER OF PARIS, is one on which the Plasterer very much depends for giving the precise form and finish to all the better parts of his work; with it he makes all his ornaments and cornices, besides mixing it in his lime to fill up the finishing coat to the walls and ceilings of rooms.

The stone from which the plaster is obtained, is known to professional men by several names, as *sulphate of lime, selenite, gypsum,* &c.; but its common name seems to have been derived from the immense quantities which have been taken from the hill named *Mont-Martre*, in the environs of Paris. The stone from this place is, in its appearance, similar to common free-stone, excepting its being replete with small specular crystals. The French break it into fragments of about the size of an egg, and then burn it in kilns, with billets of wood, till the crystals lose their brilliancy; it is then ground with stones, to different degrees of fineness, according to its intended uses. This kind of specular gypsum is said to be employed in Russia, where it abounds, as a substitute for glass in windows.

According to the chemists, the specific gravity of gypsum, or Plaster of Paris, is from 1.872 to 2.311, requiring 500 parts of cold and 450 of heat to dissolve it; when calcined, it decrepitates, becomes very friable and white, and heats a little with water. In the process of burning, or calcination, it loses its water of crystallization, which, according to Fourcroy, is 22 per cent.

The plaster commonly made use of in London is prepared from a sulphate of lime, produced in Derbyshire, and called alabaster. Eight hundred tons are said to be annually raised there. It is brought to London in a crude state, and afterwards calcined, and ground in a mill for use, and vended in brown paper bags, each containing about half a peck; the coarser sort is about fourteen-pence per bag, and the finest from eighteen to twenty-pence. The figure-makers use it for their casts of anatomical and other figures; and it is of the greatest importance not only to the plasterer, but to the sculptor, mason, &c.

The working-tools of the plasterer consist of a *spade*, of the common sort, with a *two or three-pronged rake*, which he uses for the purpose of mixing his mortar and hair together. His *trowels* are of two sorts, one kind being of three or four sizes. The first sort is called the *laying* and *smoothing-tool*; its figure consists in a flat piece of hardened iron, very thin, of about ten inches in length, and two inches and a half in width, ground to a semi-circular shape at one end, while the other is left square; on the back of the plate, and nearest to the square end, is rivetted a piece of small rod-iron, with two legs, one of which is fixed to the plate, and the other, adapted for being fastened in a round wooden handle. With this tool all the first coats of plastering are put on; and it is also used in setting the finishing coat.

The trowels of the plasterer are made more neatly than the tools of the same name used by other artificers. The largest size is about seven inches long on the plate, and is of polished steel, two inches and three-quarters at the heel, diverging to an apex or point. To the wide end is adapted a handle, commonly of mahogany, with a deep brass ferrule. With this trowel the plasterer works all his fine-stuff, and forms cornices, mouldings, &c. The other trowels are made and fitted-up in a similar manner, varying gradually in their sizes from two or three inches in length.

The plasterer likewise employs several small tools, called *stopping* and *picking-out tools*; these are made of steel, well polished, and are of different sizes, commonly about seven or eight inches long, and half an inch wide, flattened at both ends, and ground away till they are somewhat rounding. With these he models and finishes all the mitres and returns to the cornices, and fills up and perfects the ornaments at their joinings.

The workman in this art should keep all his tools very clean; they should be daily polished, and never put away without being wiped and freed from plaster.

In the practice of plastering many rules and models of wood are required. The rules, or *straight-edges*, as they are called, enable the plasterer to get his work to an upright line; and the models guide him in running plain mouldings, cornices, &c.

The CEMENTS made use of, for the interior work, are of two or three sorts. The first is called *lime* and *hair*, or coarse stuff; this is prepared in a simliar way to common mortar, with the addition of hair, from the tan-yards, mixed in it. The mortar used for lime and hair is previously mixed with the sand, and the hair added afterward. The latter is incorporated by the labourers with a three-pronged rake.

FINE-STUFF, is pure lime, slaked with a small portion of water, and afterwards well saturated, and put into tubs in a semi-fluid state, where it is allowed to settle, and the water to evaporate. A small proportion of hair is sometimes added to the fine-stuff.

STUCCO, for inside walls, called *trowelled* or *bastard stucco*, is composed of the fine-stuff above described, and very fine washed sand, in the proportion of one of the latter to three of the former. All walls intended to be painted, are finished with this stucco.

MORTAR, called, *guage-stuff*, consists of about three-fifths of fine-stuff and one of Plaster of Paris, mixed together with water, in small quantites at a time : this renders it more susceptible of fixing or setting. This cement is used for forming all the cornices and mouldings, which are made with wooden moulds. When great expedition is required, the plasterers guage all their mortar with Plaster of Paris. This enables them to hasten the work, as the mortar will then set as soon as laid on.

PLASTERERS have technical words and phrases, by which they designate the quality of their work, and estimate its value.

BY LATHING is meant the nailing up laths, or slips of wood, on the ceiling and partitions. The laths are made of fir or oak, and called *three-foots* and *four-foots*, being of these several lengths : they are purchased by the bundle or load.

There are three sorts of laths ; viz. *single laths, lath and half*, and *double laths.* Single laths are the cheapest and thinnest ; lath and half denotes one-third thicker than the single lath ; and double laths twice their thickness. The laths generally used in London are made of fir, imported from Norway, the Baltic, and America, in pieces called *staves.* Most of the London timber-merchants are dealers in laths ; and there are many persons who confine themselves exclusively to this branch of trade.

The fir-laths are generally fastened by cast-iron nails, whereas, the oaken ones require wrought-iron nails, as no nail of the former kind would be found equal to the perforation of the oak, which would shiver it in pieces by the act of driving.

In lathing ceilings, it is advisable that the plasterer should make use of laths of both the usual lengths, and so manage the nailing of them, that the joints should be as much broken as possible. This will tend to strengthen the plastering laid thereon, by giving it a stronger key or tie. The strongest laths are adapted for ceilings, and the slightest or single laths for the partitions of buildings.

LAYING consists in spreading a single coat of lime and hair all over a ceiling or partition ; taking care that it is very even in every part, and quite smooth throughout : this is the cheapest manner of plastering.

PRICKING-UP is similar to *laying*, but is used as a preliminary to a more perfect kind of work. After the plastering has been put up in this manner, it is *scratched* all over with the end of a lath, in order to give a key or tie to the *finishing coats*, which are to follow.

Lathing, Laying, and Set, are applied to work that is to be lathed as already described, and covered with one coat of lime and hair; and, when sufficiently dry, finished by being covered over with a thin and smooth coat of lime only, called by the plasterer *putty* or *set*. This coat is spread with the smoothing trowel, and the surface finished with a large flat hog's hair brush. The trowel is held in the right hand, and the brush in the left. As the plasterer lays on the set, he draws the brush backwards and forwards over it, till the surface is smooth.

Lathing, Floating, and Set, consists of lathing and covering with a coat of plaster, which is pricked up for the floated work, and is thus performed: The plasterer provides himself with a strong rule, or straight-edge, often from ten to twelve feet in length; two workmen are necessarily employed therein. It is began by plumbing with a plumb-rule, and trying if the parts to be floated are upright and straight, to ascertain where filling up is wanting. This they perform by putting on a trowel or two of lime and hair only; when they have ascertained these preliminaries, the *screeds* are prepared.

A Screed, in plastering, is a stile formed of lime and hair, about seven or eight inches wide, guaged exactly true. In floated-work these screed are made at every three or four feet distance, vertically round a room, and are prepared perfectly straight by applying the straight-edge to them to make them so; and, when all the screeds are formed, the parts between them are filled up flush with lime and hair, or *stuff*, and made even with the face of the screeds. The straight-edge is then worked horizontally upon the screeds, to take off all superfluous *stuff*. The floating is thus finished by adding *stuff* continually, and applying the rule upon the screeds till it becomes, in every part, quite even with them.

Ceilings are floated in the same manner, by having screeds formed across them, and filling up the intermediate spaces with *stuff*, and applying the rule as for the walls.

Plastering is good or bad, in proportion to the care taken in this part of the work; hence the most careful workmen are generally employed therein.

The Set to the floated work is performed in a similar way to that already described for the laid plastering; but floated plastering, for the best rooms, is performed with more care than is required in an inferior style of work. The setting, for the floated work, is frequently prepared by adding to it about one-sixth of Plaster of Paris, that it may fix more quickly, and have a closer and more compact appearance. This, also, renders it more firm, and better adapted for being whitened, or coloured when dry. The drier the pricking-up coat of plastering is, the better for the floated stucco-work; but if the floating is too dry before the last coat is put on, there is a probability of its peeling off, or cracking, and thus giving the ceiling an unsightly appearance. These cracks, and other disagreeable appearances in ceilings, may likewise arise from the weakness of the laths, or from too much plastering, or from strong laths and too little plastering. Good floated work, executed by a judicious hand, is very unlikely to crack, and particularly if the lathing be properly attended to.

RENDERING AND SET, OR RENDERING, FLOATED, AND SET, includes a portion of the process employed in both the previous modes, with the exception that no lathing is required in this branch of the work. By *rendering* is meant that one coat of lime and hair is to be plastered on a wall of brick or stone; and the *set* implies that it is again to be covered and finished with fine stuff, or putty. The method of performing this is similar that already described for the setting of ceilings and partitions. The *floated* and *set* is performed on the rendering in the same manner as it is on the partitions and ceilings of the best kind of plastering, which has been described.

TROWELLED-STUCCO is a very neat kind of work, much used in dining-rooms, vestibules, stair-cases, &c., especially when the walls are to be finished by painting. This kind of stucco requires to be worked upon a floated ground, and the floating should be as dry as possible before the stuccoing is began. When the stucco is made, as before described, it is beaten and tempered with clean water, and is then fit for use. In order to use it, the plasterer is provided with a small *float*, which is merely a piece of half-inch deal, about nine inches long and three inches wide, planed smooth, and a little rounded away on its lower edge; a handle is fitted to the upper side, to enable the workman to move it with ease. The stucco is spread upon the ground, which has been prepared to receive it, with the largest trowel, and made as even as possible. When a piece, four or five feet square, has been so spread, the plasterer, with a brush, which he holds in his left hand, sprinkles a small part of the stucco with water, and then applies the float, alternately sprinkling and rubbing the face of the stucco, till he reduces the whole to a perfect smooth and even surface. The water has the effect of hardening the face of the stucco; so that, when well floated, it feels to the touch as smooth as glass.

CORNICES are plain or ornamented, and sometimes include a portion of both; in the ornamented, superior taste has latterly prevailed, on principles derived from the study of the *antique*. The preliminaries, in the formation of cornices in plastering, consist in the examination of the drawings or designs, and measuring the projections of the members: should the latter be found to exceed seven or eight inches, *bracketing* will be necessary.

BRACKETING consists of pieces of wood fixed up at about eleven or twelve inches from each other, all round the place intended to have a cornice; on these brackets laths are fastened, and the whole is covered with one coat of plastering, making allowance in the brackets for the stuff necessary to form the cornice; for this about one inch and a quarter is generally found sufficient. When the cornice has been so far forwarded, a mould must be made of the profile or section of the cornice, exactly representing all its members; this is generally prepared, by the carpenters, of beach-wood, about a quarter of an inch in thickness; all the quirks, or small sinkings, being formed in brass. When the mould is ready, the process of running the cornice begins : two workmen are required to perform this operation ; and they are provided with a tub of set, or putty, and a quantity of Plaster of Paris ; but before they begin with the mould, they guage a straight line, or screed, on the wall and ceiling, made of putty and plaster, extending so far on each as to answer to the bottom and top of the cornice, for it to fit into. This is the guide for moving the mould upon. The putty is then mixed with about one-third of Plaster of Paris, and incorporated in a semi-fluid state, by being diluted with clean water. One of the workmen then takes two or three trowels full of the prepared putty upon his hawk, which he holds in his left hand, having in his right hand a trowel, with which he plasters the putty over the parts where the cornice is to be formed ; the other workman applying the mould to ascertain where more or less of it is required ; and, when a sufficient quantity has been put on to fill up all the parts of the mould, the other workman moves the mould backwards and forwards, holding it up firmly to the ceiling and wall ; thus removing the superfluous stuff, and leaving in plaster the exact contour of the cornice required. This is not effected at once, but the other workman keeps supplying fresh putty to the parts which want it. If the stuff dries too fast, one of the workmen sprinkles it with water from a brush.

When the cornices are of very large proportions, three or four moulds are requisite, and they are applied in the same manner until the whole of their parts are formed. The mitres, internal and external, and also small returns or breaks, are afterwards modelled and filled up by hand.

ORNAMENTAL CORNICES are formed previously, and in a similar way to those described, excepting that the plasterer leaves indents or sinkings in the mould for the casts to be fixed in. The plasterers of the present day cast all their ornaments in Plaster of Paris ; whereas, they were formerly the work of manual labour, performed by ingenious men, then known in the trade as *ornamental-plasterers*. The casting of ornaments in moulds has almost superseded this branch of the art ; and the few individuals now living, by whom it was formerly professed, are chiefly employed in modelling and framing of moulds.

All the ornaments which are cast in Plaster of Paris, are previously modelled in clay. The clay-model exhibits the power and taste of the designer, as well as that of the sculptor. When it is finished, and becomes rather firm, it is oiled all over, and put into a wooden frame. All its parts are then retouched and perfected, for receiving a covering of melted wax, which is poured warm into the frame and over the clay-mould. When cool, it is turned upside down, and the wax comes easily away from the clay, and is an exact reversed copy. In such moulds are cast all the enriched mouldings, now prepared by common plasterers. The waxen models are made so as to cast about one foot in length of the ornaments at a time ; this quantity being easily removed out of the moulds, without the danger of breaking.

The casts are all made with the finest and purest Plaster of Paris, saturated with water. The casts, when first taken out of the moulds, are not very firm, and are suffered to dry a little, either in the air, or in an oven adapted for the purpose ; and when hard enough to bear handling, they are scraped and cleaned up for the workmen to fix in the places intended.

THE FRIEZES AND BASSO-RELIEVOS are performed in a manner exactly similar, except that the waxen moulds are so made as to allow of grounds of plaster being left behind the ornaments, half an inch, or more, in thicknesses ; and these are cast to the ornaments or figures, which strengthen and secure the proportions.

CAPITALS to columns are prepared in a similar way, but require several moulds to complete them.   The Corinthian capital will require a shaft or bell to be first made exactly shaped, so as to produce graceful effects in the foliage and contour of the volutes ; all of which, as well as the other details, require separate and distinct reversed moulds when intended for capitals made to order.

The plasterers, as before-mentioned, in forming cornices, in which ornaments are to be used, take care to have projections in the running moulds ; which have the effect of grooves or indents in the cornices ; and into these grooves are put the ornaments after they are cast, which are fixed in their places by having small quantities of liquid Plaster of Paris spread at their backs.   Friezes are prepared for cornices, &c., in a similar way, by leaving projections in the running moulds, at those parts of the cornices where they are intended to be inserted, and they are also fixed in their places with liquid plaster.   Detached ornaments, when designed for ceilings, or any other parts, to which running moulds have not been employed, are cast in pieces exactly corresponding with the designs, and are fixed upon the ceilings, or other places, with white-lead.

Plasterers require numerous models in wood, and very few or any of their best works can be completed without them.   But, with moulds, good plasterers are capable of making the most exquisite mouldings, possessing sharpness and breadths unequalled by any other modes now in practice.   This, however, is, in some measure, dependent on the truth of the moulds.   Good plastering is known by its exquisite appearance, as to its regularity, correctness, solid effect, and without any cracks or indications of them.

ROMAN CEMENT, OR OUTSIDE STUCCO.—The qualities of this valuable cement is now generally known in every part of the *United Kingdom*.   It was first introduced to public notice by the late JAMES WYATT, Esq. eminent for having planned and executed some of the most magnificent and useful structures in these countries.   It was originally known as *Parker's Patent Cement*, and was sold by Messrs. Charles Wyatt and Co., Bankside, London, at *five shillings* and *sixpence* per bushel : it is now vended by different manufacturers in the Metropolis at *three shillings* per bushel, and even less, when the casks are returned.   Equal quantities of this cement and sharp clean grit-sand, mixed together, will form very hard and durable coverings for the outsides of public and private edifices.   If the sand is wet or damp, the composition should be used immediately.   When the works are finished, they should be frescoed, or coloured, with washes, composed in proportions of five ounces of copperas to every gallon of water, and as much fresh lime and cement as will produce the colours required. Where these sorts of works are executed with judgment, and finished with taste, so as to produce picturesque effects, they are drawn and jointed to imitate well-bonded masonry, and the divisions promiscuously touched with rich tints of umber, and occasionally with vitriol; and, upon these colours mellowing, they will produce the most pleasing and harmonious effects; especially if dashed with judgment, and with the skill of a painter who has profitted by watching the playful tints of nature produced by the effects of time in the mouldering remains of our ancient buildings.

One bushel of cement, used with discretion, care, and judgment, will perform from three to four yards superficial; that is, mixed with an equal portion of clean sharp grit-sand; and, in procuring the latter article, great pains should be taken to select such qualities as are of a lively and binding description, and free from all slime or mud. As soon as the sand and cement is mixed with clean water, the composition should be used as quick as possible, and not a moment lost in floating the walls which will require incessant labour, until the cement is set, which is almost instantaneous.

ROUGH-CASTING is an outside finishing cheaper than stucco. It consists in giving the wall to be rough-casted a pricking-up coat of lime and hair; and when this is tolerably dry, a second coat of the same material, which is laid on the first, as smooth and even as can be. As fast as this coat is finished, a second workman follows the other with a pail of rough-cast, which he throws on the new plastering. The materials for rough-casting are composed of fine gravel, with the earth washed cleanly out of it, and afterwards mixed with pure lime and water, till the entire together is of the consistence of a semi-fluid; it is then spread or rather splashed, upon the wall by a float made of wood. This float is five or six inches long, and as many wide, made of half-inch deal, to which is fitted a rounded deal handle. The plasterer holds this in his right hand, and in his left a common white-wash brush; with the former he lays on the rough-cast, and with the latter, which he dips in the rough-cast, he brushes and colours the mortar and rough-cast that he has spread, to make them, when finished and dry, appear of the same colour throughout.

SCAGLIOLA.—The practice of forming columns with SCAGLIOLA is a distinct branch of plastering. It originated in Italy, and was thence introduced into France, then into England. For its first introduction here, our country is indebted to the late Henry Holland, Esq. who was for many years the favourite architect of his present Majesty, who caused artists to be invited from Paris to perform such works in Carlton Palace; some of whom, from finding a considerable demand for their works, remained with us, and taught the art to our British workmen.

In order to execute columns and their antæ, or pilasters, in Scagliola, the following remarks and directions are to be observed: when the architect has furnished the drawing, exhibiting the diameter of the shafts, a wooden cradle is made about two and a half inches less in diameter than that of the projected column. This cradle is lathed all round, as for common plastering, and afterwards covered by a pricking-up coat of lime and hair : when this is quite dry, the workers in Scagliola commence their peculiar labour.

The Scagliola is capable of imitating the most scarce and precious marbles ; the imitation taking as high a polish, and feeling to the touch as cold and solid as the most compact and dense marble.   For the composition of it the purest gypsum must be broken in small pieces, and then calcined till the largest fragments have lost their brilliancy.   The calcined powder is then passed through a very fine seive, and mixed up with a solution of Flanders glue, isinglass, &c., with the colours required in the marble they are about to imitate.

When the work is to be of various colours, each colour is prepared separately, and they are afterwards mingled and combined nearly in the same manner as a painter mixes, on his pallet, the primitive colours which are to compose his different shades When the powdered gypsum, or plaster, is prepared, and mingled for the work. it is laid on the shaft of the column, &c., covering over the pricked-up coat, which has been previously laid on it, and is floated, with moulds of wood to the sizes required. During the floating, the artist uses the colours necessary for the marble intended to be imitated, which thus become mingled and incorporated in it.   In order to give his work the polish or glossy lustre, he rubs it with a pumice-stone, and cleanses it with a wet sponge.   He next proceeds to polish it with tripoli and charcoal, and fine soft linen ; and, after going over it with a piece of felt, dipped in a mixture of oil and tripoli, finishes the operation by the application of pure oil.

This is considered as one of the finest imitations in the world ; the Scagliola being as strong and durable as real marble for all works not exposed to the effects of the atmosphere, retaining its lustre as long and equal to real marble, without being one-eighth of the expense of the cheapest marble imported.

COMPOSITION.—Besides the composition, before adverted to, for covering the outsides of buildings, plasterers use a finer species of composition for inside orna-mental works.   The material alluded to is of a brownish colour, exceedingly compact, and, when completely dry, very strong.   It is composed of powdered whitening, glue in solution, and linseed-oil ; the proportions of which are to two pounds of whitening, one pound of glue, and half a pound of oil.   These are placed in a cop-per and heated, being stirred with a spatula till the whole becomes incorporated.   It is then suffered to cool and settle ; after which it is taken and laid upon a stone, covered with powdered whitening, and beaten till it becomes of a tough and firm consistence.   It is then put by for use, and covered with wetted cloths to keep it fresh.

The ornaments to be cast in this composition are modelled in clay, for common plastering, and afterwards carved in a block of box-wood.   The carving must be done with great neatness and truth, as on it depends the exquisiteness of the orna-ment.   The composition is cut with a knife into pieces, and then closely pressed by hand into every part of the mould ; it is then placed in a press, worked by an iron screw, by which the composition is forced into every part of the sculpture.   After being taken out of the press, by giving it a tap upside down, it comes easily out of mould. One foot in length is as much as is usually cast at a time; and when this is first taken out of the mould, all the superfluous composition is removed by cutting it off with a knife; the waste pieces being thrown into the copper to assist in making a fresh supply of composition.

This composition, when formed into ornaments, is fixed upon wooden or other ground, by a solution of heated glue, white-lead, &c. It is afterwards painted or gilded, to suit the taste and style of the work for which it is intended.

PLASTERER'S MEASURING AND VALUATION.

The *measuring* and *valuation* of plasterer's work is conducted by surveyors. All common plastering is measured by the yard square, of nine feet; this includes the partitions and ceilings of rooms, stuccoing, internally and externally, &c. &c. Cornices are measured by the foot superficial, girting their members to ascertain their widths, which, multiplied by their lengths, will produce the superficial contents. Running measures consist of beads, quirks, arrises, and small mouldings. Ornamental cornices are frequently valued in this way; that is, by the running foot.

The labour in plasterer's work is frequently of more consideration than the materials; hence it becomes requisite to note down the exact time which is consumed in effecting particular portions, so that an adequate and proper value may be put upon the work.

GLOSSARY OF TECHNICAL TERMS.

FROM NICHOLSON'S NEW PRACTICAL BUILDER.

AARON'S ROD; an ornamental figure, representing a rod with a serpent twined about it, and, called by some, though improperly, the *Caduceus* of Mercury.

Abacus; the upper member of a capital of a column, serving as a kind of crown piece in the Grecian Doric, and a collection of members or mouldings in the other Orders.

Abreuvoir or Abrevior, in Masonry; the joint or junction of two stones; or the space or interstice to be filled up with mortar or cement. *Abreuvoir* also signifies a Bathing House or Place.

Abutment or Butment; *See Groin Arches.*

Acanthus; a plant, the English *Bear's Breech*, the leaves of which are represented in the capital of the Corinthian Order, &c. *Acanthine* means ornamented with leaves of the acanthus.

Accessories; in architectural composition, those parts or ornaments, either designed or accidental, which are not apparently essential to the use and character of a building.

Accompaniments; subordinate buildings or ornaments.

Accouplement, in carpentry; a tie or brace, or the entire work when framed.

Acropolis; from the Greek: the highest part of a city, the citadel or fortress.

Acroterium; (plural, *Acroteria*) the extremity or vertex of any thing; a pedestal or base placed on the angle, or on the apex of a pediment, which may be for the support of a vase or statue.

Ædes; among the ancients, an inferior kind of temple.

Ægis; in decoration, a shield or breast-plate, particularly that of Minerva.

Ægricanés; sculptures representing the heads and skulls of rams; commonly used as a decoration of ancient altars, friezes, &c.

Æneatores; sculptures representing military musicians.

Aërial Perspective; the representation of objects, weakened and diminished in proportion to the distance from the eye.

Ætoma; a pediment, or the *tympanum* of a pediment.

Aile or Aisle; a walk in a church, on the sides of the *nave*; the wings of a choir.

Air-trap; an opening for the escape and admission of air.

Alcove; a recess or part of a chamber, separated by an *estrade*, or partition of columns, and other corresponding ornaments.

Arœostyle; the greatest interval or distance that can be made between columns.

Alto-relievo or High-relief; that kind or portion of sculpture which projects so much from the surface to which it is attached, as to appear nearly insulated. It is therefore used in comparison with *Mezzo-relievo*, or Mean-relief, and in opposition to *Basso-relievo* or Low relief.

Amphitheatre; a spacious edifice, of a circular or oval form, in which the combats and shows of antiquity were exhibited.

Amphora (plural, *Amphoræ*); a vase or earthen jar, with two handles; among the ancients, the usual receptacles of olives, grapes, oil, and wine. Hence, in decoration, *Amphoral* means shaped like an amphora or vase.

Amulet; in decoration, a figure or character to which miraculous powers are supposed to be attached, and which particularly distinguished the buildings of Egypt.

Ancon; in decoration, a curved drinking cup or horn. The arm of a chair.

Anconés; ornaments depending from the corona of Ionic door-ways, &c. The trusses, or *consoles*, or brackets, sometimes employed in the dressings of apertures, as an apparent support to the cornice, upon the flanks of the architrave.

Angels; brackets or corbels, with the figures or heads of angels.

Angle-Bar; the upright bar of a window, constructed on a polygonal plan, standing at the meeting of any two planes of the sides.

Angle-Chimney; a chimney in the angle, or in a side formed at an angle of the apartment.

Angle-Rafter; in carpentry, otherwise Hip-rafter.

Angular Capital; the modern Ionic or *scammozian* capital, which is formed alike on all the four faces, so as to return at the angles of the building.

Annular-Vault; a vault rising from two circular walls; the vault of a circular corridor.

Annulet or Fillet; a small square member in the Doric capital, under the quarter-round. It is also used to imply a narrow flat moulding, common to the various parts of the columns, particularly their bases, capitals, &c.

Antæ; a species of pilasters common in the Grecian

temples, but differing from pilasters, in general, both in their capitals and situation.

Apron, in plumbing, the same as *Flashing*.

Arabesque, or Moresque; something done after the manners of the Arabians or Moors, and destitute of human and *animal* figures.

Arcade; an aperture in a wall, with an arched head: it also signifies a range of apertures with arched heads. Arcades are frequently constructed as porticoes, instead of Colonnades, being stronger, and less expensive. In the construction, care must be taken that the piers be sufficiently strong to resist the pressure of the arches, particularly those at the extremities. The arcades of the Romans were seen in triumphal arches, in threatres, amphitheatres, and aqueducts, and frequently in temples. They are common in the piazzas and squares of modern cities, and may be employed, with great propriety, in the courts of palaces, &c.

Arc-boutants, or Boutants; arch-formed props, in Gothic churches, &c. for sustaining the vaults of the nave; their lower ends resting on the pilastered buttresses of the aisles, and their upper ends resisting the pressure of the middle vault, against the several springing points of the groins. They are, at times, called *flying-buttresses, arched buttresses,* and *arch-butments.*

Arch; a part of a building supported at its extremities only, and concave towards the earth or horizon: but arches are either circular, elliptical, or *straight*: the last being so termed, but improperly, by workmen. The terms *arch* and *vault* properly differ only in this, that the arch expresses a narrower, and the vault a broader, piece of the same kind.

Arches, straight; heads of apertures which have a straight intrados in several pieces, with radiating joints, or bricks tapering downwards.

Architectonic; something endowed with the power and skill of building, or calculated to assist the architect.

Architrave; a beam; that part of an entablature which lies immediately upon the capital or head of the columns.

B.

Back; generally that side of an object which is opposite to the face, or breast: but the *back of a hand-rail,* is the upper side of it; that of a rafter, is the upper side of it in the sloping plane of one side of a roof.

Back-shutters, or back-flaps; additional breadths hinged to the front-shutters, for completely closing the aperture when the window is to be shut.

Bagnio; the Italian name for a bath, or bathing-house: answering to the Greek *Balaneia,* and the Latin *Balneum.*

Balcony (from the French *Balcon*); an open gallery, projecting from the front of a building, and commonly constructed of iron or wood. When a portico or porch is surmounted with a balcony, it is commonly of stone, with iron or wood.

Baluster; a small kind of column or pillar, belonging to a *Balustrade.*

Balustrade; a range of *Balusters,* supporting a cornice, and used as a parapet or screen, for concealing a roof or other object.

Bande or Band; a narrow flat surface, having its face in in a vertical plane: hence *Bandelet,* a little band, any flat moulding or fillet.

Bandel Column; a column encircled with *Bands,* or annular *rustics.*

Barge Course; that part of the tiling which projects over the gable of a building, and is made up below with mortar.

Base; the lowest part of a figure or body, and finish of rooms, &c.

Bay-Window; a window projecting from the front, in two or more planes, and not forming the segment of a circle.

Beaking Joint, in Carpentry; a provincial term, denoting that the heading joints of the boards of a floor fall in the same straight line.

Beam-filling; filling up the space, with stones or bricks, from the level of the under edges of the beams to that of their upper edges, &c.

Bearing-Wall or partition; in a building, is a wall resting upon the solid, and supporting some other part, as another wall, &c.

Belfry, anciently the *campanile;* the part of a steeple in which the bells are hung.

Belvedere; a turret, look out, or observatory, commanding a fine prospect, and generally very ornamental.

Binding-Joists; those beams in a floor which support transversely the bridgings above, and the ceiling joists below.

Binding-Rafters. The same as Purlins. See *Purlins.*

Boasting; in stone-cutting, paring the stone irregularly with a broad chisel and mallet; in carving, the rough cutting of the outline, before the incisions are made for the minuter parts.

Boning; in carpentry and masonry, the art of making a plane surface by the guidance of the eye. Joiners try up their work by *boning* with two straight-edges, which determine whether it be in or out of *Winding*; that is to say, whether the surface be twisted or a plane.

Bosse or Boss, in sculpture; relief or prominence: hence *Bossage,* the projection of stones laid rough, to be afterwards carved into mouldings, capitals, or other ornaments. *Bossage* is also that which is otherwise called *Rustic work*; consisting of stones which seem to advance beyond the naked of a building, from indentures or channels left in the joinings; these are used chiefly in the corners of edifices and thence called *Rustic quoins.*

Boulder-Walls; those constructed of flints or pebbles, laid in strong mortar.

Bow-Window; a window forming the segment of a circle.

Broad-stone; the same as Free-stone.

Buffet; an ornamented cupboard, or cabinet for plate, glasses, china, &c.

Burrs; clinker bricks.

Butment, see *Abutment*.

Butt-end of timber; the largest end next to the root.

Buttery; a store-room for provisions.

Buttress or Plaster Bricks; those made with a notch at one end, half the length of the brick, and used for binding work built with *great brick*.

Buttresses, flying, &c. see *Arc-boutants*.

C

CADUCEUS, an emblem or attribute of Mercury; a rod entwined by two-winged serpents.

Camber; an arch on the top of an aperture, or on the top of a beam : whence *Camber-windows*, &c.

Campana; the body of the Corinthian capital.

Campanæ, or Campanula, or Guttæ; the drops of the Doric architrave.

Campanile; ancient name for a belfry.

Cant-moulding; a bevelled surface, neither perpendicular to the horizon, nor to the vertical surface to which it may be attached.

Cap, in joinery; the uppermost of an assemblage of parts; as the capital of a column, the cornice of a door, &c.

Carcase roofing; that which supports the covering by a grated frame of timber-work.

Caryatidæ or Caryatides; so called from the Caryatides, a people of Caria; an order of columns or pilasters, under the figure of women dressed in long robes, after the manner of the Carian people, and serving to support an entablature. This order is styled the *Caryatic*.

Case of a Door; the frame in which the door is hung.

Casements; sashes or glass frames, opening on hinges, and revolving upon one of the vertical edges.

Castellated; built in imitation of an ancient castle.

Catacomb; a subterraneous place for the interment of the dead.

Cement; a composition.

Chain-timber, in brick building; a timber of large dimensions placed in the middle of the height of a story, for imparting strength.

Chancel; the communion place, or that part of a Christian church between the altar and balustrade which encloses it.

Chantry; a small chapel, on the side of a church, &c.

Chapiter; the same as *Capital*.

Chaplet; a small carved or ornamented fillet.

Clamping, in joinery; securing boards with clamps.

Cloacæ; the Roman name for sewers, drains, and sinks, conveying filth from the city into the river.

Coffer-dam; a hollow space, formed by a double range of piles, with clay rammed in between, for the purpose of constructing an entrance-lock to a canal, dock, or basin. See also *Batterdeau*.

Cogging. See *Cocking*.

Coin, or Quoin; a corner or angle made by the two surfaces of a stone or brick building, whether external or internal.

Collar; a ring or cincture.

Colonnade; a range of columns, whether attached or insulated, and supporting an entablature.

Comparted; divided into smaller parts; or partitioned into smaller spaces.

Conservatory; a superior kind of Greenhouse, for valuable plants, &c., arranged in beds of earth, with ornamental borders.

Console; a bracket or projecting body, shaped like a curve of contrary flexure, scrolled at the ends, and serving to support a cornice, bust, vase, or other ornament. Consoles are also called, according to their form, *ancones* or *trusses, mutules*, and *modillions*.

Continued; uninterrupted; unbroken; as a continued attic, pedestal, &c., not broken by pilasters or columns.

Contour; a French word for *Outline*.

Coping; the stones laid on the top of a wall, to strengthen and defend it from injury.

Corbeils; carved work, representing baskets filled with fruit or flowers, and used as a finish to some elegant part of a building. This word is sometimes used to express the bell or vase of the Corinthian capital.

Corbels; a horizontal row of stones or timber, fixed in a wall or on the side of a vault, for sustaining the timbers of a floor or of a roof; the ends projecting out six or eight inches, as occasion may require, in the manner of a shoulder-piece, and cut at the end according to fancy, in form of an ogee, &c., the upper side being flat. In the castellated style of architecture, the *Corbels* are a range of stones, projecting from a wall, for the purpose of supporting a parapet or superior part of the wall, which projects beyond the inferior part.

Cornice; a crowning; any moulded projection which crowns or finishes the part to which it is attached. The Cornice of an order is a secondary member of the order itself, or a primary member of the entablature. The latter is divided into three principal parts, and the upper one is the *cornice*.

Cornucopia; the horn of plenty; represented in sculpture under the figure of a large horn out of which issue fruits, flowers, grain, &c.

Corridor; a long gallery or passage around a building, and leading to the several apartments.

Counter-forts; projections of masonry from a wall, at certain regular distances, for strengthening it or resisting a pressure.

Counter-gauge, in carpentry; a method of measuring joints by transferring the breadth of a mortice to the place of the other timber where the tenon is to be made.

Counter-lath, in tiling; a lath placed, by eye, between every two gauged ones, so as to divide every interval into two equal parts.

Country-house. *See Villa*.

Coupled Columns; those disposed in pairs, so as to form a narrow and wide interval alternately.

Couples; rafters framed together in pairs, with a tie, which is generally fixed above the feet of the rafters.

Course ; a continued level range of stones or bricks, in a wall, &c.

Coursing Joint ; the joint between two courses.

Cove ; any kind of concave moulding ; also the concavity of a vault. Hence, a *coved and flat ceiling* is a ceiling of which the section is a portion of a circle, springing from the walls, and rising to a flat surface.

Cover, in slating ; the part of the slate that is hidden : the exposed part being called the margin.

Cover-way, in roofing ; the recess or internal angle left to receive the covering.

Covered-way ; a passage arched over.

Coving ; an exterior projecture, in an arched form, now disused. The covings of a fire-place are the inclined vertical parts on the sides, so formed for contracting the space, &c.

Crockets ; in the pointed style of architecture, the small ornaments placed equi-distantly along the angles of pediments, pinnacles, &c.

Crosettes, in decoration ; the trusses or consoles on the flanks of the architrave, under the cornice.

Cross-springers ; in groins of the pointed style, the ribs that spring from one diagonal pier to the other.

Crown ; the uppermost member of a cornice, including the corona, &c. Of an arch, its most elevated line or point.

Crypt ; an ancient name for the lowest part or apartment of a building.

Cupola ; a dome, arched roof, or turret.

Cusps ; the pendents of a pointed arch, &c., two of which form a trefoil, three a quadrefoil, four a cinquefoil, &c.

Cylindro-spheric groin. See *Groin*.

D.

Dead-shoar ; an upright piece of wood, built up in a wall which has been broken through, in order to make some alteration in the building.

Demi, or Semi, or Hemi, signifies one half. Hence Semi-circle, Hemi-sphere, &c.

Demi-relievo, in carving or sculpture, denotes that the figure rises one half from the plane. See *Alto-relievo*.

Die of a pedestal ; the part comprehended between the base and cornice.

Diglyph ; a tablet with two engravings or channels.

Diminished Bar, in joinery ; the bar of a sash that is thinnest on the inner edge.

Dish-out ; to form coves by means of ribs, or wooden vaults for plastering upon.

Distemper ; in painting, the working up of colours with something besides mere water or oil, as size, or other glutinous or unctuous substances.

Ditriglyph ; having two triglyphs over an intercolumn.

Double-hung sashes ; in joinery, those of which the window contains two, and each moveable by means of weights and lines.

Dove-tailing ; in joinery, a method of fastening one piece of wood to another, by projecting bits, cut in the form of dove-tails in one piece, and let into corresponding hollows in another.

Dressings ; all mouldings projecting beyond the naked of walls or ceilings.

Drops ; in ornamental architecture, small pendent cylinders, or frustrums of cones attached to a surface vertically, with the upper ends touching a horizontal surface, as in the cornice of the Doric order.

Drum or Vase, of the Corinthian and Composite capitals ; the solid part to which the foliage and stalks, or ornaments, are attached.

Dwarf-wainscoting ; that wainscoting which does not reach to the usual height.

Dwarf-walls ; those of less height than the story of a building.

Dye ; the plain part of a pedestal, between the base and cornice.

E.

Eaves ; the margin or edge of a roof, overhanging the walls.

Elbows of a Window ; the two flanks of panelled work, one under each shutter, and generally tongued or rebatted into the back.

Embattled ; a building with a parapet, having embrasures, and therefore resembling a battery or castle.

Embossing ; forming work in relievo, whether cast, moulded, or cut with a chisel. See *Alto* and *Demi-relievo*.

Epistylium, or architrave of the entablature.

Estrade ; a French word for a public walk. In a room, a small elevation of the floor, frequently encompassed with a rail or alcove.

F.

Façade ; the face or front of a building.

Facings ; in joinery, those fixed parts of wood-work which cover the rough work of the interior sides of walls, &c.

Falling-moulds ; in joinery, the two moulds which are to be applied to the vertical sides of the rail-piece, in order to form the back and under surface of the rail, and finish the squaring.

Flyers ; steps, of which the treads are all parallel.

Flying buttresses. See *Arc boutant*.

Framing of a house ; all the timber work, comprehending the carcase flooring, partitioning, roofing, ceiling, beams, &c.

Franking ; in sash-making, is the operation of cutting a small excavation on the side of a bar for the reception of the transverse bar, so that no more of the wood be cut away than may suffice to show a mitre when the two bars are joined together.

Fret ; a species of ornament, commonly composed of straight grooves or channelures at right rangles to each other. The *labyrinth fret* has many turnings or angles, but in all cases the parts are parallel and perpendicular with each other.

Frosted ; a species of rustic work, representing ice formed by irregular drops of water.

Frowey timber ; such as works freely to the plane, without tearing.

G.

GABLE; the triangular part of the wall of a house or building immediately under the roof.

Galilee; a porch constructed at or near the west end of the great abbey churches, where the monks and clergy assembled on proceeding to, and returning from, processions, &c.

Gangway; in building, the temporary rough stair, set up for ascending or descending, before the regular stair is built.

Gathering of the wings, in a chimney: the sloping part above the fire-place, where the funnel contracts or tapers.

Gauge or Gage; in carpentry and joinery, a tool for drawing a line or lines on any side of a piece of stuff, parallel to one of the arrises of that side.

Girt. The same as *Fillet*.

Gorge; a concave moulding, much less recessed than a *scotia*. This word is sometimes used for the *cyma-recta*.

Gothic, more properly British, architecture.

Greek Orders of architecture; the Doric, Ionic, and Corinthian. See these names respectively.

Griffin, or Griffon; a fabulous animal, sacred to Apollo, and mostly represented with the head and wings of an eagle, and the body, legs, and tail, of a lion. It was a common ornament of ancient temples.

Groin; the hollow formed by the intersection of two or more simple vaults, crossing each other at the same height. Groins of different forms are distinguished by particular designations, as follow:

Conic Groin is a groin formed by the intersection of one portion of a cone with another.

Cono-conic Groin is one which is formed by the intersection of one conic vault piercing another of greater altitude.

Cylindric Groin; that which is formed by the intersection of one portion of a cylinder with another.

Cylindroidic Groin; that which is formed by the intersection of one portion of a cylinder with another.

Cylindro-cylindric Groin is that which is formed by the intersection of two unequal cylindric vaults.

Equi-angular Groin is that in which the several axes of the simple vaults form equal angles around the same point, in the same horizontal plane.

Multangular Groin is that which is formed by three or more simple vaults piercing each other.

Rectangular Groin is that which has the axis of the simple vault in two vertical planes, at right angles to each other.

Spheric Groin is that which is formed by the intersection of one portion of a sphere with another.

Cylindro-spheric Groin; that which is formed by the intersection of a cylindric vault with a spheric vault; the spheric portion being of less height than the cylindric.

Sphero-cylindric Groin is that which is formed by the intersection of a cylindric vault with a spheric vault, the spheric portion being greater in height than the cylindric.

Groined ceiling; a cradling constructed of ribs, lathed and plastered.

Groins and Arches, in carpentry.

Groins of Bricks, construction in masonry; a small recess made with a plane.

Grotesque; the light, gay, and beautiful, style of ornament, practised by the ancient Romans in the decoration of their palaces, baths, villas, &c. It is supposed to have originated from the hieroglyphics of Egypt, where the human body may be seen fantastically attached to foliage, vases, and other figures.

H.

HALF-SPACE or resting place, in stairs, &c.

Hall; a word commonly denoting a mansion or large public building, as well as the large room at the entrance.

Hammer-Beam; a transverse beam at the foot of the rafter, in the usual place of a tie.

Hanging of doors and shutters. See *Hingeing*.

Heart-bond; in masonry, the lapping of one stone over two others, together making the breadth of a wall.

Helix; little scrolls in the Corinthian capital, also called *Urillæ*.

Hem; the projecting and spiral parts of the Ionic capital.

Hollow-wall; a wall built in two thicknesses, leaving a cavity between, which may be either for saving materials, or for preserving a uniform temperature in apartments.

Housing; the space excavated out of one body for the insertion of some part of the extremity of another, in order to unite or fasten the same together.

Hoveling; carrying up the sides of a chimney, so that when the wind rushes over the mouth, the smoke may escape below the current or against any one side of it.

I.

IMPOST; the footing of an arch, &c.

Intaglios; the carved work of an order or any part of an edifice, on which heads or other ornaments may be sculptured.

Intercolumn; the open area or space between two columns.

Inter-dentils; the space between dentils.

Inter-fenestration; the space between windows.

Inter-joist; the space between joists.

Inter-pilaster; the space between pilasters.

Inter-quarter; the space between two quarters.

Intersole or Mezzanine.

Intrados, of a vault, the concavity or interior surface. See *Extrados*.

Involution or Raising of Powers.

Isodomum. See *Wall*.

J.

JAMBS, the vertical sides of an aperture, as of doors, windows, &c.

Jamb-lining; the lining of a jamb.

Jamb-post; a post fixed on the side of a door, &c. and to which the jamb-lining is attached

Jamb-stones; in walls, those used in building the sides of an aperture, and of which every alternate stone should have the whole thickness of the wall.

Jettee or Jetty, in masonry.

Joggle; the joint of two substances, as of wood, &c. so formed as to prevent their sliding past each other.

Joggle-piece, in carpentry.

K.

KEEP; in a castle, the middle or principal tower.

Kerf, in carpentry.

Keyed-dado; dado, secured from warping by bars grooved into the back.

Keyes; in naked flooring, are pieces of timber framed in, between every two joists, by mortise and tenon. If driven fast between each pair, with the ends butting against the grain of the joists, they are denominated *strutting pieces.*

Keyes; in joinery, pieces of wood let transversely into the back of a board, especially when made of several breadths of timber, either by dove-tailing or grooving.

Knotting; in painting, the process for preventing knots from appearing in the finish.

L.

LABEL; an ornament placed over a window or other aperture, generally in a castellated building, and consisting of a horizontal portion over the head, with a part at each end returning downwards at a right angle: the latter may be terminated by a bead, but it more frequently returns again at a right angle outwards or horizontally.

Labyrinth; an intricate building, so contrived by its meandering form, as to render it difficult for those who have entered, to find the way out again. Hence a *Labyrinth-fret,* a fret with many turnings, which was a favourite ornament of the ancients. See *Fret.*

Lacunariæ, or Lacunars; panels or coffers formed on the ceilings of apartments, and sometimes on the soffits of coronæ in the Ionic, Corinthian, and Composite, orders.

Lancet-arch; the same as *pointed-arch.*

Landing of Stairs. See *Stairs.*

Lantern; a turret raised above the roof, with windows round the sides, constructed for lighting an apartment beneath.

Larmier, or Larmer. See *Corona.*

Lath-bricks; a sort of bricks, much longer than the ordinary sort, and used for drying malt upon.

Ledgers; in scaffolding for brick buildings, the horizontal pieces of timber parallel to the wall, and fastened to the *standards* by cords, for supporting the *put-logs.* On the last are laid the boards for working upon.

Lever-boards; a set of boards, parallel to each other, so connected together that they may be turned to any angle, for the admission of more or less air or light; or so as to lap upon each other and exclude both.

Lining; the covering of the interior surface of a hollow body, and used in opposition to *casing* the exterior surface.

Lining out; drawing lines on a piece of timber, &c. so as to cut it into boards, planks, or other figures.

Lintels, in carpentry, and in masonry; pieces of wood or stone over apertures in walls.

Listing; in carpentry or joinery, the act of cutting away the sap-wood from one or both edges of a board.

Lobby; a small hall or waiting room, or the entrance into a principal apartment.

Luffer-boarding; a series of boards placed in an aperture, very frequently in lanterns, so as to admit air into the interior, and to exclude rain.

Lunette; an aperture in a cyldrinic, cylindroidic, or spherical, ceiling; the head of the aperture being also cylindric or cylindroidic.

Luthern; a kind of window, over the cornice, in the roof of a building, formed perpendicularly over the naked of the wall, for the purpose of illuminating the upper story. They are denominated according to their forms, as square, semi-circular, bull's eyes, &c.

M.

Mansion; a large dwelling house or habitation: the chief house of a manor, &c.

Mantles of fire-places; the embellishments or furniture of a fire-place.

Mantle-tree; the lower part of the breast of a chimney, now by law, in disuse; an iron bar, or brick, or stone, being substituted.

Marble; a species of lime-stone, too well known to require description. It is found in almost every part of the world, more especially Italy, but there are many fine varieties in Great Britian and Ireland.

Mechanical Powers; such implements or machines as are used for raising greater weights, or overcoming greater resistances, than could be effected by the natural strength without them. The simple machines, called *Mechanical powers,* are six in number; viz., the lever, the wheel and axle, the pulley, the inclined plane, the wedge, and the screw: and of these all the most compound engines consist.

The general principle is, that the power or advantage gained by any of these machines, be it ever so simple or ever so compound, is as great as the space moved through by the working power is greater than the space through which the weight or resistance moves during the time of working. Thus, if that part of the machine to which the working power is applied moves through 10, 20, or 1000, times as much space as the weight moves through in the same time, a person who has just strength enough to work the machine will raise 10, 20, or 1000, times as much by it as he could do by his natural strength without it: but then *the time lost will be always as great as the power gained*: for it will require 10, 20, or 1000, times as much time for the power to move through that number of feet or inches as it would do to move through one foot, or one inch, &c.

Medallion; a circular tablet, ornamented with embossed or carved figures, bustos, &c.

Member; any part of an edifice or of a moulding.

Meros; the middle part of a trigliph. See *Trigliph.*

Metope ; in the Doric frieze, the square piece or interval between the trigliphs, or between one trigliph and another. The metopes are sometimes left naked, but are more commonly adorned with sculpture. When there is less space than the common metope, which is square, as at the corner of the frieze, it is called a *semi* or *demi-metope.*

Mezzo-relievo or Demi-relievo ; sculpture in half relief. See *Alto-relievo.*

Middle Post ; in a roof, the same as *King Post.*

Minnaret ; a Turkish steeple with a balcony.

Mitreing angles, joining an angle by way of a mitre-box.

Monopteron, or Monoptral, Temple ; an edifice consisting of a circular colonnade, supporting a dome, without any inclosing wall.

Monotrigliph ; having only one trigliph between two adjoining columns : the general practice in the Grecian Doric.

Moresque, or Moresk. See *Arabesque.*

Mosaic, or Mosaic Work ; an assemblage or combination of small pieces of marble, glass, stones, &c., of various colours and forms, cemented on a ground so as to imitate paintings. Mosaic work of marble, which is, from its nature, very expensive, may be frequently found in the pavements of temples, palaces, &c.

Museum ; originally, a palace at Alexandria, which occupied a considerable part of the city ; it was thus named from its being dedicated to the *Muses,* and appropriated to the cultivation of the sciences and of general knowledge.

N.

Naked of a wall or column ; the plain surface, in distinction from the ornaments. Thus the *Naked of a wall* is the flat plain surface that receives the mouldings ; and the naked of a column or pilaster is its base surface.

Nave ; the body of a church, reaching from the choir or chancel to the principal door.

Nebule ; a zigzag ornament, but without angles, frequently found in the remains of Saxon architecture.

Neck of a capital ; the space between the channelures and the annulets of the Grecian Doric capital. In the Roman Doric, the space between the astragal and annulet.

Nerves ; the mouldings of the groined ribs of Gothic vaults.

Newel ; a post at the starting or landing of a stair.

Niche ; from an Italian word, signifying a *shell* ; a hollow formed in a wall, for receiving a statue, &c. An *Angular Niche* is one formed in the corner of a building ; a *Ground Niche,* one having its rise from the ground, without a base or dado.

Niches ; in carpentry, and masonry.

Nogs ; a provincial term, signifying what are otherwise called *Wood-bricks.*

O.

Obelisk ; a quadrangular pyramid, high and slender, raised as a monument or ornament, and commonly charged with inscriptions and ornaments.

Odeum ; among the ancients, a place for the rehearsal of music and other particular purposes.

Ogee ; a moulding of two members, one concave, the other convex. It is otherwise called a *cymatium.*

Opened-newelled stairs ; a stair with newels at the starting and angles of the well-hole.

Oriel-window ; a projecting angular window, commonly of a triagonal or pentagonal form, and divided by mullions and transoms into different bays and compartments.

Orthogonal ; the same as *Rectangular.*

Orthography ; an elevation. showing all the parts of a building in true proportion.

Ova ; an ornament in form of an egg. *Oviculum* is its diminutive.

Out of winding ; perfectly smooth and even, or forming a true plane.

Out to out ; to the extremities or utmost bounds ; as in taking dimensions.

P.

Pagoda, or Pagod ; an Indian temple, common in Hindoostan and the countries to the east. These structures, dedicated to idolatry, are mostly of stone, square, not very lofty, without windows, and crowned with a cupola.

Palace ; a name generally given to the dwellings of kings, princes, bishops, &c.

Pale ; a pointed stake, and piece of board, used in making enclosures. Hence a *Paling Fence* is that sort of fence which is constructed with pales. See *Post and Paling.*

Paling for trees ; a sort of fencing for separate trees, formed by three small posts, connected with cross bars.

Palisade ; pales or stakes set up for an enclosure.

Pallier. or Paillier ; a French term, signifying a landing-place in a stair-case, which, being broader than the rest of the stairs, serves as a resting-place.

Pallification, or Piling ; the act of piling ground work, or strengthening it with piles.

Pantheon ; a temple of a circular form, originally pagan.

Parapet ; a dwarf wall, generally raised to prevent accidents.

Parget ; the several kinds of gypsum or plaster stone of which *Plaster of Paris* is composed.

Paternosters ; a sort of ornament in form of beads, round or oval, on astragals, &c.

Pavilion ; a kind of turret or building, usually insulated and contained under a single roof ; sometimes square, and sometimes in the form of a dome : thus called from the resemblance of its roof to a tent.

Pedestal ; a square body of stone or other material, raised to sustain a column, statue, &c. It is, therefore, the base or lowest part of an order of columns. A *Square Pedestal* is that of which the height and width are equal : a *Double Pedestal,* that which supports two columns, and therefore is greater in width than height: a *Continued Pedestal* is that which supports a row of columns, without any break.

Pediment; an ornament, properly of a low triangular figure, crowning the front of a building, and serving often also as a decoration over doors, windows, and niches. Though the original and natural form of the pediment be triangular, it is sometimes formed as a segment of a circle, and sometimes broke to let in busts or figures. The pediment consists of its *tympanum* and *cornice*; the tympanum is the panel, which may be either plain or ornamented. The cornice crowns this tympanum.

Pendent Bridge; a wooden bridge supported by posts and pillars, and suspended only by butments at the ends.

Pendentive; the whole body of a vault, suspended out of the perpendicular of the walls, and bearing against the *arc-boutants*.

Pendentive Cradling; the timber-work, in arched or vaulted ceilings, for sustaining the lath and plaster. The term *Dishing-out* is sometimes used instead of *Cradling*.

Pendentive Bracketing. See *Pendentive Arch.*

Pentastyle; a work containing five rows of columns.

Periptere; a building encompassed with columns, which form a kind of aisle all round it. It is thus distinguished from a building which has columns only before it, by the Greeks called a *Prostyle*, and from one that has none at the sides, called an *Amphi-prostyle*. The space, or aisle, in a periptere, between the columns and the wall, was called the *Peridrome*.

Peristyle; among the ancients, the converse of Periptere, a continued row of columns *within* the buildings: among the moderns, a range of columns, either within or without the same.

Persians; statues of men, serving instead of columns to support entablatures. They differ from the *Caryatides*, inasmuch as the latter represent women only.

Piazza; a portico or covered walk, supported by arches.

Pier; a square pillar, without any regular base or capital.

Pilasters; a pilaster, in Roman architecture, has the same proportion in diameter and mouldings as the column. The Grecian pilaster is generally called *Antæ*, and differs in diameter, bases, and capital. A *Demi-pilaster* is one that supports an arch.

Pile-planks; planks of which the ends are sharpened, so as to enter into the bottom of a canal, &c.

Pillar; a column of an irregular make; not formed according to rules, but of arbitrary proportions; free or insulated in every part, and always deviating from the measures of regular columns. This is the distinction of the *pillar* from the *column*. A square pillar is commonly called a *pier*. A butting pillar is a butment or body of masonry, erected to prop, or to sustain, the thrust of a vault, arch, &c.

Pinnacle; the top or roof of a building, terminating in a point.

Planting; laying the first courses of stone in a foundation, with all possible accuracy.

Platband; any flat square moulding, of which the height much exceeds its projecture. Se *Fasciæ*. The *Platband of a door or window*, is used for the lintel, where that is made square or not much arched. *Platbands of flutings* are the lists or fillets between the flutings of columns.

Platform; a row of beams, supporting the timber-work of a roof, and lying at the top of the wall where the entablature ought to be raised: also a flat terrace on the top of a building.

Plinth; the square piece under the mouldings in the bases of columns. The *plinth* terminates the column with its base at the bottom, as the *abacus* does with its capital at the top: but the abacus, in the Tuscan order, being plain, square, and massy, has been called the plinth of that capital. The plinth of a statue, &c., is a base serving to support it and its pedestal.

Plugs; pieces of timber, driven perpendicularly into a wall, and having the projecting part sawed away, so as to be flush with the face.

Pointed-arch; an arch so pointed at the top as to resemble the point of a lance.

Pointed architecture; that style vulgarly called *Gothic*, more properly English.

Porch; the kind of vestibule at the entrance of temples, halls, churches, &c.

Portail; the face of a church, on the side in which the great door is formed; also the gate of a castle, palace, &c.

Portal; a little gate, where there are two of a different size: also a kind of arch, of joiner's work, before a door.

Portico; a covered walk, porch, or piazza, supported by columns.

Post and Paling; a close wooden fence, constructed of posts set into the ground and pales nailed to rails between them. The part of the post intended to be inserted in the ground should be charred, or superficially burnt, in order to prevent decay.

Post and Railing; an open wooden fence, consisting of posts and rails only.

Posticum; a postern gate or back-door.

Postcenium; in an ancient theatre, a back room or place for dressing in, &c.

Powderings; a species of device for filling up vacant spaces in carved works, &c.

Priming; in painting, the laying on of the first colour.

Principal Brace; a brace immediately under the chief rafters or parallel to them. See *Brace.*

Principal Rafters. See *Rafters.*

Priory; a religious house or institution, at the head of which is a prior or prioress.

Profile; the figure or draught of a building, &c.; also the general contour or outline.

Projecture; the outjetting, or prominence, which the mouldings and other ornaments have beyond the naked of the wall, &c.

Pronaos; an ancient name for a porch to a temple or other spacious building.

Proscenium; in a theatre, the stage or the front of it.

Prostyle; a range of columns in front of a temple.

Prothyrum; a porch or portal at the outer door.

Pudlaies; pieces of timber, for stages, &c.

Pug-piling; dove-tailed or pile-planking.

Purfled; ornamented in a manner resembling drapery, embroidery, or lace-work.

Putlogs or Putlocks; in scaffolding, the transverse pieces, at right angles to the wall.   See *Ledgers*.

Puzzolana; a substance composed of volcanic ashes, named from *Puzzuolo* in Italy, where it abounds, and celebrated as a principal ingredient in cements. When mixed with a small proportion of lime it quickly hardens, and this induration takes place even under water.   See *Cements*.

Pycnostyle; columns thick set.

Pyramid; a solid massive structure, which, from a square, triangular, or other base, rises diminishing to a vertex or point.

Q.

QUADRA; any square border or frame encompassing a basso relievo, panel, &c.

Quadrangle; a figure having four sides and four angles : a square is, therefore, a regular quadrangle, and a trapezium an irregular one.

Quarry a pane of glass, in a lozenge or diamond form.

Quink; a piece of ground taken out of any regular ground-plot or floor.   Thus, if the ground-plot were oblong or square, a corner-piece separated from it, to make a court, yard, &c. is called a *quink*.

Quirk; a recess member in mouldings.

Quirk-mouldings are the convex parts of Grecian mouldings, where they recede at the top, and form a re-entient angle with the soffit which covers the moulding.

Quoin, external or internal.   The name is particularly applied to the stones at the corners of brick buildings.   When these stand out beyond the brickwork, with edges chamfered, they are called *Rustic Quoins*.

R.

RABETTING, or Rebating; a recess made in door-jambs, &c.

Raiser; a board set on edge under the foreside of a step or stair.

Raising pieces; pieces that lie under the beams and over the posts or punchions.

Raising-plates or Top-plates; plates in brick walls to lay the beams on, or plates to fix the beams, principal rafters, &c., to.

Raking moulding; a moulding whose arrises are inclined to the horizon in any given angle.

Ramp; in hand-railing, a concavity on the upper side, formed over risers, or over a half or quarter space, by a sudden rise of the steps above.

Rampant arch; an arch, of which the abutments spring from an inclined plane.

Reglet, or Riglet; a flat narrow moulding, used chiefly in compartments and panels to separate the parts or members, and to form knots, frets, &c.

Regrating; in masonry, taking off the outer surface of an old hewn stone, so as to make it look new again.

Rejointing; in masonry, the filling up of the joints of stones in old buildings, when worn hollow by time and weather.

Relievo, Relief, or Embossment.   See *Alto-relievo*, &c.

Resault; a French word signifying projecting or receding from a line or general range.

Return-bead; a bead which appears on the edge and face of a piece of stuff in the same manner, forming a *double quirk*.

Revels, pronounced *Reveals*; the vertical retreating surface of an aperture, as the two vertical sides between the front of the wall and the windows or door-frame.

Rib; a curved or arch-formed timber.

Ribbing; the whole of the timber-work for sustaining a vaulted or coved ceiling.

Ridge-piece; a piece running from one king-post to the other, to receive the ends of the jack-rafters.

Rood-loft; in ancient cathedral and abbey churches, the gallery over the entrance into the choir.

Rose; an ornament in the form of a rose, found chiefly in cornices, friezes, &c.

Rotondo or Rotunda; a common name for any circular building.

Rubble-wall; a wall built of unhewn stone, whether with or without mortar.

Rudenture; the figure of a rope, or of a staff, whether plain or carved, with which a third part of the fluting of columns is frequently filled up.   It is sometimes called *cabling* ɪ hence the columns are said to be *cabled* or *rudented*.

Ruderated; in paving, &c., laid with pebbles or little stones.

Rustic building; one constructed in the simplest manner, and apparently more agreeably to the face of nature than the rules of art.   Rustic work and rustic quoins are commonly used in the basement part of a building.

Rusticating; incisions made in the stone work, either by a recess at right angles, or an angle of forty-five degrees to the surface; the former making a groove of three sides, the latter two.

Rustic-work; that exhibited on the face of stones, which, instead of being smooth, are hatched or picked (*frosted* or *vermiculated*,) with a point of a tool, &c.

S.

SAGGING; bending downwards in the middle, from a horizontal direction; as a long plank laid horizontally, and supported at each end only.

Sagitta; a name by some used for the key-piece o an arch.

Sally; a projection or sort of bird's-mouth to rafter, &c.

Saloon; a spacious, lofty, and elegant hall or apartment, vaulted at top, and generally having two ranges of windows. A state-room common in the palaces of Italy.

Sarcophagus; a tomb of stone, in general highly decorated, and used by the ancients to contain the dead bodies of distinguished personages.

Sash; a frame for holding the panes or squares of glass in windows: too well known to require description.

Scaffolding. See *Ledgers*.

Scribing; adjusting the edge of a board, so that it shall fit and correspond with a given surface. In joinery, the act of fitting one piece of wood upon another, so that the fibres of one may be perpendicular to those of the other. See *Mitring*.

Scroll. See *Volute*, or *Stavis*.

Sealing; fixing a piece of wood or iron in a wall, with mortar. lead, or other binding, for staples, hinges, &c.

Section of a building; a representation of it, as vertically divided into two parts, so as to exhibit the construction of the interior.

Sesspool, or Cesspool; a deep hole or well under the mouth of a drain, for the reception of sediment, &c., by which the drain might be choked.

Sewer; a common drain or conduct for conveying foul water, &c.

Shaft of a column, the part between the base and capital.

Sham-door; in joinery, a panel of frame-work that appears like a door, but does not open.

Shanks; the intersticial spaces between the channels of the triglyph, in the Doric frieze: sometimes called *Legs*.

Shoar; an oblique prop, acting as a brace upon the side of a building.

Shoar, dead. See *Dead-shoar*.

Shoe; the part at the bottom of a water trunk or pipe, for turning the course of the water.

Side-posts; in roofing, a sort of truss-posts, placed in pairs, each post being fixed at the same distance as the rest from the middle of the truss.

Single-hung; in window-sashes, when one only is moveable.

Single-measure: in doors, means square on both sides, in opposition to *double-measure*, which signifies moulded on both sides. If moulded on one side, and square on the other, it is expressed by *measure and half*.

Slit-deal; an inch deal cut into two leaves or boards.

Socle, or Zocle; a square piece, broader than it is high, placed under the bases of pedestals, &c., to support vases, and other ornaments. As there is a *Continued Pedestal*, so is there, also, a Continued Socle. See *Pedestal*.

Soffita, or Soffit; any timber ceiling, formed of cross-beams of flying cornices, the square compartments or pannels of which are enriched with sculpture or painting. *Soffit* also means the under side of an architrave, and that of the corona, or drip, &c.; also, the horizontal undersides of the heads of apertures, as of doors and windows.

Soffit, of stairs.

Sommering; the continuation of the joints of arches towards a centre or meeting point.

Span of an arch, or building; the extremities of the inner or outer sides, as the case may be.

Span-roof; a simple roof, consisting of two inclined sides.

Spherical and Spherodial Bracketing; brackets formed to support lath and plaster, so that the outer surface shall be spherical, or spheroidal.

Sphinx; a favourite ornament in Egyptian architecture, representing the monster, half woman and half beast, said to have been born of Typhon and Echidna.

Splayed; one side making an oblique angle with the other, as Splays or Splaying Jambs.

Springing-course; the horizontal course from which an arch begins to spring, or the rows of stones upon which the first arch-stones are laid.

Square in geometry, but, among workmen, it commonly means that one side or surface is perpendicular to another. In joinery, the work is said to be framed square, when the framing has all the angles of its styles, rails, and mountings, square, without mouldings.

Square of building, is 100 superficial feet measured on the surface of the ground.

Squaring hand-rails; the method of cutting a plank to the form of a rail for a stair-case, so that all the vertical sections may be rectangles.

Standards; the upright poles used in scaffolding. In joinery, the upright pieces of a plate-rack.

Staves; in joinery, the boards that are united laterally, in order to form a hollow cylinder, cone, &c. In stables, the cylinders or *rounds* forming the hay-rack.

Story-posts; upright timbers, chiefly in sheds and workshops, and so disposed, with a beam over them, as to support the superincumbent part of the exterior wall.

Striæ; the fillets or rays separating the furrows or grooves of fluted columns.

Striges; the channels of a fluted column.

String-board; in stairing, a board placed next to the well-hole, and terminating the ends of the steps.

Summer-tree; a beam full of mortises to receive the ends of joists, and to which the girders are framed.

Sunk-shelves; in pantries, &c., shelves having a groove to prevent the plates, set up on edge, from sliding off.

Surbases, a horizontal finish, around rooms, immediately under the windows.

Swallow-tail; a mode of uniting two pieces of timber so strongly that they cannot fall asunder. See *Dovetail*.

Systyle, an intercolumniation of two diameters.

T.

TABLE, projecting or raised; a flat surface, sometimes ornamented, which projects from the surface of a wall.

Table, raking; one not perpendicular to the horizon.

Table rusticated. See *Rusticated*.

Table of Glass; the circular plate, before it is cut or divided. Twenty-four such make a *case*.

Tabled; cut into, or formed like, tables.

Tænia, or Tenia; a small square fillet, at the top of the architrave, in the Doric capital.

Tail in; to fasten any thing into a wall at one end, as steps, &c. In joinery, commonly called *housing*.

Tail-trimmer; a trimmer next to the wall, into which the ends of joists are fastened.

Tailing; the part of a projecting brick, &c. inserted in a wall.

Talus; the slope or inclination of a wall, among workmen called *Battering*. If the wall inclines beyond the perpendicular of its base, it is called *hanging*.

Tambour; from a word signifying a drum, and meaning the naked of a Corinthian or Composite capital: also the wall of a circular temple, surrounded with columns. The same word signifies a place inclosed with folding doors, to break the current of air from without, at the entrances of churches, &c.

Tarras, or Terras; a strong mortar or plaster, used in aquatic works.

Tassels; the pieces of timber that lie under the mantletree; common in the country. See *Torsel*.

Teaze-tenon; a tenon upon the top of a post for supporting two level pieces of timber at right angles to each other.

Telamones; a Roman term for the figures of men supporting a cornice, &c. The same as the Atlantidæ and Persians of the Greeks. See *Persians*.

Terminus (plural *Terminii*); a trunk or pedestal, sculptured at top into the figure of the head of a man, woman, or satyr, whose body seems to be inclosed in the trunk, as in a sheath. The latter is called the *Vagina*.

Terrace; an elevated area for walking upon, and sometimes meaning a balcony.

Terrace-roofs; roofs flat on the top.

Tesselated pavement; a curious pavement of Mosaic work, composed of small square stones, bricks, &c. called *tesselæ*.

Tessera; a cube or dye; also a modern composition for covering flat roofs.

Testudinal Ceilings; those formed like the back of a tortoise.

Tetrastyche; a gallery with four rows of pillars.

Tie-beam, a beam running from one wall to the other, on which a pair of principal rafters may be placed.

Tiles; the artificial stones used in covering buildings. *Plane-tiles* and *Crown-tiles* are of a rectangular form, with a flat surface, of which the dimensions are about 10½ inches long, 6 broad, and five-eights thick: weight from 2lbs. to 2½lbs.

Ridge-tiles, or *Roof-tiles*, are those of a cylindric form, and used for covering the ridges of houses. Of these the dimensions are 12 inches long, 10 broad,

and five-eighths thick: weight, about 4½lbs. Those covering the angle formed by two sloping sides are called hip-tiles.

Gutter-tiles, formed according to the purpose for which they are intended, are of the same weight as the ridge-tiles.

Pan-tiles are those having each surface, both concave and convex; they are hung on the lath, by means of a ledge formed on the upper end. The usual size is 14½ inches long and 10 broad. Weight from 5 to 5¼lbs.

Tile-creasing; two rows of tiles fixed horizontally under the coping of a wall, for discharging rain-water.

Tondino; a round moulding resembling a ring. See *Torus*.

Tongue; a projecting part, on the edge of a board, to be inserted in a groove ploughed in the edge of another.

Top-beams; the collar beam of a truss; the same as formerly called *wind-beam* or *strut-beam*, and now *collar-beam*.

Top-rail; the upper rail of a piece of framing or wainscotting.

Torsel; a piece of wood laid into a wall for the end of a timber or beam to rest on.

Torus, a semi-bead.

Trabs; an ancient name for wall-plates or rising-plates, for supporting the rafters.

Transept; the cross-ailes of a church of a cruciform structure.

Transom; a cross-beam: the horizontal piece framed across a double-lighted window.

Transom windows; a window or light, over a door, &c. Improperly called fan-lights.

Tread of a step; the horizontal part of it.

Trellis-work; reticulated or net-like framing, made of thin bars of wood.

Trigliph or Triglyph, an ornament in the frieze of a Doric entablature.

Trimmed; cut into shape, or fitted in between parts previously executed, as in partition-walls, &c.

Tripod; a three-legged seat, from which the priests of antiquity delivered their oracles, and frequently represented in architectural ornaments.

Trophy; an ornament representing the trunk of a tree, supporting military weapons, colours, &c.

Truncated; cut short or divided parallel to the base. The frustrum of a cone, pyramid, &c., is therefore *truncated*.

Truss-partition; one with a truss, generally consisting of a quadrangular frame, two braces, and two queen-posts, with a straining piece between the queen-posts, opposite the top of the braces.

Trussels, small stands upon which carpenters saw.

Trussing-pieces; such timbers in a roof as are in a state of compression.

Turning-piece; a board with a circular edge, for turning a thin brick arch upon.

Tuscan Order, an order in architecture, invented in Tuscany.

Tympanum, or Tympan. See *Pediment*. Tympan also signifies the panel of a door and the dye of a pedestal.

V.

VALLEY ; the internal angle of two inclined sides of a roof.

Valley-rafter, a rafter at the internal angle of a roof. The valley-board is a board fixed upon this rafter, for the leaden gutter to lie on.

Vault; an interior concavity extending over two parallel opposite walls. The *axis* of a vault is the same as the axis of a geometrical solid. See *Arch* and *Groin*. The *Reins* of a vault are the sides or walls which sustain the arch.

Vellar cupola ; a cupola or dome, terminated by four or more walls.

Venetian Door ; a door lighted on each side.

Venetian Window ; a window having three separate apertures.

Ventiduct ; a passage or place for wind or fresh air.

Vermiculated Rustics ; stones worked or tooled so as to appear as if eaten by worms.

Volute ; the scroll or principal ornament of the Ionic capital.

W.

WAINSCOTING ; in joinery, the lining of walls ; mostly pannelled.

Wall-plates. See *Raising and Top-plates*.

Water-table, the uppermost stone, and shield to a wall.

Weather-boarding ; feather-edged boards, lapped and nailed upon each other, so as to prevent rain or drift from passing through.

Weather-tiling ; the covering of a wall or upright with tiles.

Well-hole of stairs, the entire space occupied by a stair, as also the opening between front strings, either straight or circular.

Wood-bricks ; blocks of wood, shaped like bricks, and inserted in walls as holds for the joinery.

Wreathed columns ; such as are twisted in the form of a screw. *Now obsolete*.

Z.

ZOCLE. See *Socle*.

Zystos ; among the ancients, a portico or aisle of unusual length, commonly appropriated to gymnastic exercises.

Fig. 1.

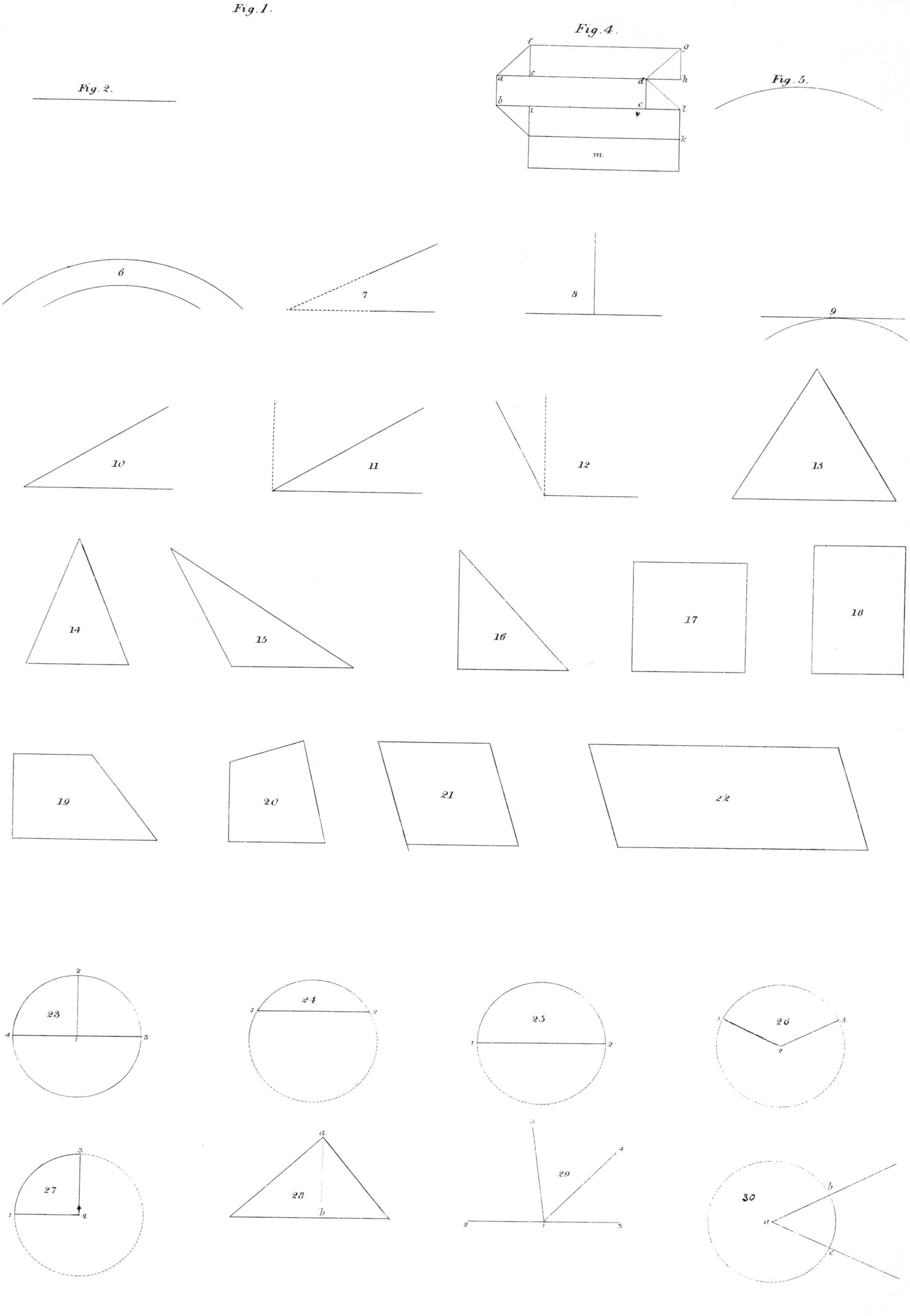

Fig. 2.

Fig. 4.

Fig. 5.

6

7

8

9

10

11

12

13

14

15

16

17

18

19

20

21

22

23

24

25

26

27

28

29

30

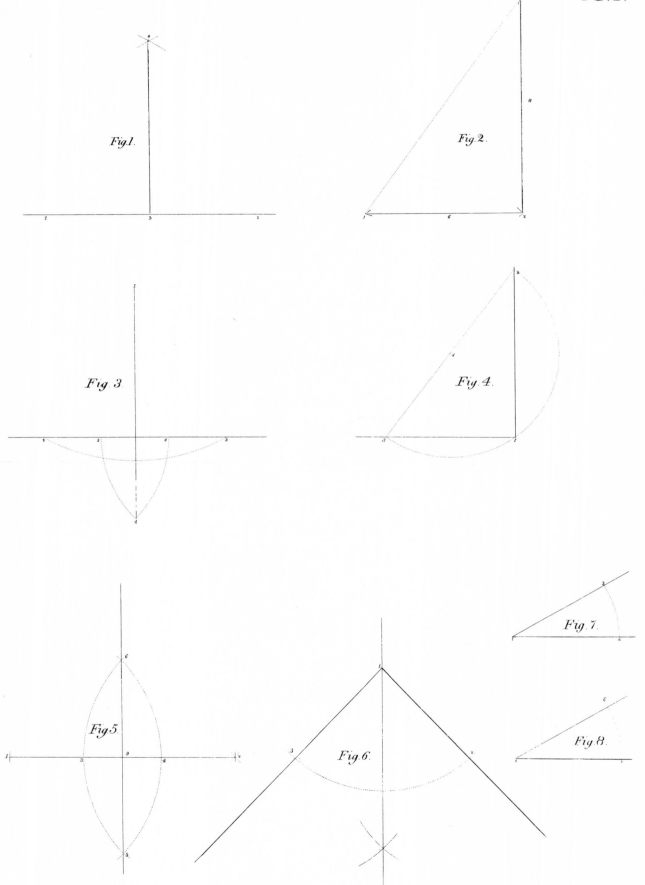

Fig.1.

Fig.2.

Fig.3.

Fig.4.

Fig.5.

Fig.6.

Fig.7.

Fig.8.

Pl. 3.

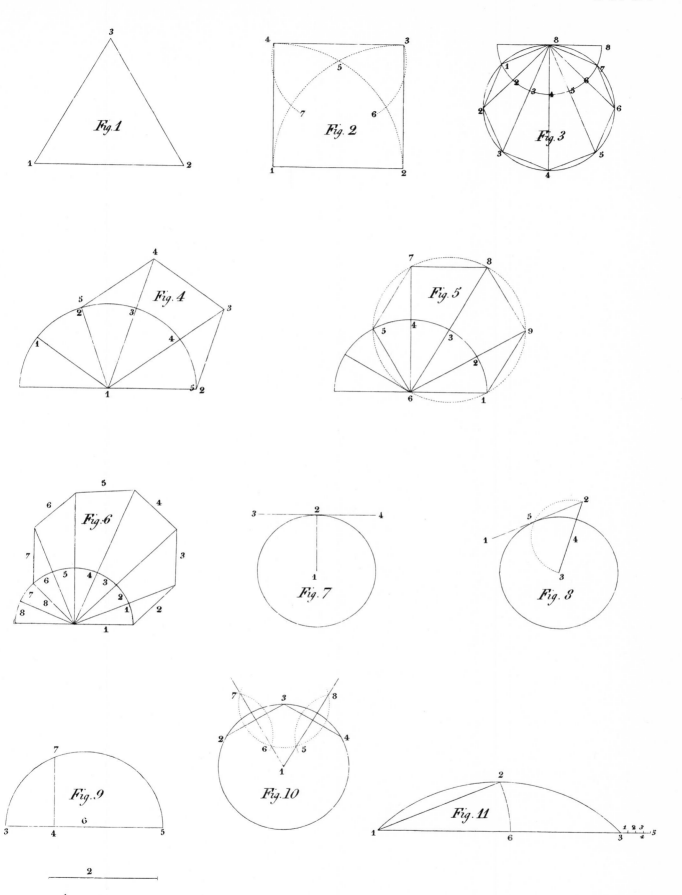

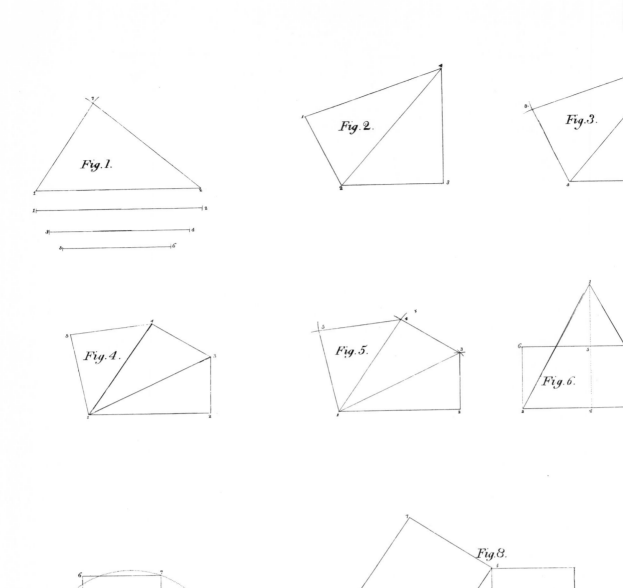

Fig.1.

Fig.2.

Fig.3.

Fig.4.

Fig.5.

Fig.6.

Fig.7.

Fig.8.

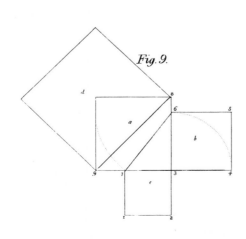

Fig.9.

Fig.1.

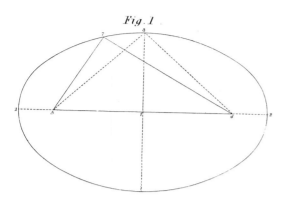

Fig.2.

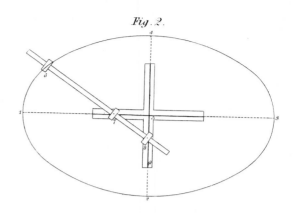

Fig.3.

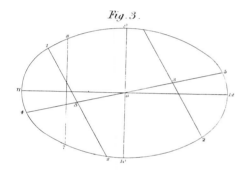

Fig.4.

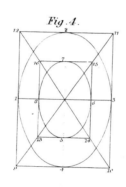

Fig.5.

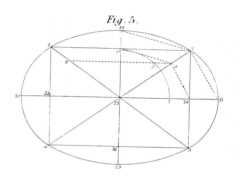

Fig.6.

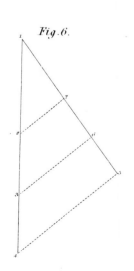

Fig.7.

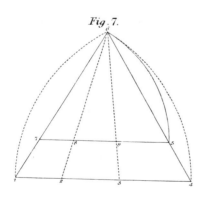

Fig.8.

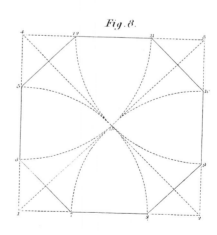

Fig.1.

Fig.2.

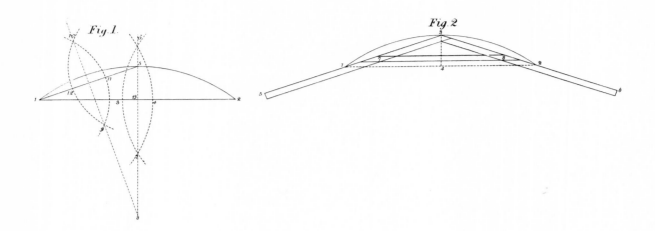

Fig.3.

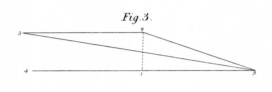

Fig.4.

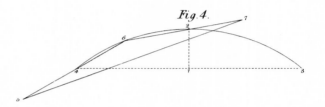

Fig.5.

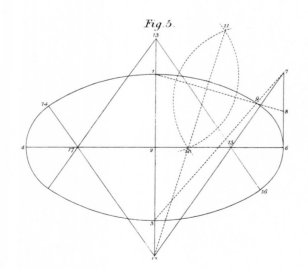

Fig.6.

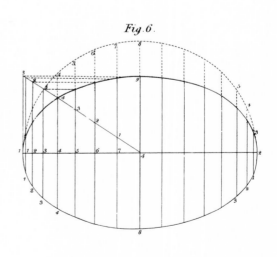

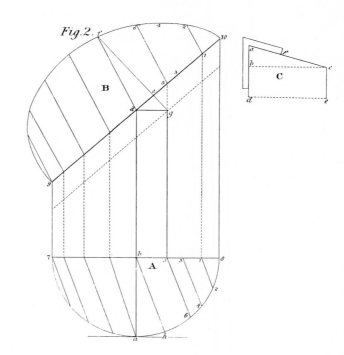

Fig.1.

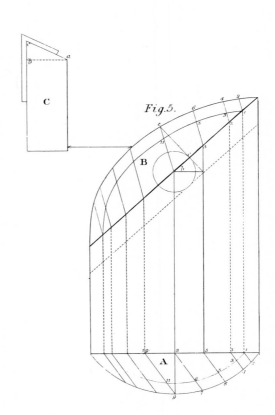

Fig.2.

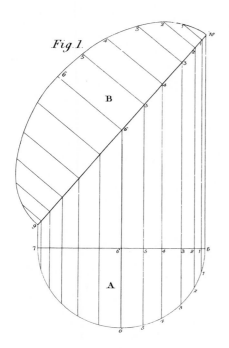

Fig.3.

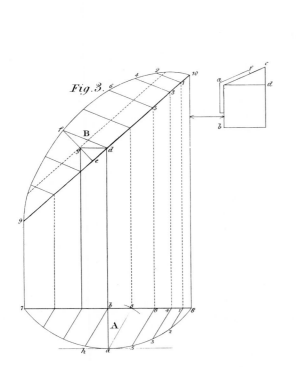

Fig.5.

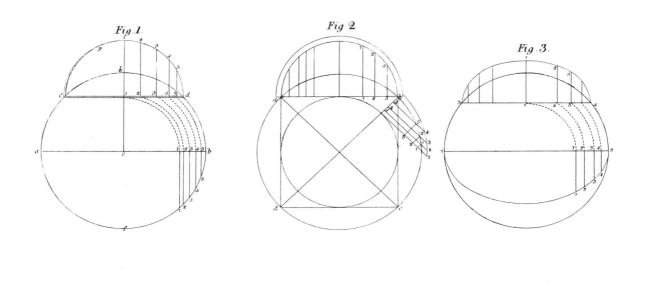

Fig.1. Fig 2. Fig 3.

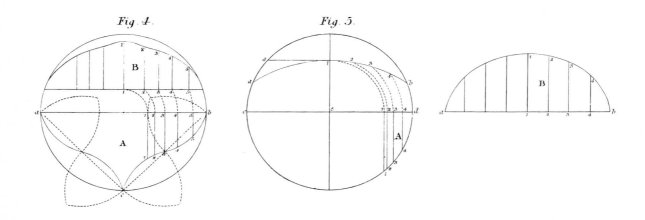

Fig.4. Fig.5.

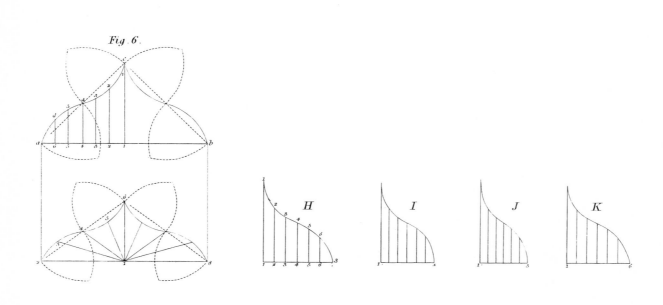

Fig.6.

H   I   J   K

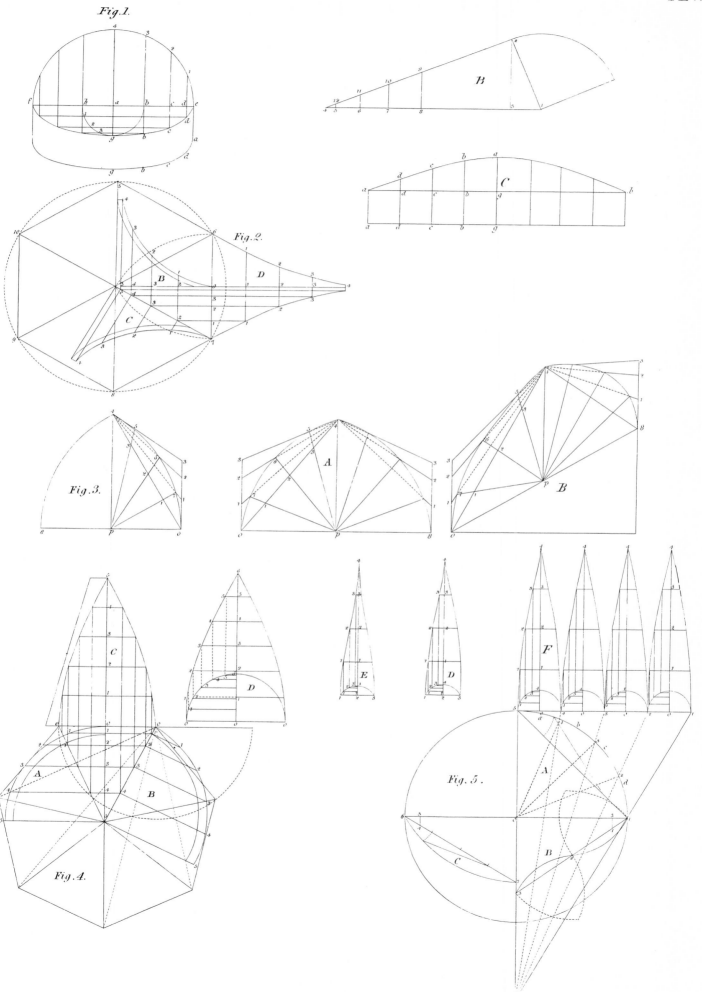

Fig.1.

Fig.2.

Fig.3.

Fig.4.

Fig.5.

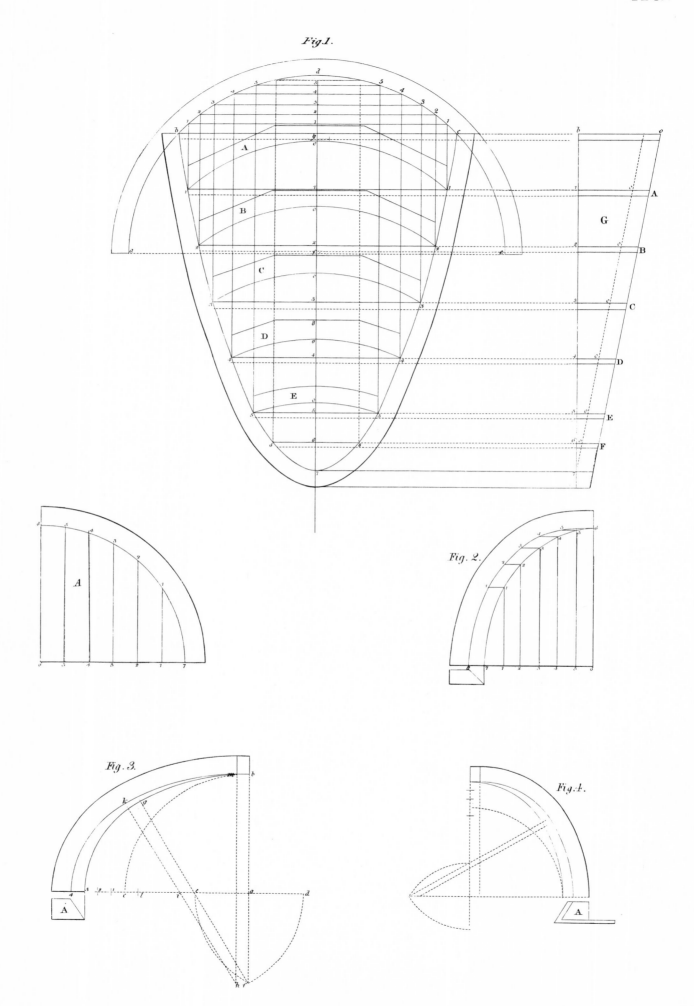

Fig.1.

Fig.2.

Fig.3.

Fig.4.

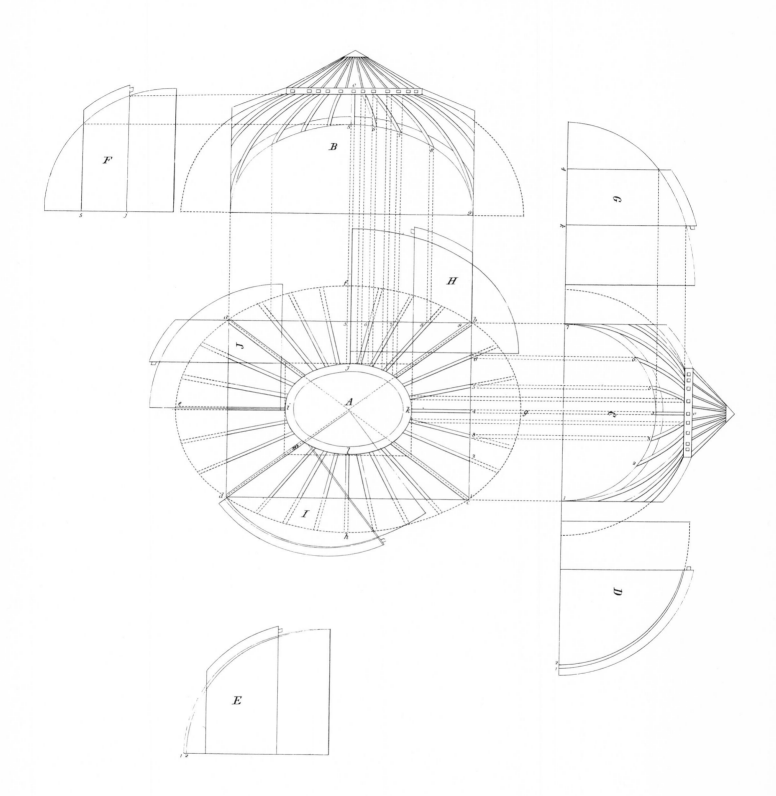

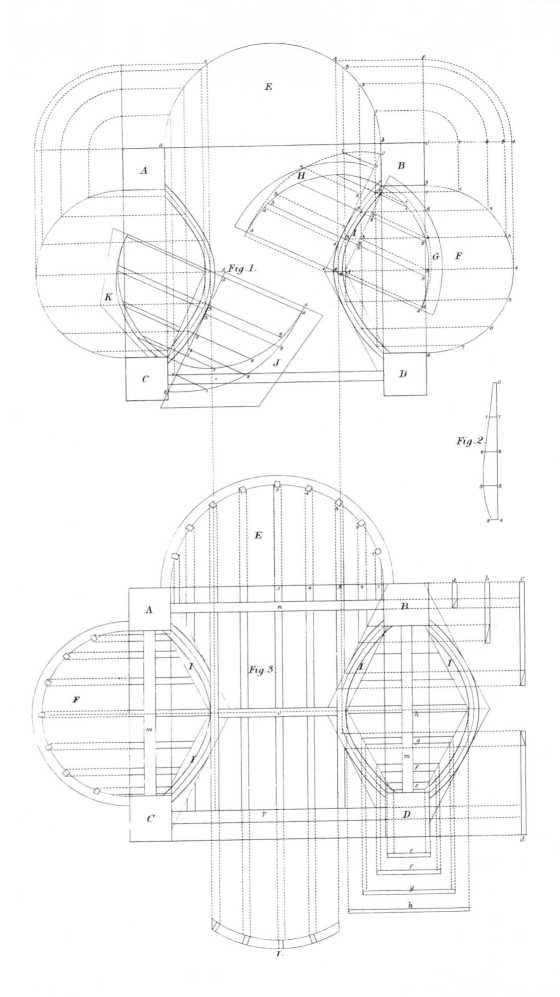

Fig.1.

Fig.2.

Fig.3.

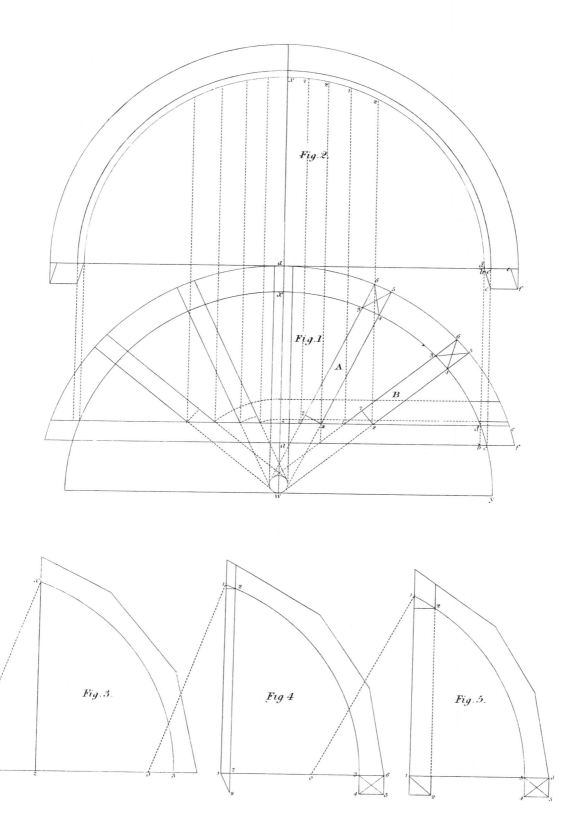

Fig.2.

Fig.1.

A

B

Fig.3.

Fig 4

Fig.5.

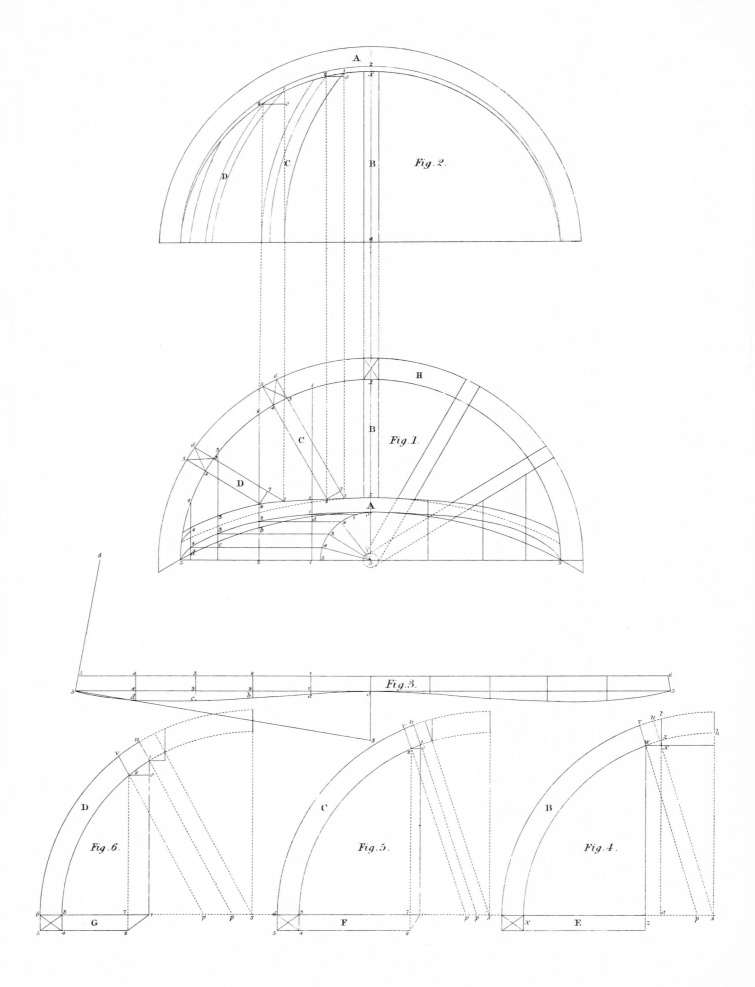

PL.14.

Fig.2.

Fig.1.

Fig.3.

Fig.6. Fig.5. Fig.4.

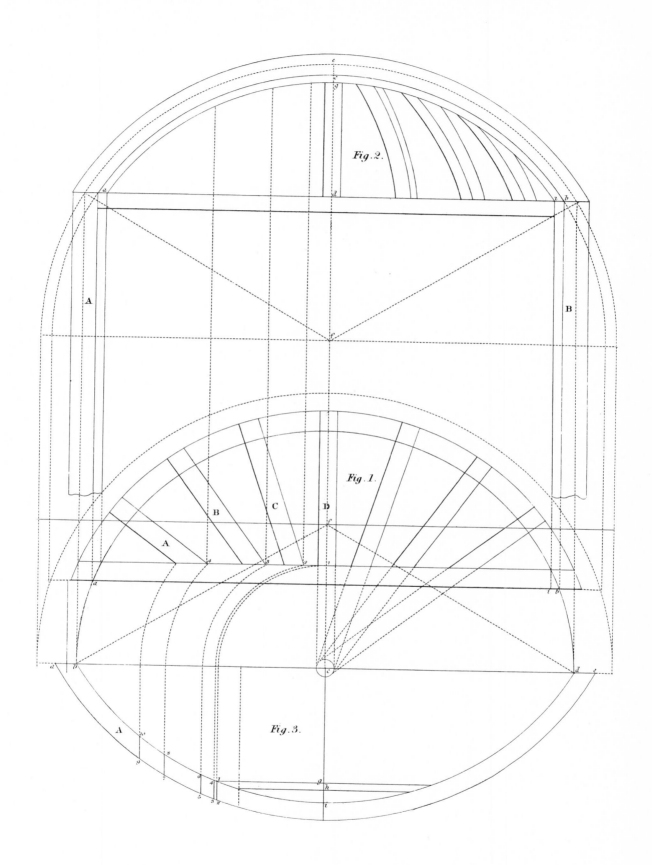

Fig.2.

A

B

Fig.1.

B   C   D

A

Fig.3.

A

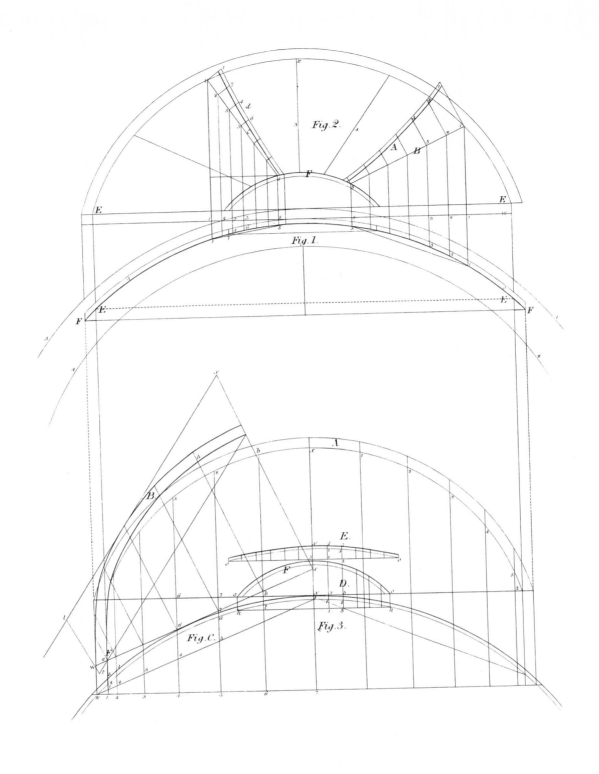

Fig.2.

Fig.1.

Fig.C.   Fig.3.

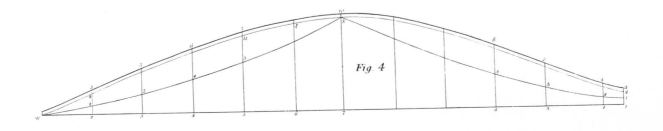

Fig. 4

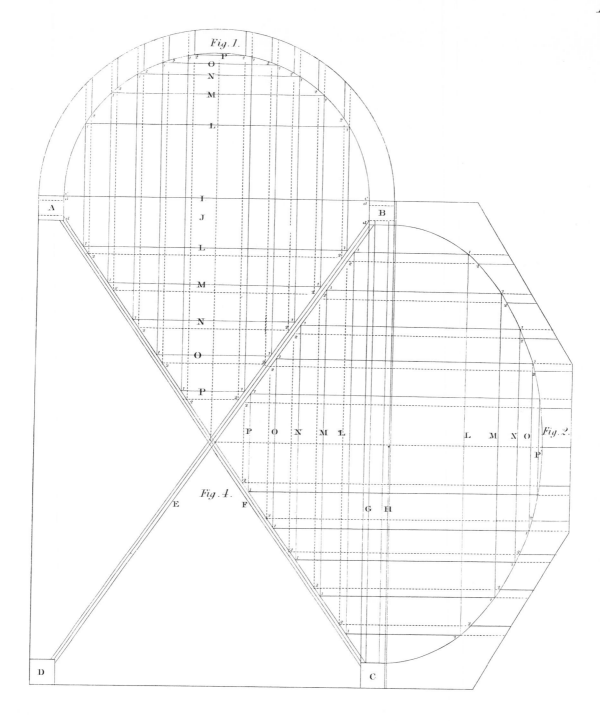

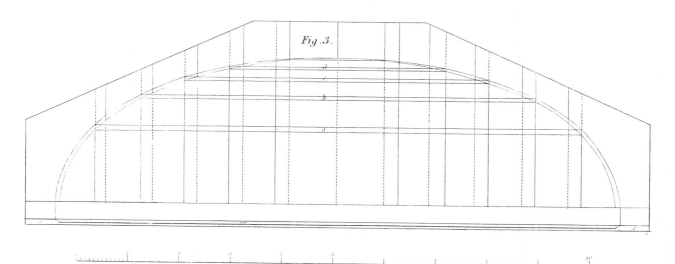

N.º 1. Fig. A.

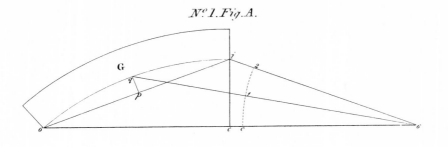

N.º 2. Fig. A.

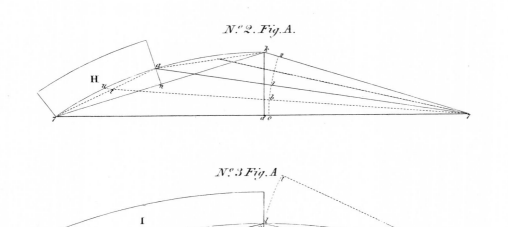

N.º 3 Fig. A.

Fig. K.

Fig. A.

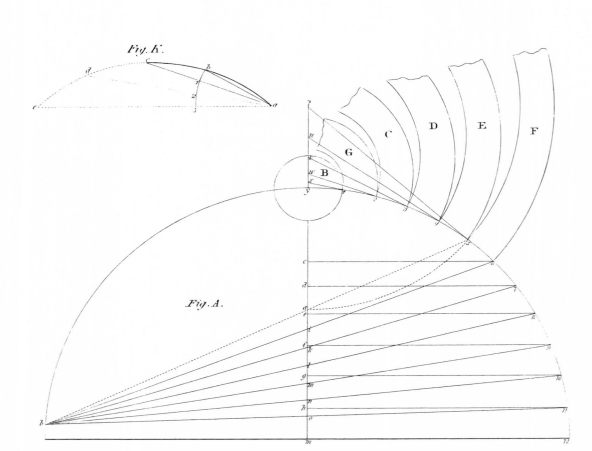

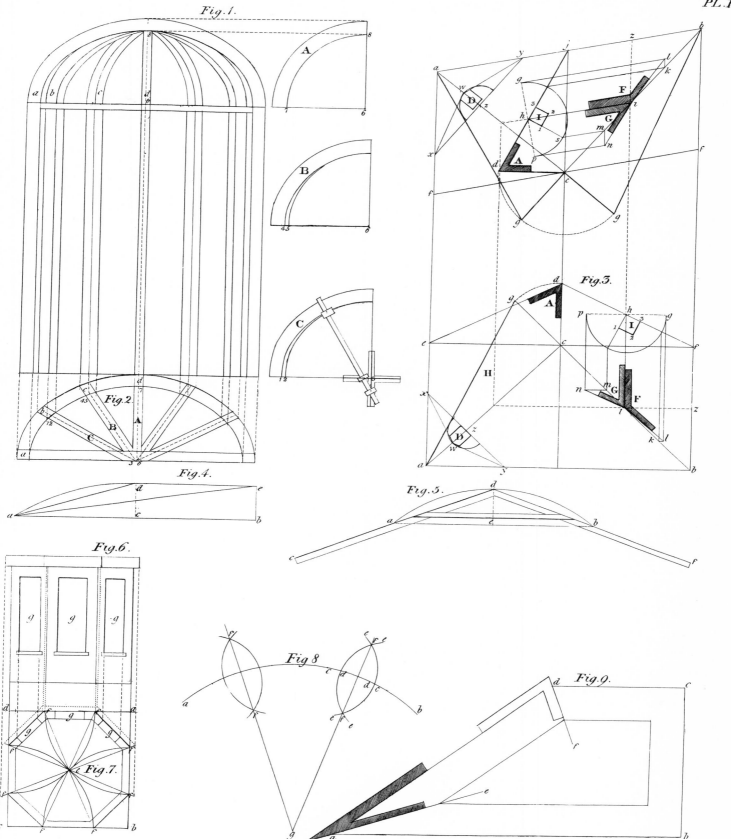

Fig. 1.

A

B

C

Fig. 2.

Fig. 3.

Fig. 4.

Fig. 5.

Fig. 6.

Fig. 7.

Fig 8

Fig. 9.

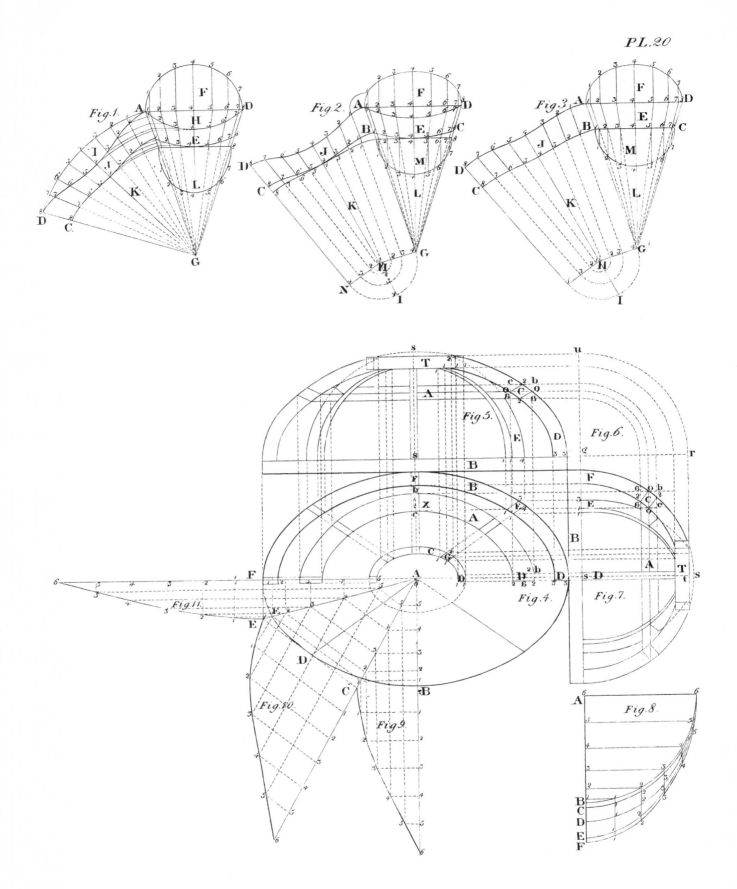

Fig.1.

Fig.2.

Fig.3.

Fig.5.

Fig.6.

Fig.4.

Fig.7.

Fig.11.

Fig.10.

Fig.9.

Fig.8.

PL. 21.

Fig. 1.

Fig. 2.

Fig. 3.

Fig. 4.

Fig. 5.

Fig. 6.

Fig. 7.

Fig. 8.

Given
Rib

Fig. 9.

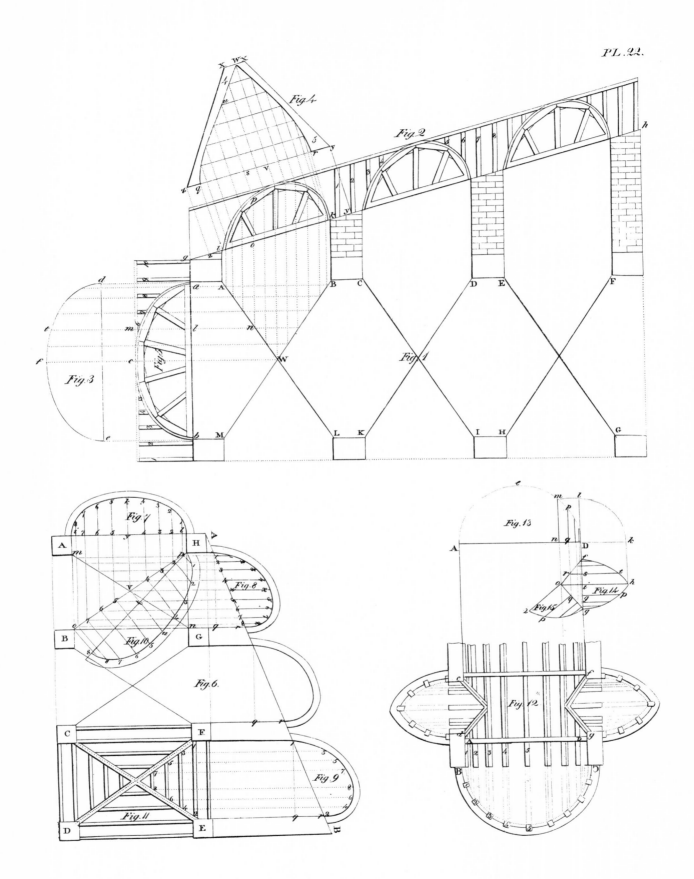

PL.22.

Methods for Obtaining Soffits in oblique & circular Walls.

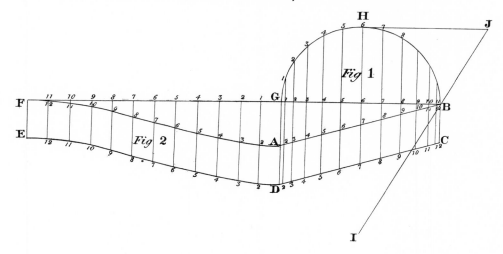

Fig 1

Fig 2

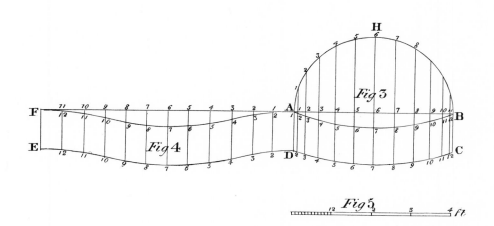

Fig 3

Fig 4

Fig 5

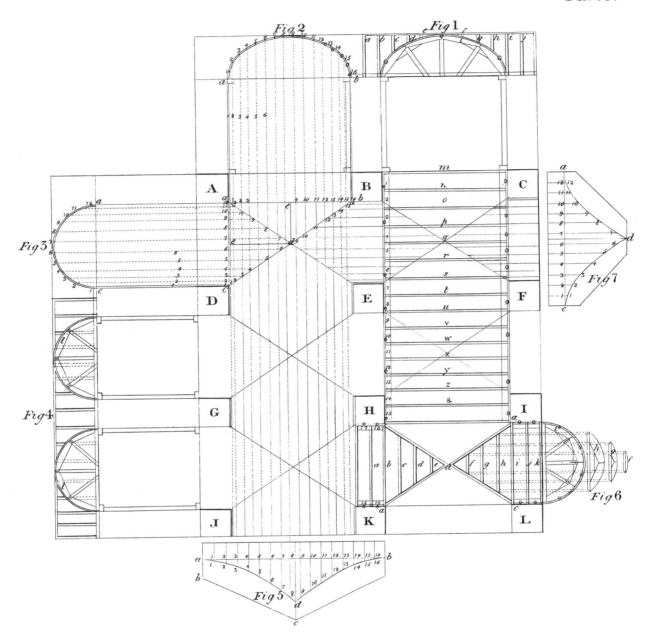

PL. 24.

Fig 2   Fig 1

Fig 3

Fig 4

Fig 7

Fig 6

Fig 5

10   20   30

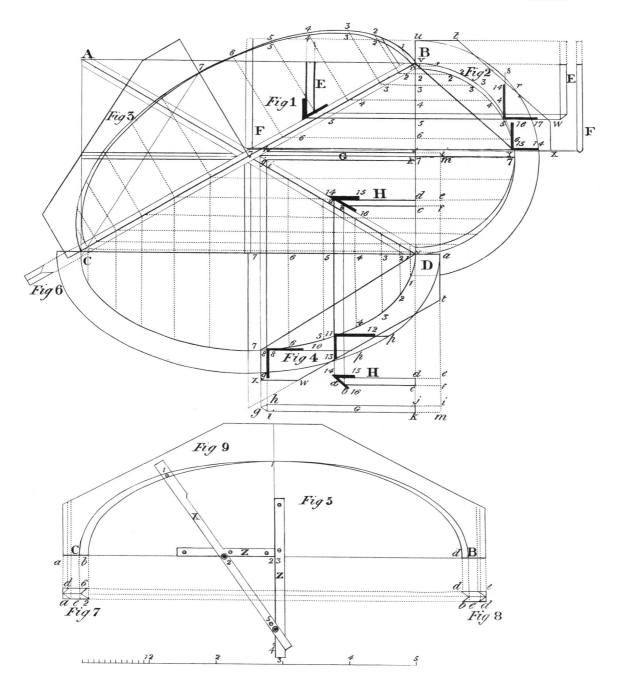

Fig 1
Fig 2
Fig 3
Fig 4
Fig 5
Fig 6
Fig 7
Fig 8
Fig 9

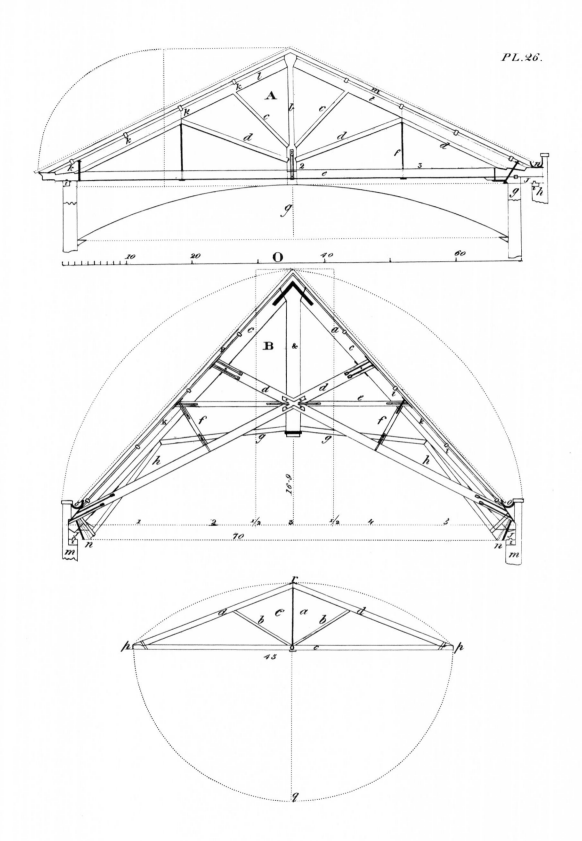

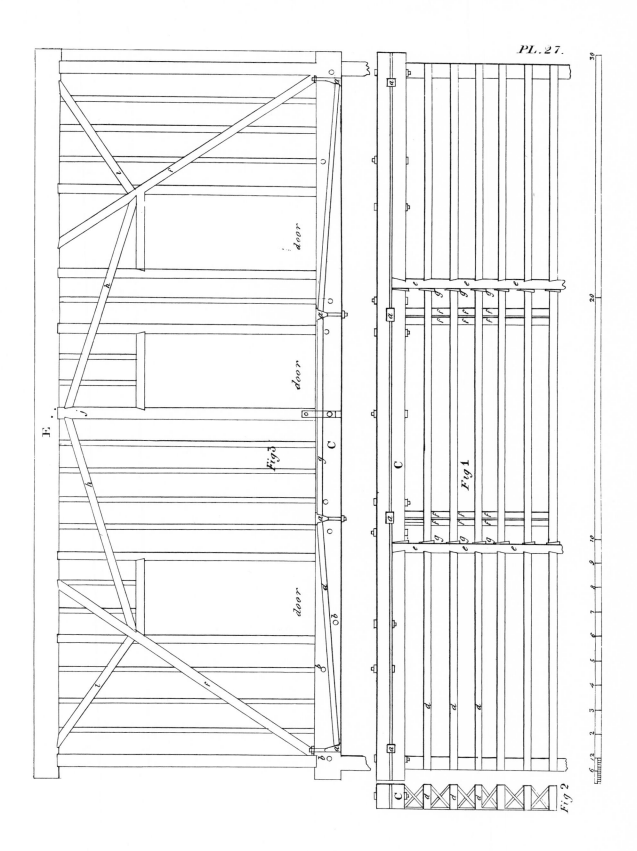

PL.27.

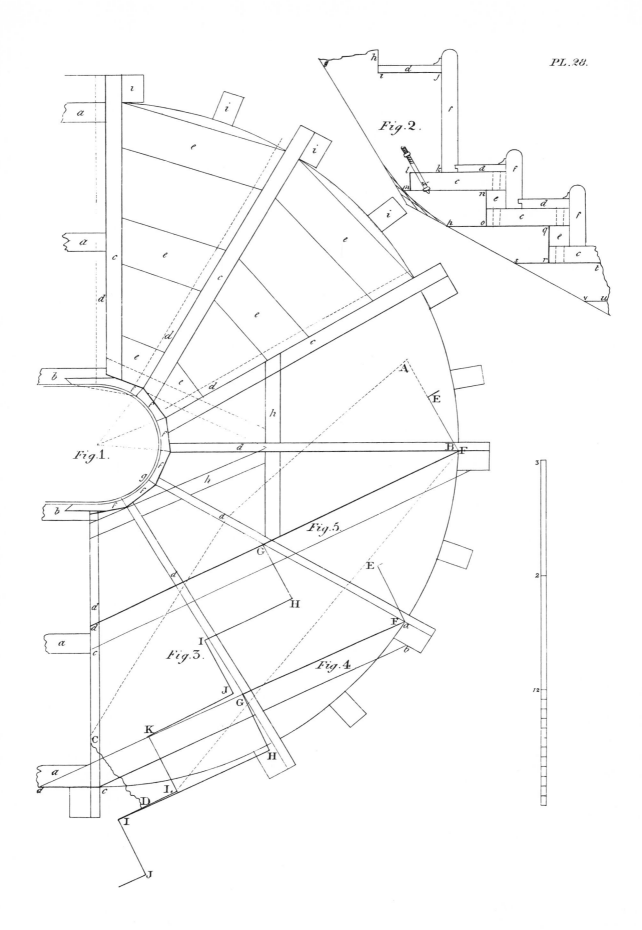

Fig. 2.

Fig. 1.

Fig. 5.

Fig. 3.

Fig. 4.

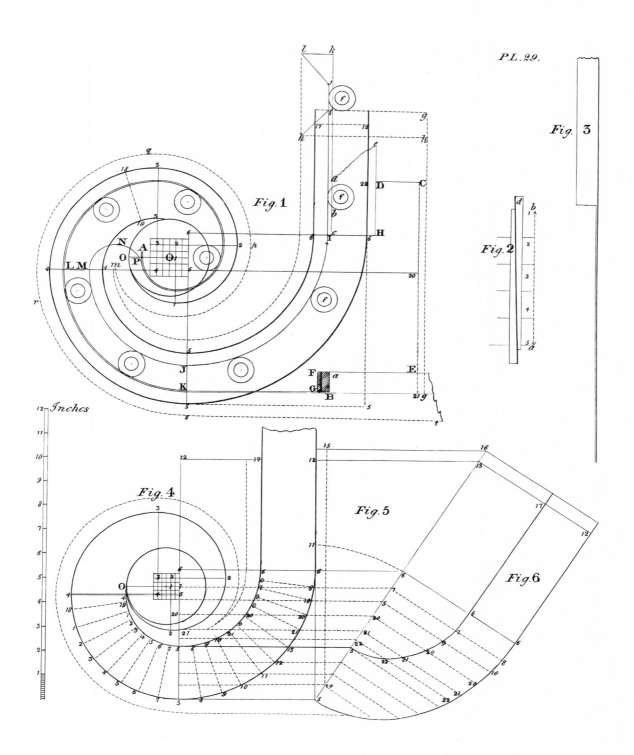

PL.29.

Fig. 1

Fig. 2

Fig. 3

Fig. 4

Fig. 5

Fig. 6

Inches

Fig 1

Fig 2

Fig 3

Fig 4

Fig 5

Fig 6

Inches

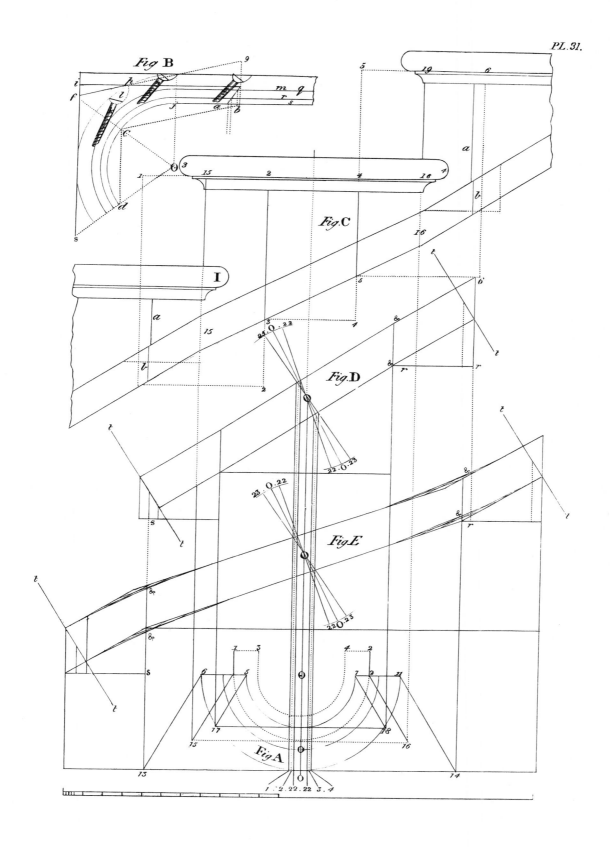

Fig B

*Fig.*C

I

*Fig.*D

*Fig*E

*Fig*A

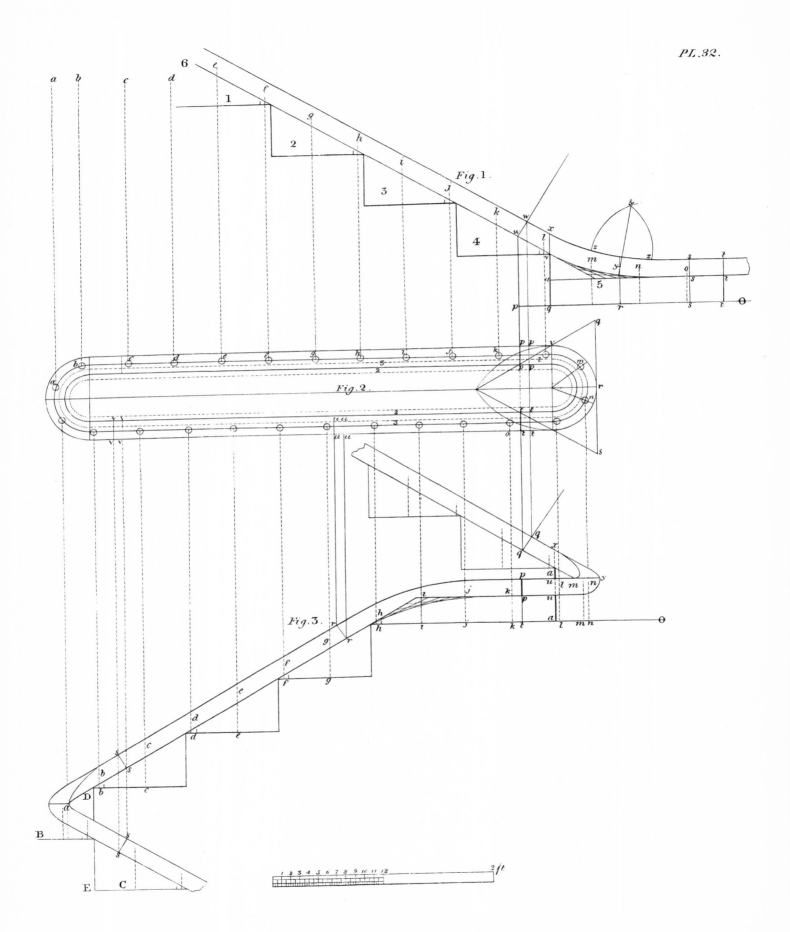

PL.32.

Fig.1.

Fig.2.

Fig.3.

O

O

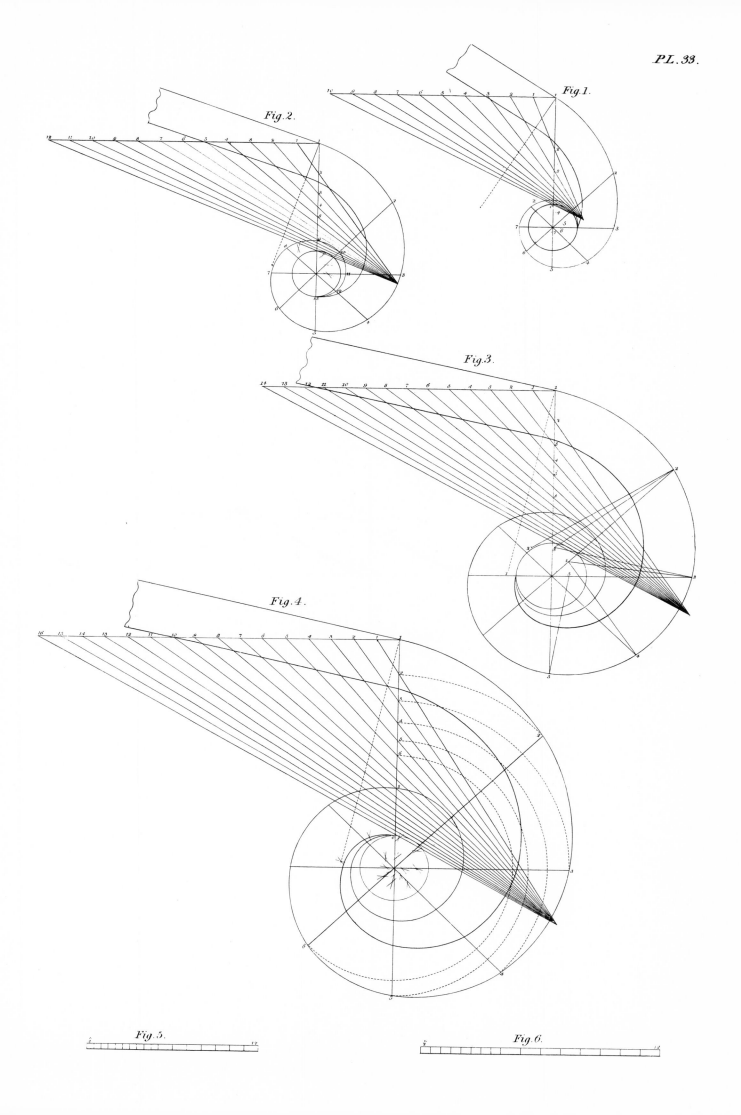

PL. 33.

Fig. 1.

Fig. 2.

Fig. 3.

Fig. 4.

Fig. 5.

Fig. 6.

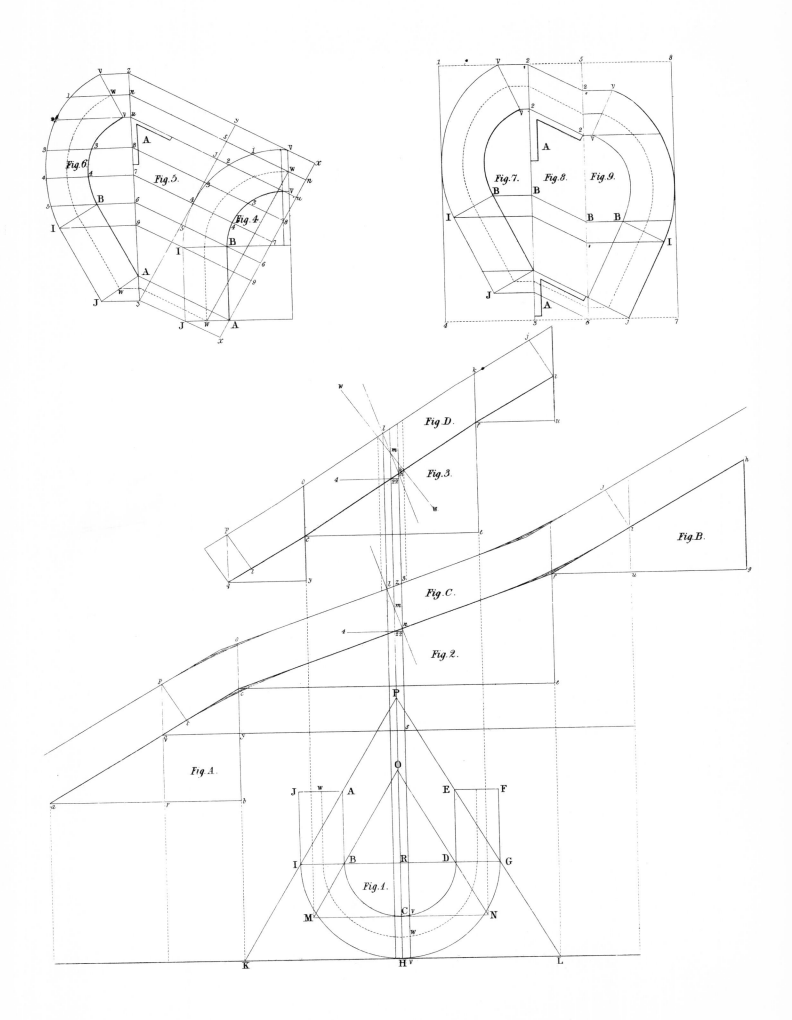

Fig.6.

Fig.5.

Fig.4.

Fig.7. Fig.8. Fig.9.

Fig.D.

Fig.3.

Fig.B.

Fig.C.

Fig.2.

Fig.A.

Fig.1.

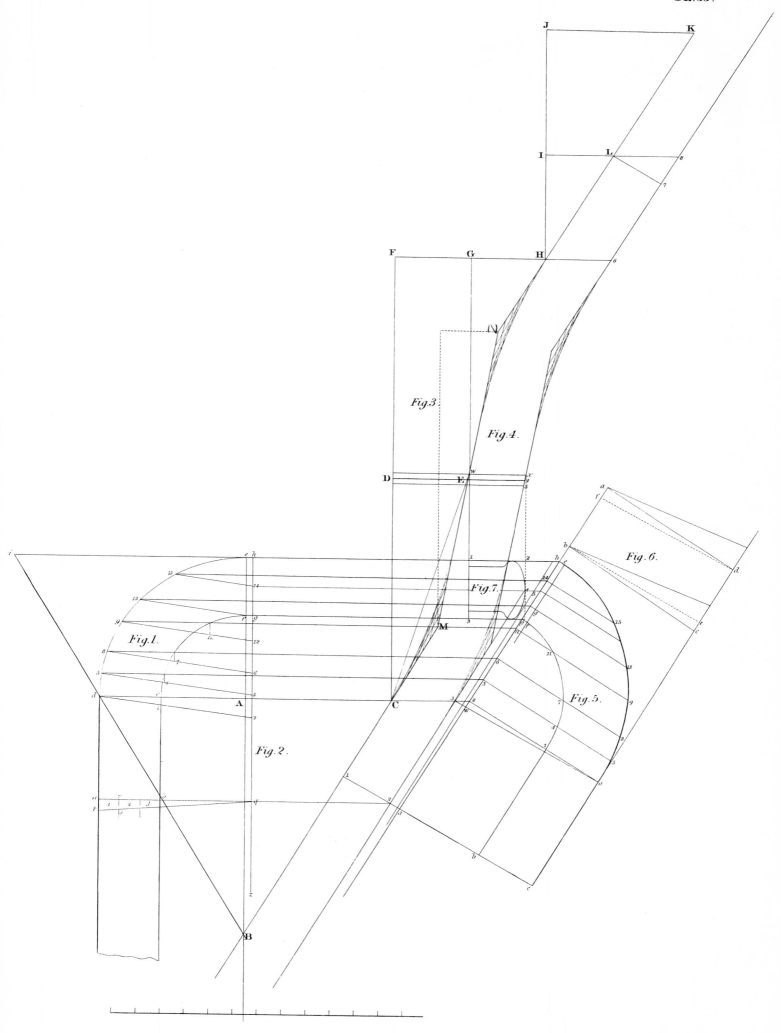

Fig. 3.

Fig. 4.

Fig. 6.

Fig. 7.

Fig. 1.

Fig. 5.

Fig. 2.

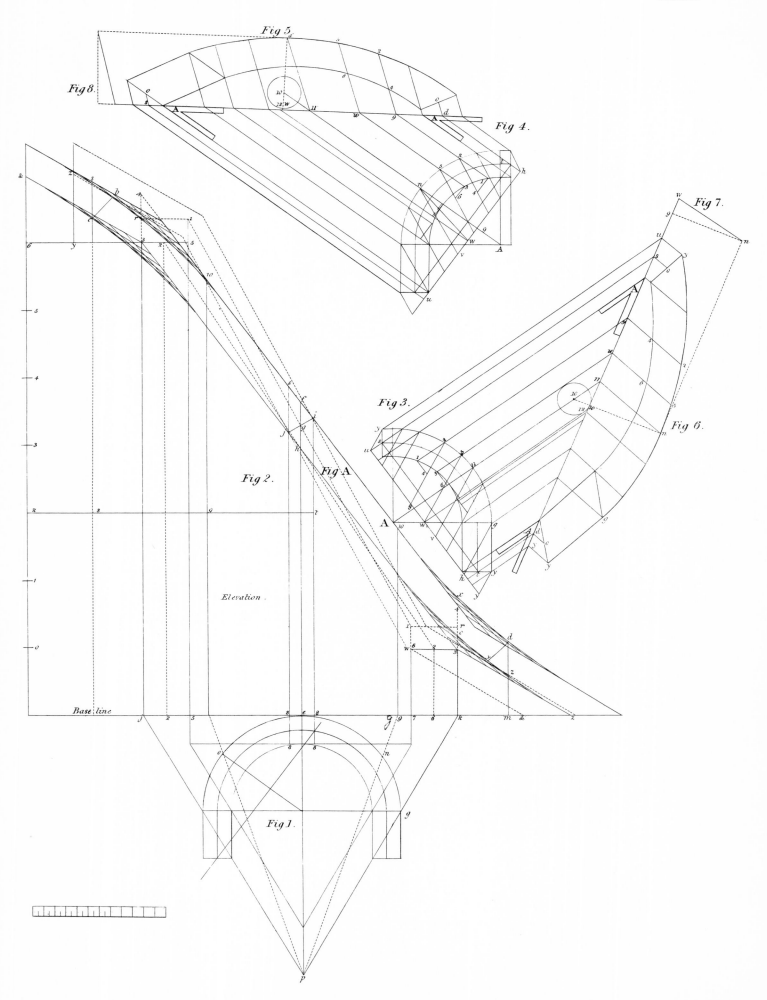

PL. 36.

Fig 5.

Fig 8.

Fig 4.

Fig 7.

Fig 3.

Fig 6.

Fig 2.

Fig A.

Elevation.

Base line.

Fig 1.

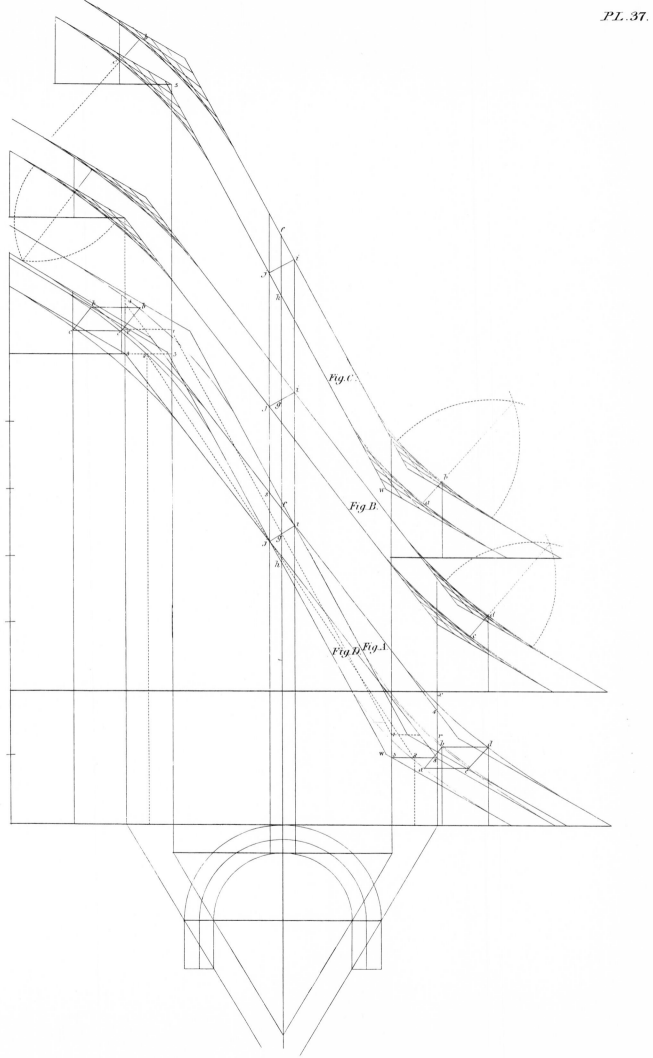

Fig. C.

Fig. B.

Fig. D. Fig. A.

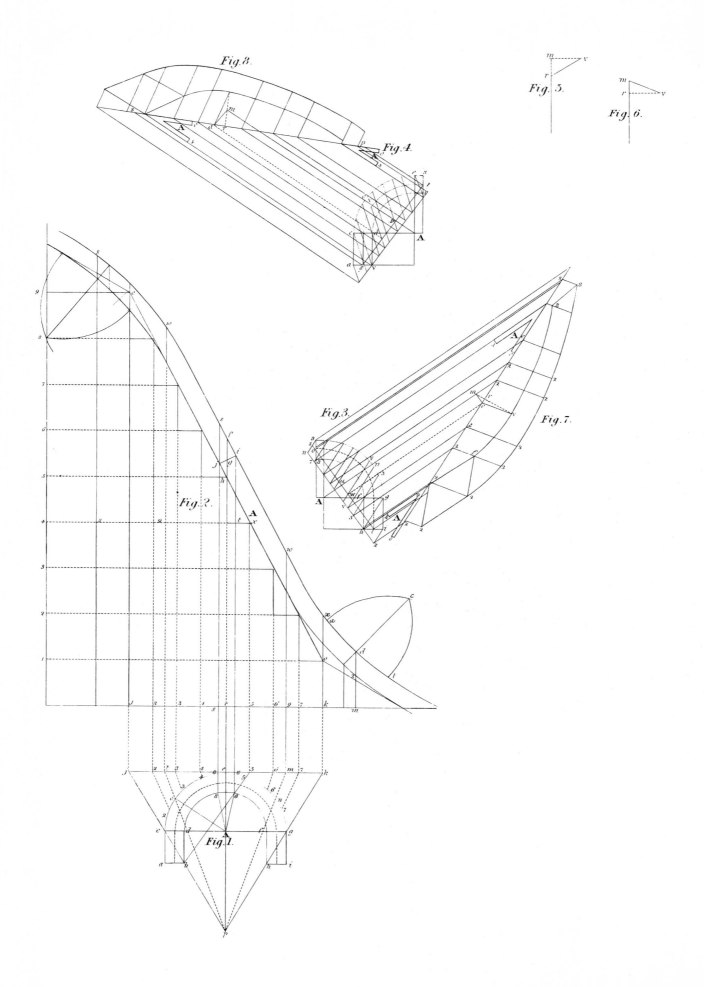

Fig. 8.

Fig. 5.

Fig. 6.

Fig. 4.

Fig. 3.

Fig. 7.

Fig. 2.

Fig. 1.

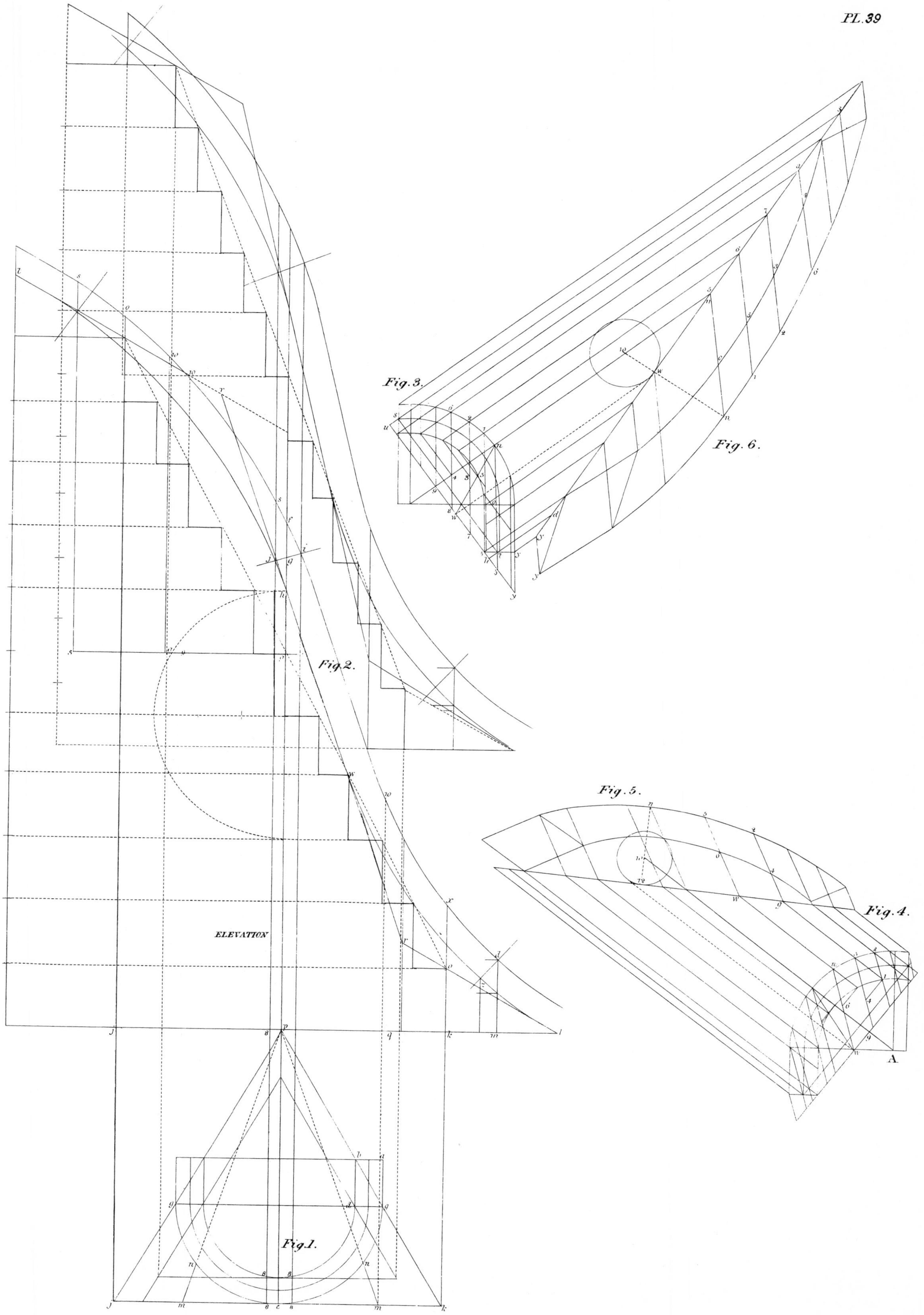

Fig. 3.

Fig. 6.

Fig. 2.

ELEVATION

Fig. 5.

Fig. 4.

A

Fig. 1.

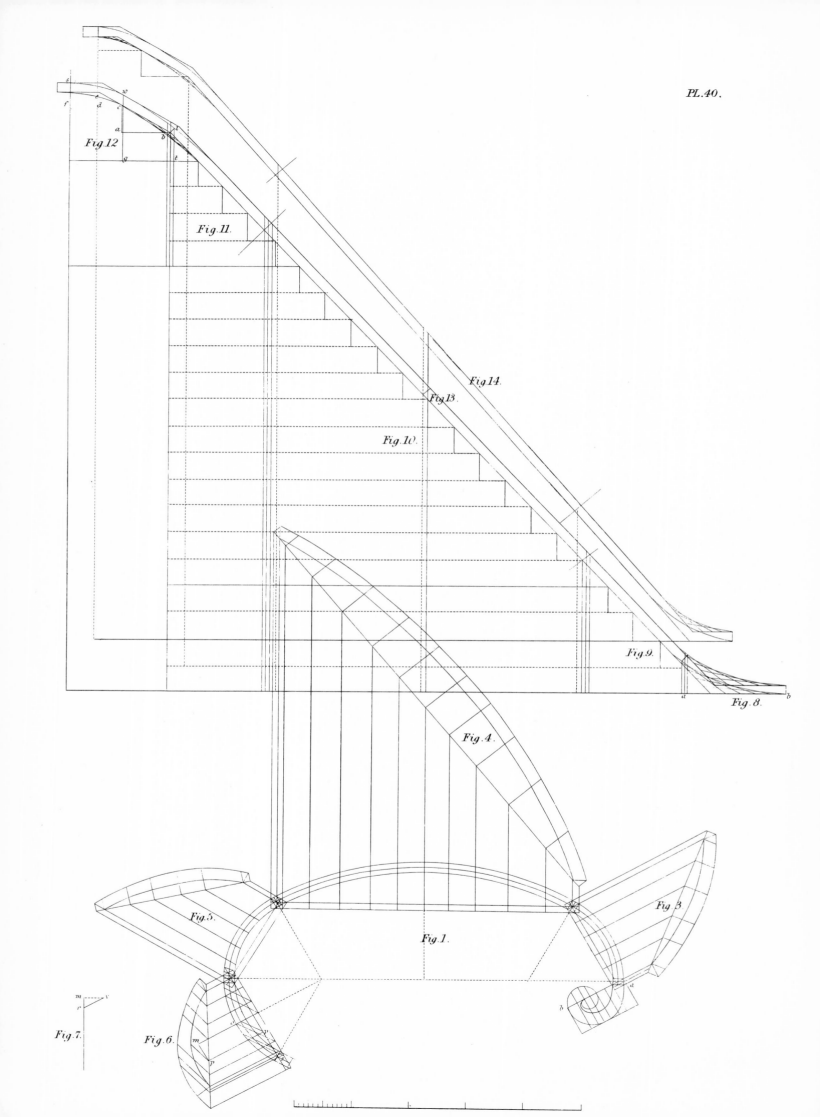

PL.40.

Fig.12.

Fig.11.

Fig.14.

Fig.13.

Fig.10.

Fig.9.

Fig.8.

Fig.4.

Fig.5.

Fig.3.

Fig.1.

Fig.7.

Fig.6.

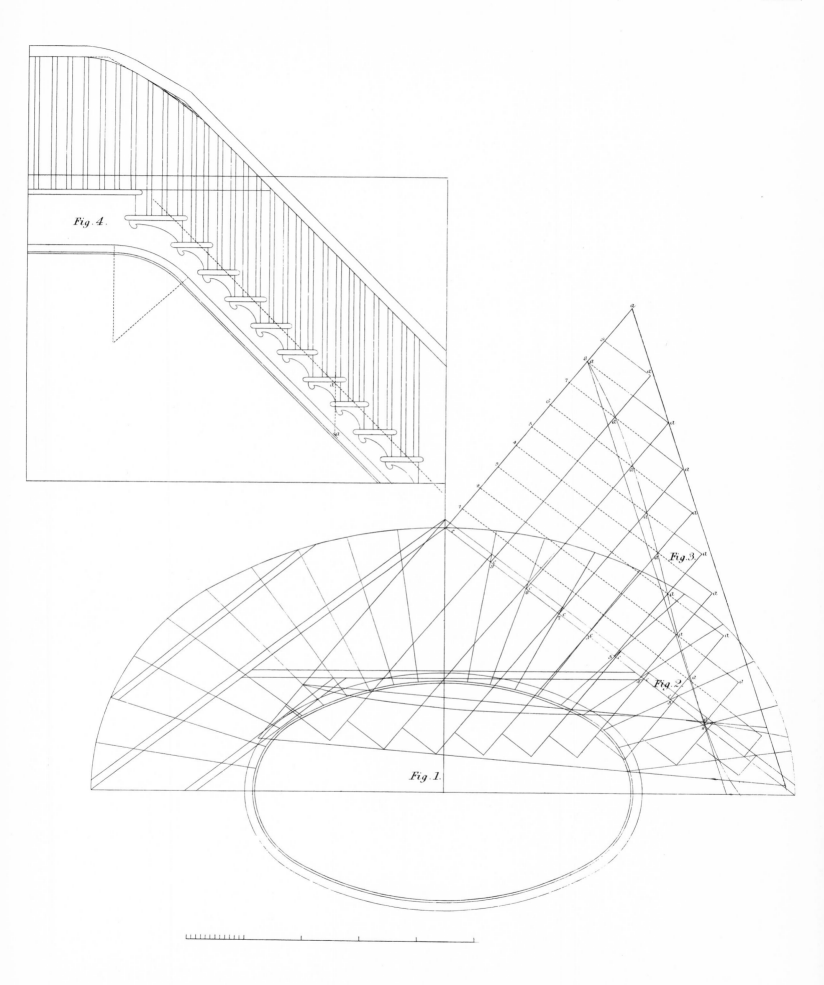

Fig. 4.

Fig. 3.

Fig. 2.

Fig. 1.

PL.42.

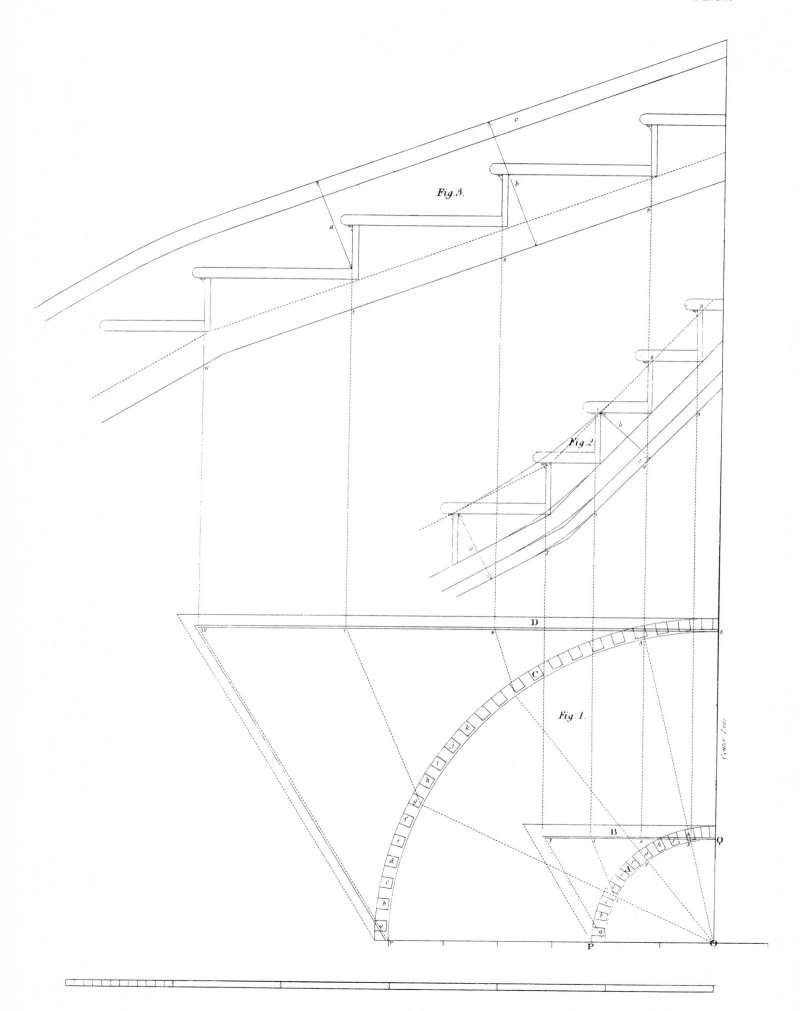

Fig.3.

Fig.2.

Fig.1.

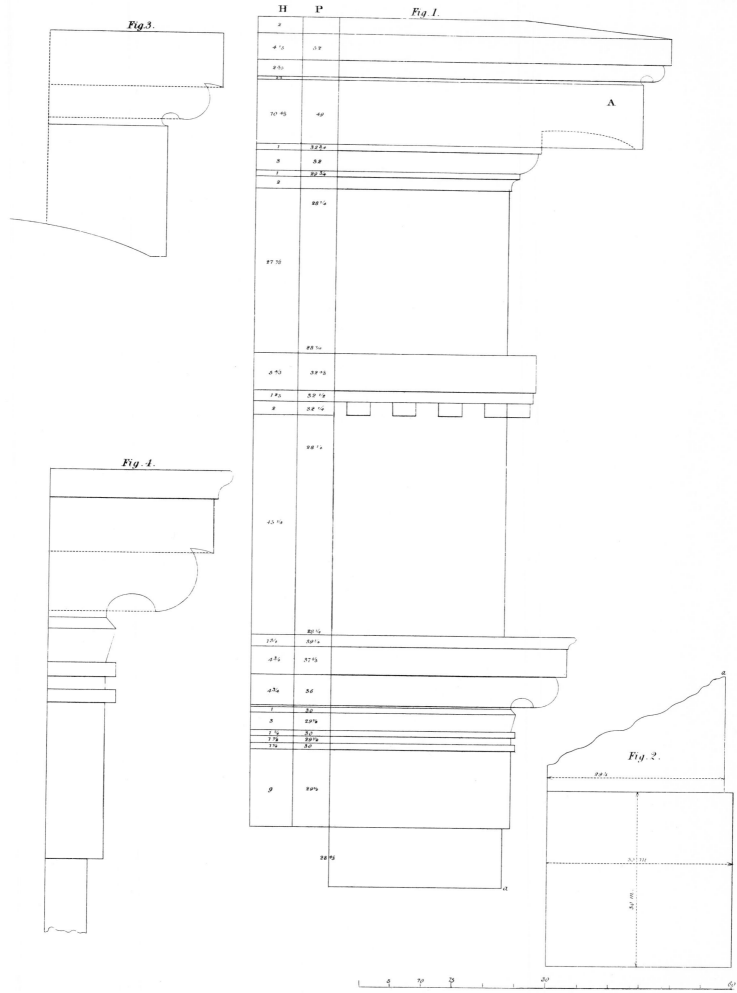

Fig. 3.

Fig. 4.

H P Fig. 1.

A

Fig. 2.

a

Pl.44.

DORIC ORDER

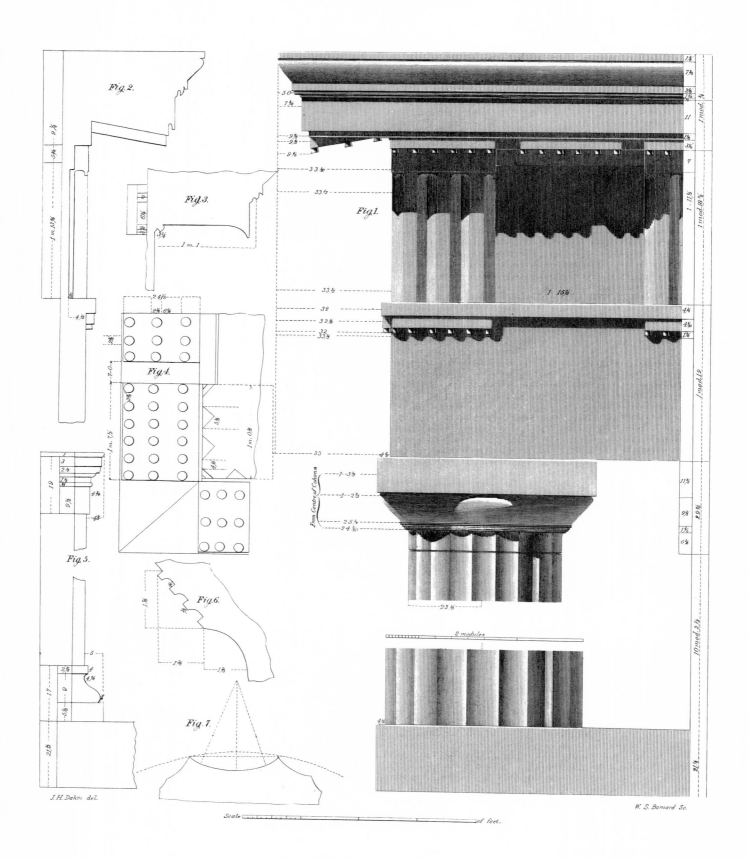

Fig. 2.

Fig. 3.

Fig. 4.

Fig. 5.

Fig. 6.

Fig. 7.

Fig. 1.

From Centre of Column

2 modules

J.H.Dakin del.

W. S. Barnard Sc.

Scale of feet.

Temple of Theseus

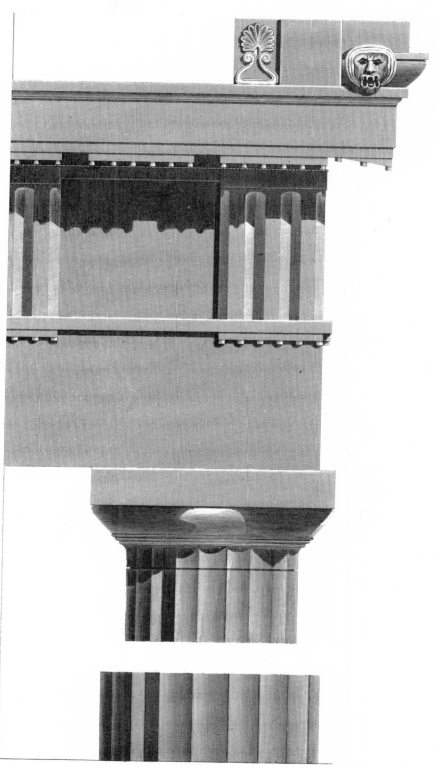

Drawn by M.Lafever.   Eng.d by Wm.D.Smith.

GRECIAN DORIC ORDER,

FROM THE TEMPLE OF MINERVA, AT ATHENS.

Pl. 46

IONIC ORDER

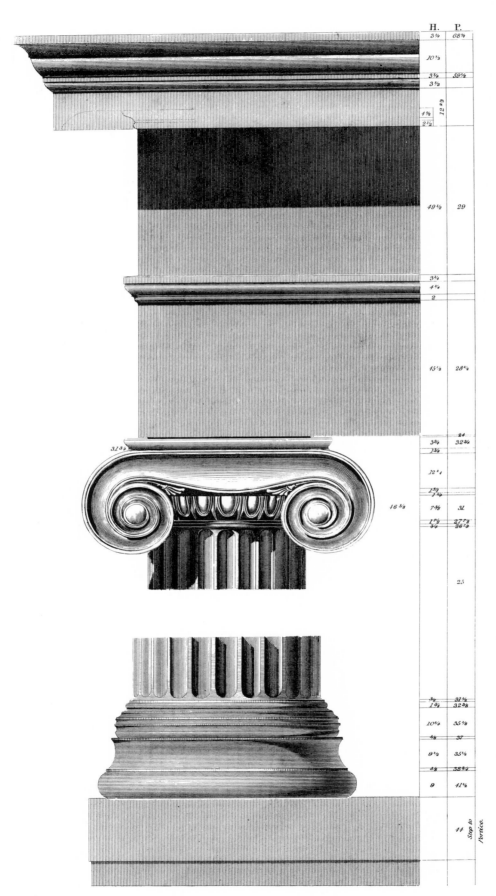

	H.	P.
	3¼	68¾
	10½	
	3¼	59½
	3½	
	12⅔	
	1⅜	
	2½	
	49½	29
	3¼	
	4¾	
	2	
	15½	28½
		24
	3¾	32¾
	1¾	
	12¼	
	1⅜	
	1¾	
16⅝	7⅞	31
	1⅞	27⅞
	¾	26⅞
		25
	¾	37½
	1¾	32⅜
	10¾	35½
	⅝	37
	9½	35¼
	⅝	38¾
	9	41½
	11	Step to Portico.

31¾

Lafever Arch.t Del.   W.S.Barnard sc.

Temple on the Ilissus.

Plate 47.

VOLUTE FROM THE IONIC TEMPLE ON THE ILISSUS,
(near Athens)

J. H. Dakin Inv. and Del. for Lafever.

W. S. Barnard Sc.

16 parts

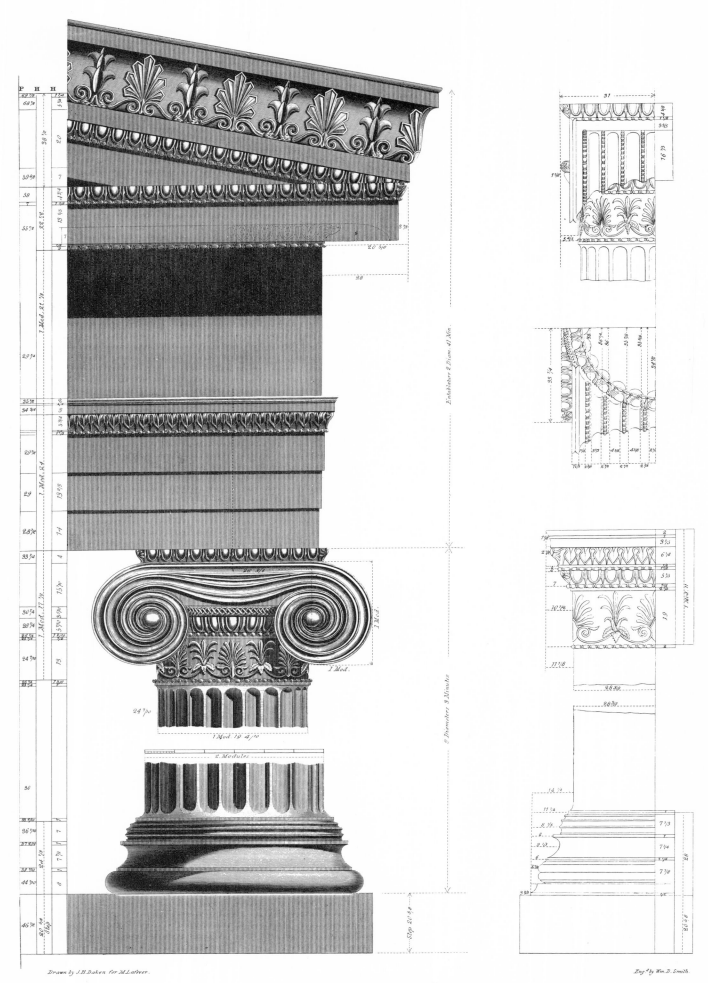

Drawn by J.H.Daken for M.Lafever.

Eng.d by Wm.D.Smith.

IONIC ORDER,

FROM THE TEMPLE OF ERECTHEUS AT ATHENS.

Plate 49.

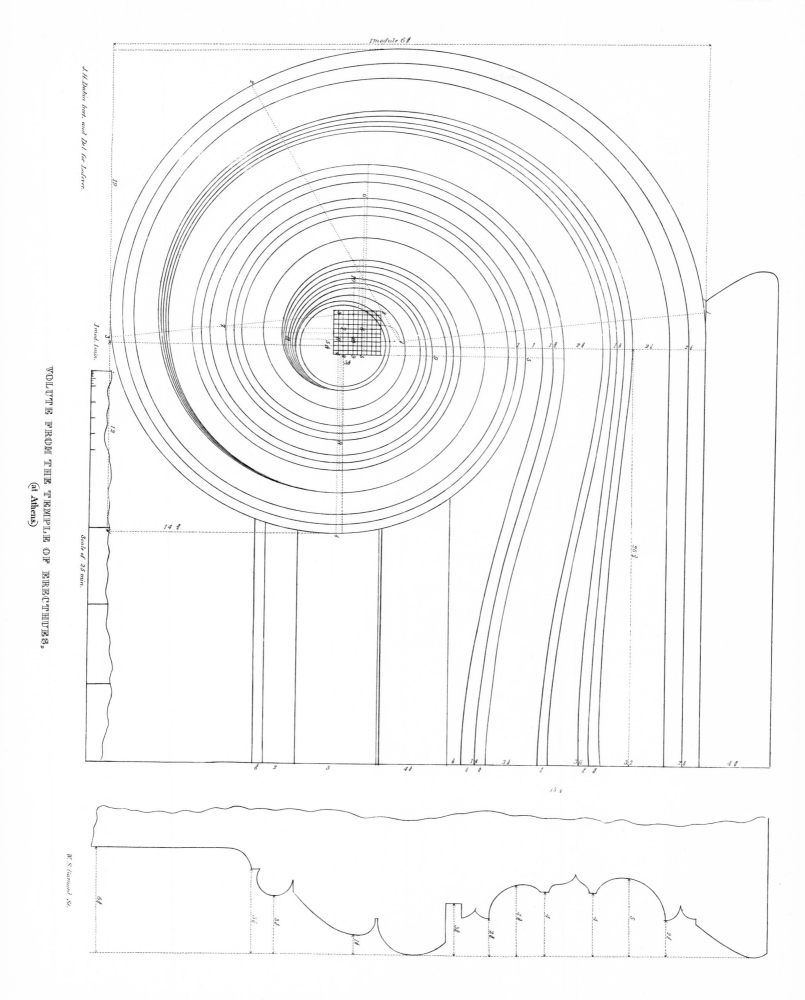

VOLUTE FROM THE TEMPLE OF ERECTHUES,
(at Athens)

J.H.Dakin. invt. and Del. for Lafevr.

W.S.Samuel Sc.

Pl.50.

Flank of the Ihssus Capitol.

Flank of the Erectheus Capitol.

Plan of the Flank.

Plan of the Flank.

Fig. 1.

Fig. 4.

Fig. 3.

2 Modules

1. Mod.

Fig. 2.

Drawn by Bakin. for Lafever.

Eng.ᵈ by Wm. D. Smith.

Scale of Feet.

CORINIHIAN ORDER,

FROM THE MONVMENT OF LYSICRATES AT ATHENS.

Pl.52

DORIC ORDER from THE TEMPLE of MINERVA at ATHENS

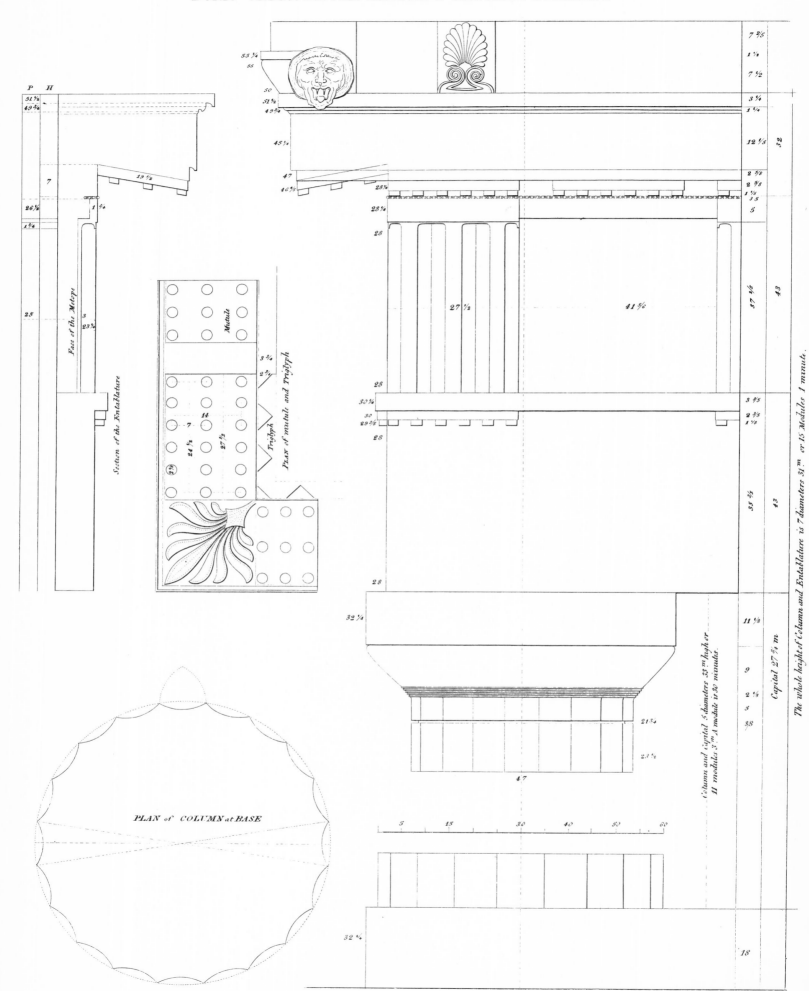

PLAN of COLUMN at BASE

Section of the Entablature

Face of the Metope

Mutule

Plan of mutule and Triglyph

Triglyph

Capital 27 ¾ m

The whole height of Column and Entablature is 7 diameters 31 ᵐ or 15 Modules 1 minute.

Column and capital 5 diameters 33 ᵐ higher 11 modules 3 ᵐ. A module is 30 minutes.

Drawn and Figured by Lafever from Stuarts Antiquities.

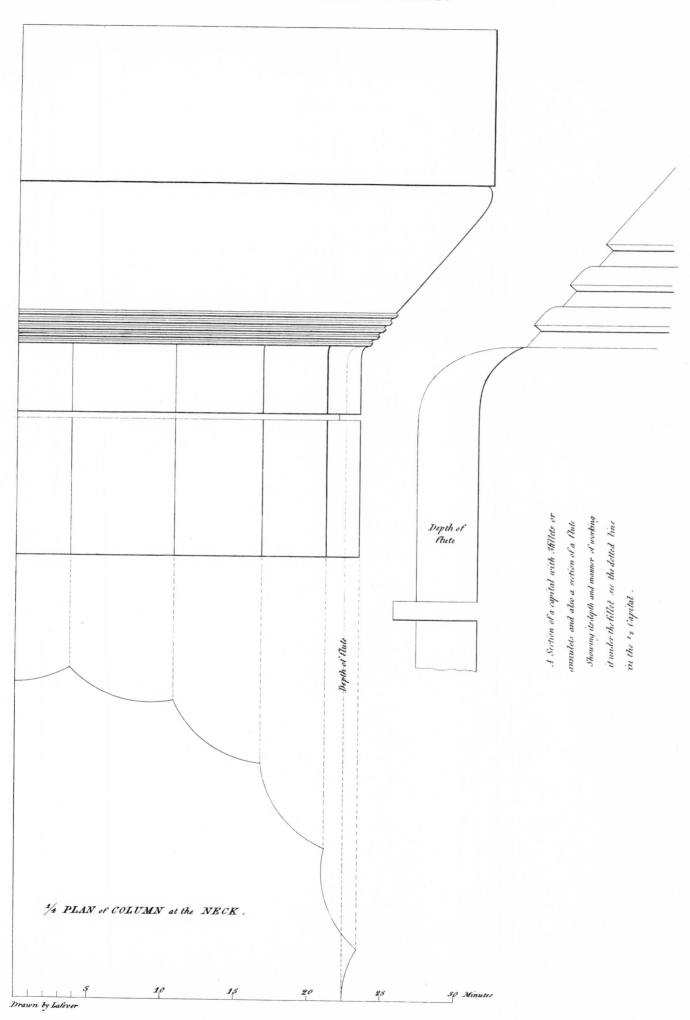

Depth of
Flute

Depth of Flute

A Section of a capital with 3 fillets or
annulets and also a section of a flute
Showing its depth and manner of working
it under the fillet see the dotted line
in the ¹/₂ Capital .

¼ PLAN of COLUMN at the NECK.

5   10   15   20   25   30 Minutes

Drawn by Lafever

PLAN AND ELEVATION OF A CHURCH,

Designed in the

GRECIAN IONIC ORDER.

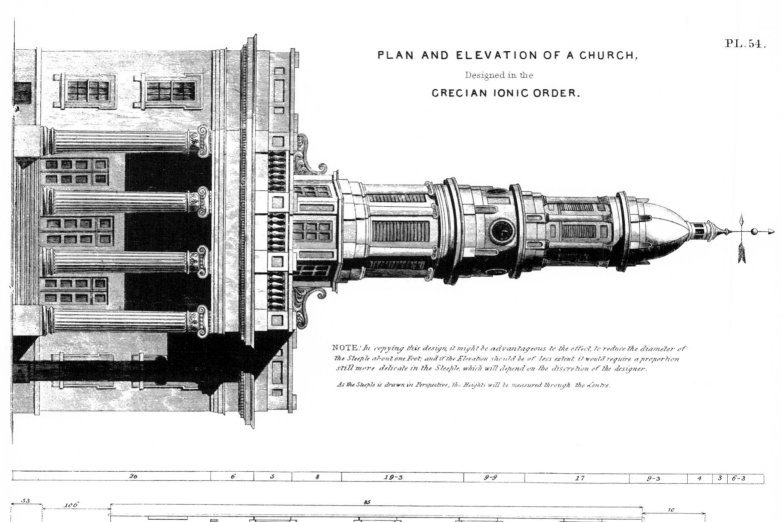

NOTE: In copying this design, it might be advantageous to the effect, to reduce the diameter of the Steeple about one Foot; and if the Elevation should be of less extent, it would require a proportion still more delicate in the Steeple, which will depend on the discretion of the designer.

As the Steeple is drawn in Perspective, the Heights will be measured through the Centre.

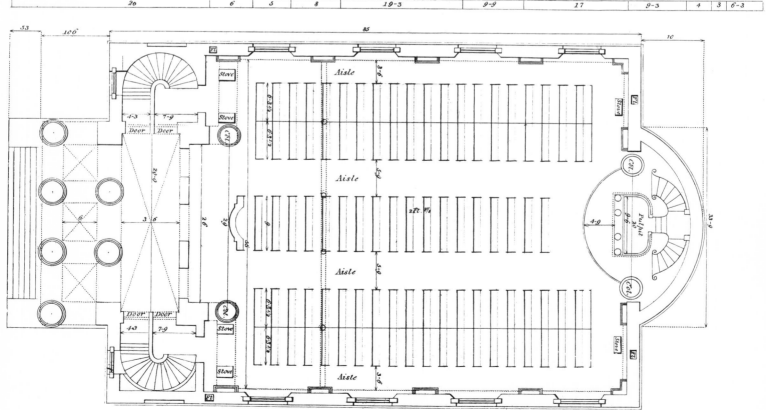

PL. 55.

PLAN AND ELEVATION OF A GOTHIC CHURCH.

And is in its Elevation, very similar to the New

NATIONAL SCOTCH CHURCH LONDON.

A Vestibule. B. Entrances to the Side Aisles, and Gallery Stairs. C. Extent of the Gallery, front Wall. D. Front line of the Gallery.
E Kneeling Step. F Communion Table. G Reading Desk. H Pulpit. I Colums to support the Organ Gallery. J Vestry Room.
K Book Case. L Wardrobe. M Rear entrances, and Stairs. N Stairs to the Organ Gallery. O Chancel.
NOTE—The size of the Apartments, Measured by the Scale.

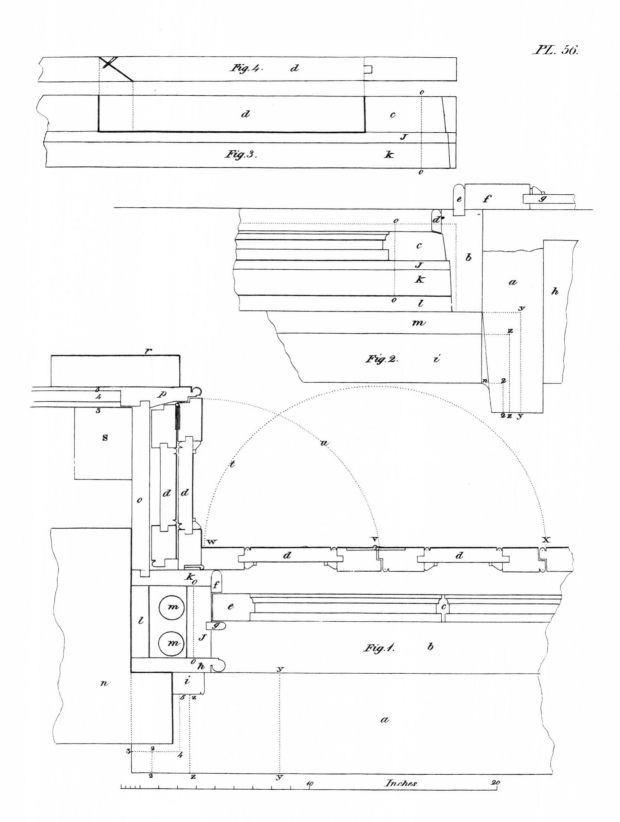

Fig.4.   d

Fig.3.

Fig.2.

Fig.1.

Inches.

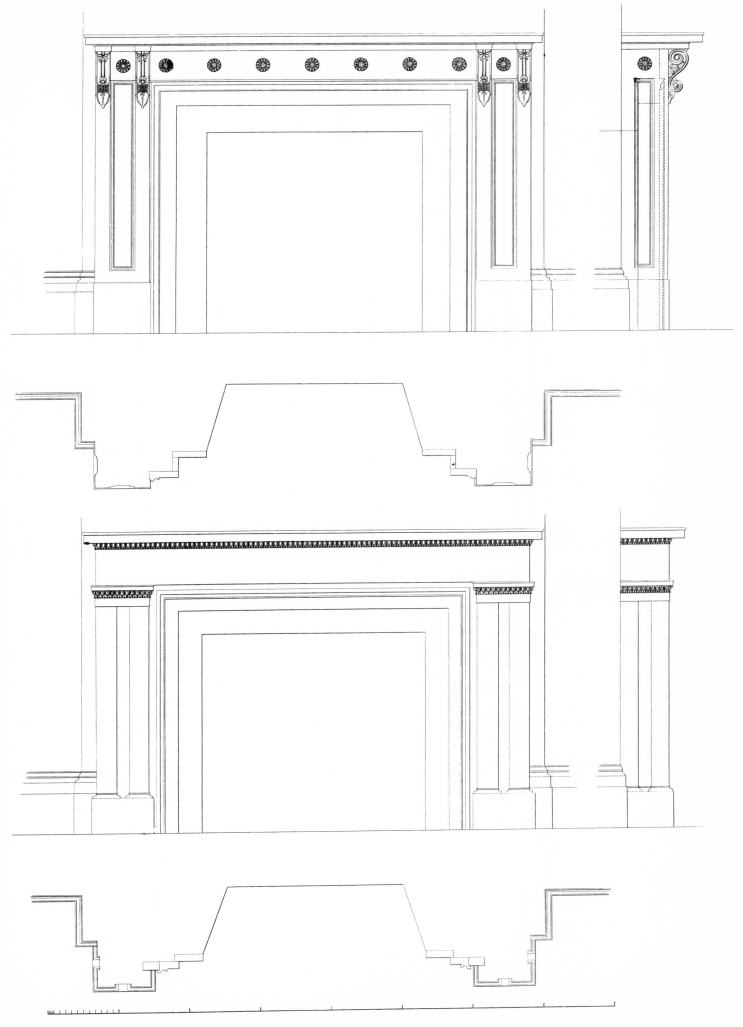

Eng.d by Wm.D.Smith

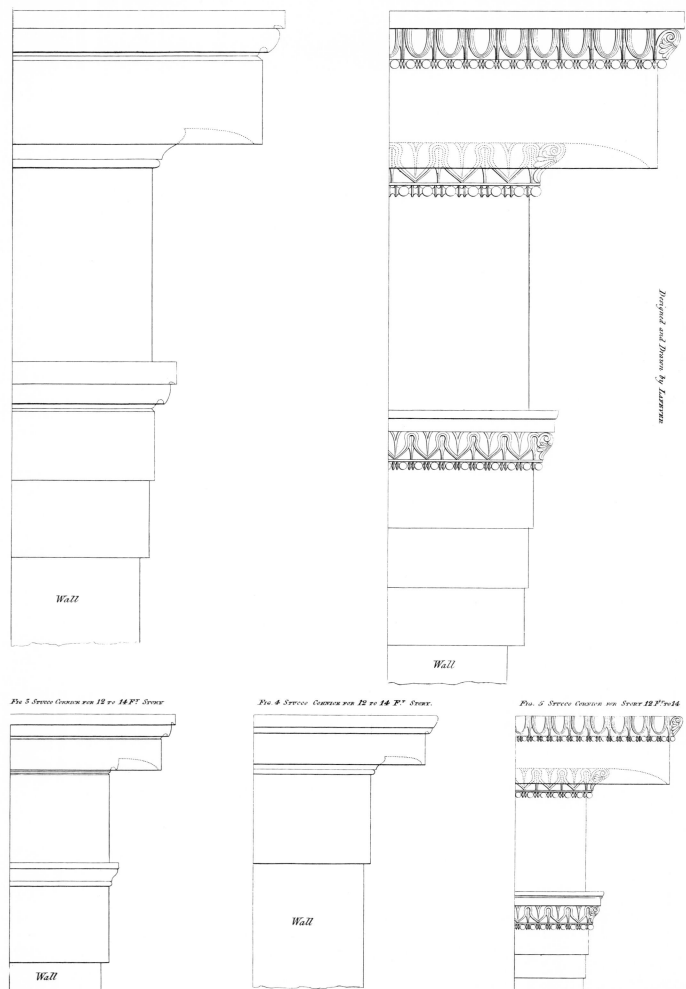

FIG. 1 EVE CORNICE FOR A 2 STORY HOUSE   FIG. 2 EVE CORNICE FOR A 3 STORY HOUSE   Pl. 58

Designed and Drawn by LAFEVER

Wall

Wall

FIG. 3 STUCCO CORNICE FOR 12 TO 14 FT. STORY   FIG. 4 STUCCO CORNICE FOR 12 TO 14 FT. STORY.   FIG. 5 STUCCO CORNICE FOR STORY 12 FT. TO 14

Wall

Wall

Wall

12   1   2   3 Ft.

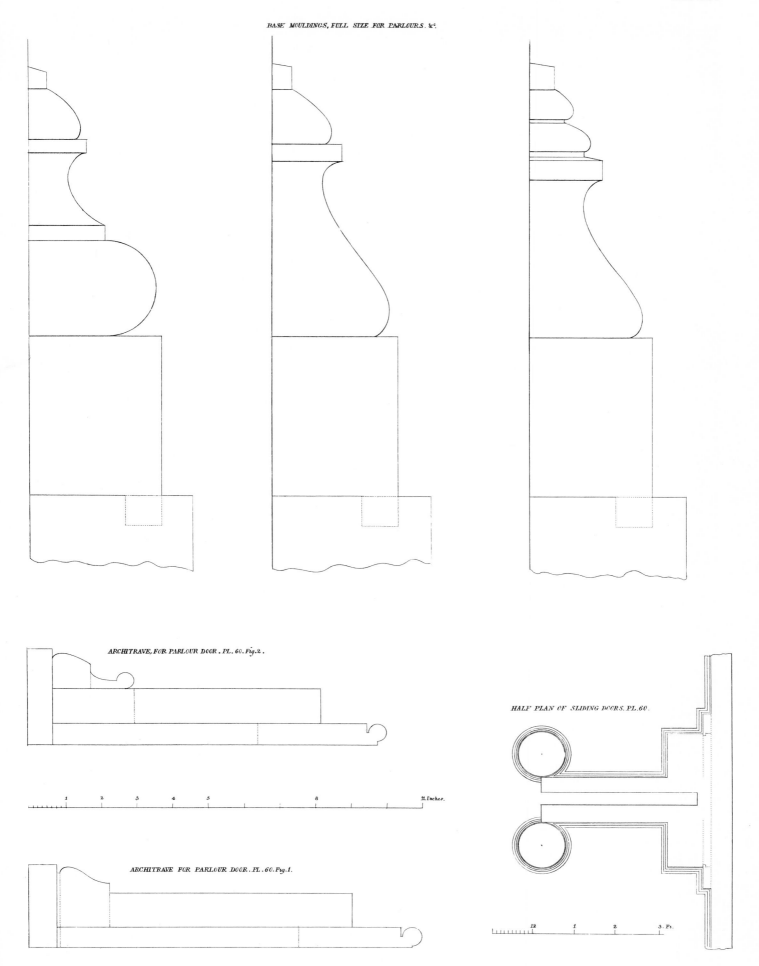

BASE MOULDINGS, FULL SIZE FOR PARLOURS, &c.

ARCHITRAVE, FOR PARLOUR DOOR. PL. 60. Fig. 2.

ARCHITRAVE FOR PARLOUR DOOR. PL. 60. Fig. 1.

HALF PLAN OF SLIDING DOORS. PL. 60.

Fig.1.

Fig.2.

DESIGNS. FOR. PARLOUR. DOORS.

Drawn by M.Lafever.

Eng.d by Wm.R.Smith.

DESIGN FOR SLIDING DOOR.

Plate 61.

Fig.1.   Fig. 2.   Fig.3.   Fig.4.   Fig.5.   Fig. 6.   Fig. 7.

W. S. Barnard. Sc.

Plate 62.

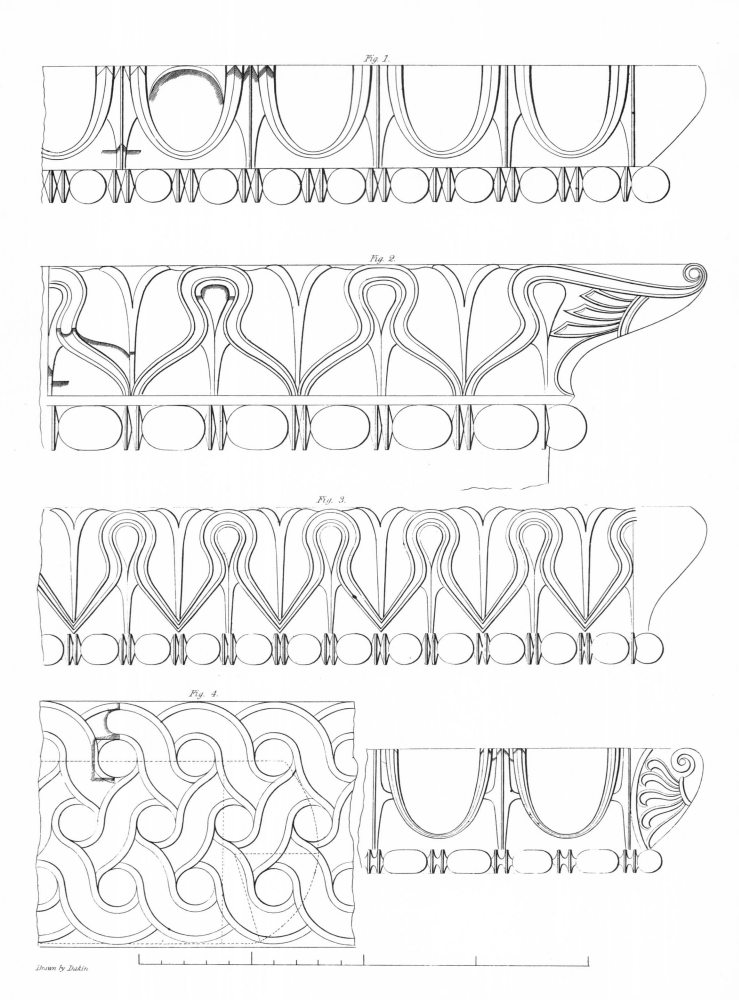

Fig. 1.

Fig. 2.

Fig. 3.

Fig. 4.

Drawn by Dakin

Designed & drawn by J.H.Dakin for Lafever.

Eng.d by W.D.Smith.

DESIGN FOR A FRONT DOOR.

Pl. 64.

Haien del for Lafever.   W.S.Barnard Sc.

Pl. 65.

Dakin del for Lafever.

W.S.B. sc.

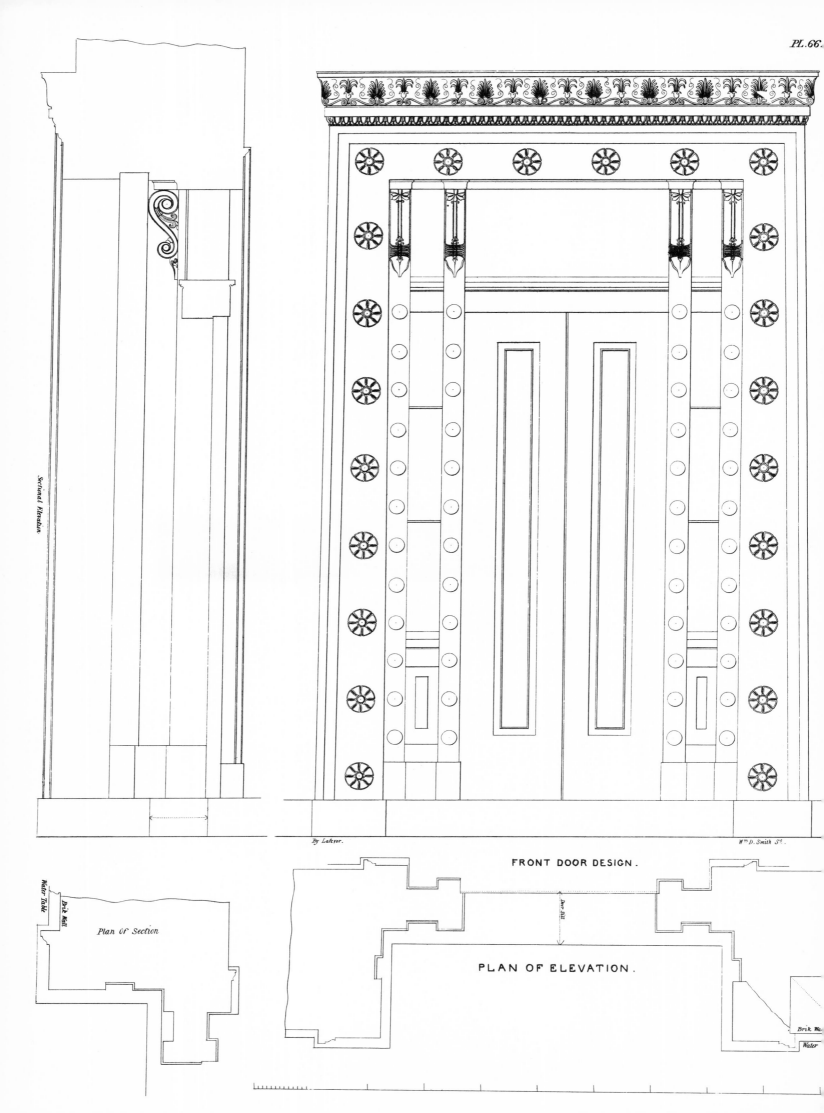

Sectional Elevation.

By Lafever.

Wm D. Smith Sc.

FRONT DOOR DESIGN.

Water Table

Brik Wall

Plan Of Section

Door Sill

PLAN OF ELEVATION.

Brik Wall

Water

Pl. 67.

INTERIOR ELEVATION OF A PARLOUR AND FRONT HALL DOOR.

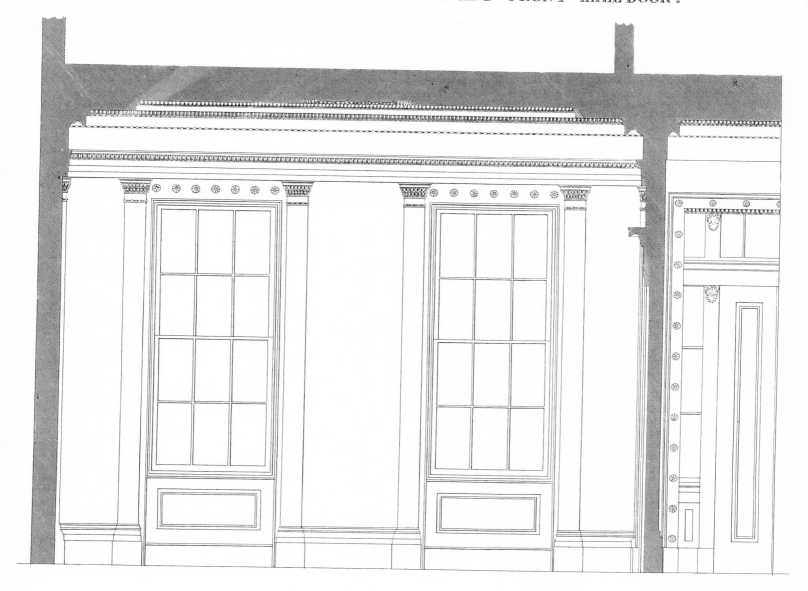

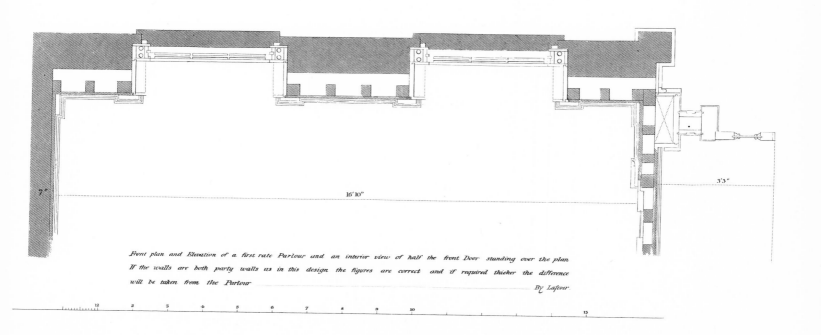

16'10"

5'3"

7"

Front plan and Elevation of a first rate Parlour and an interior view of half the front Door standing over the plan
If the walls are both party walls as in this design the figures are correct and if required thicker the difference
will be taken from the Parlour ⸺⸺⸺⸺⸺⸺⸺ *By Lafever.*

12   2   3   4   5   6   7   8   9   10   15

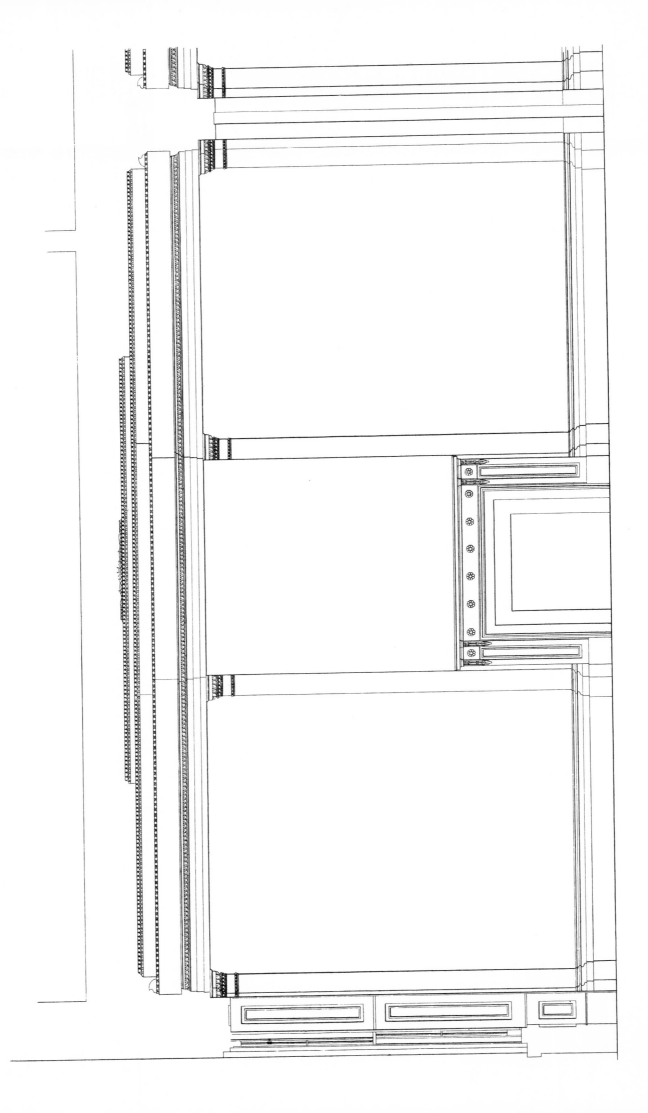

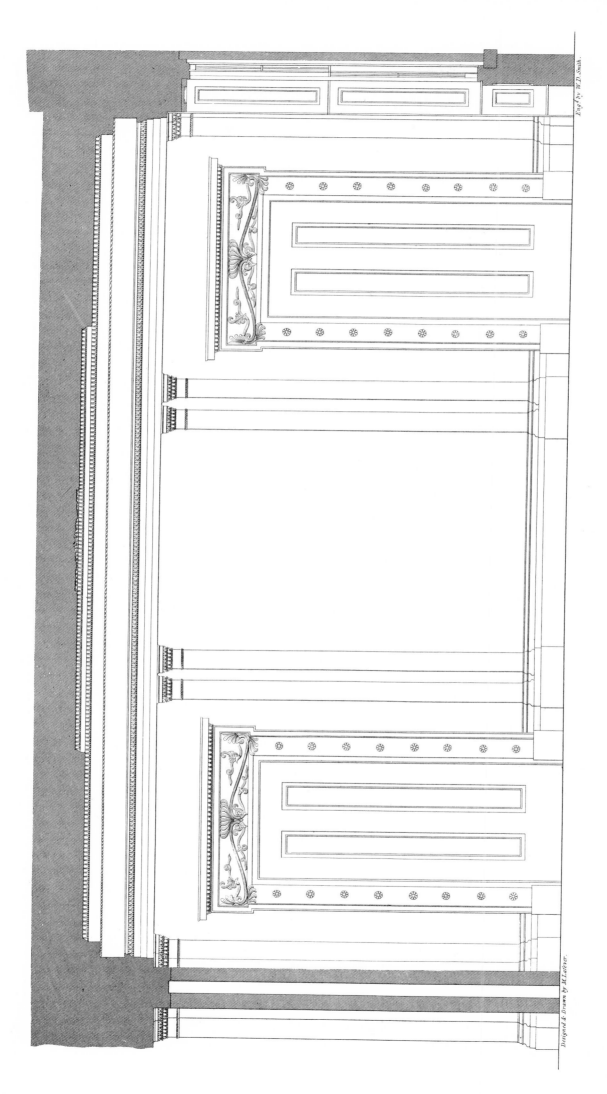

Designed & Drawn by M.Lafever.

Eng.d by W.D. Smith.

ELEVATION OF A PARLOUR NEXT THE HALL

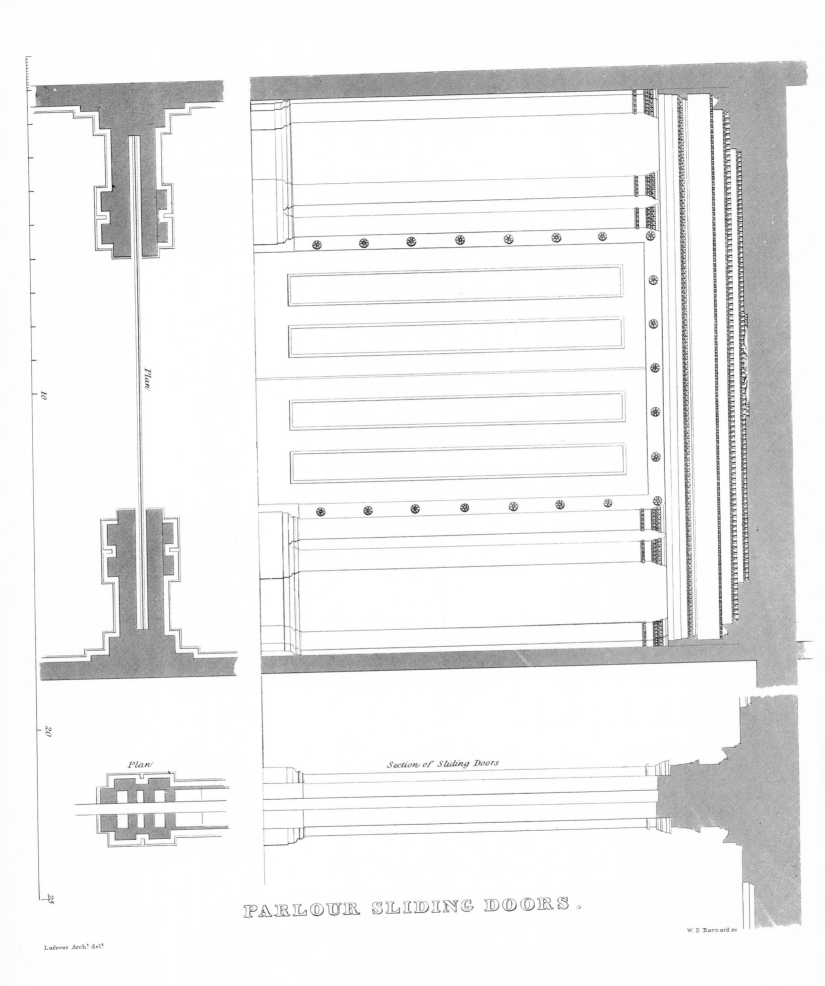

Plan

Plan

Section of Sliding Doors

PARLOUR SLIDING DOORS.

Lafever Arch.ᵗ del.ᵗ

W. S. Barnard sc

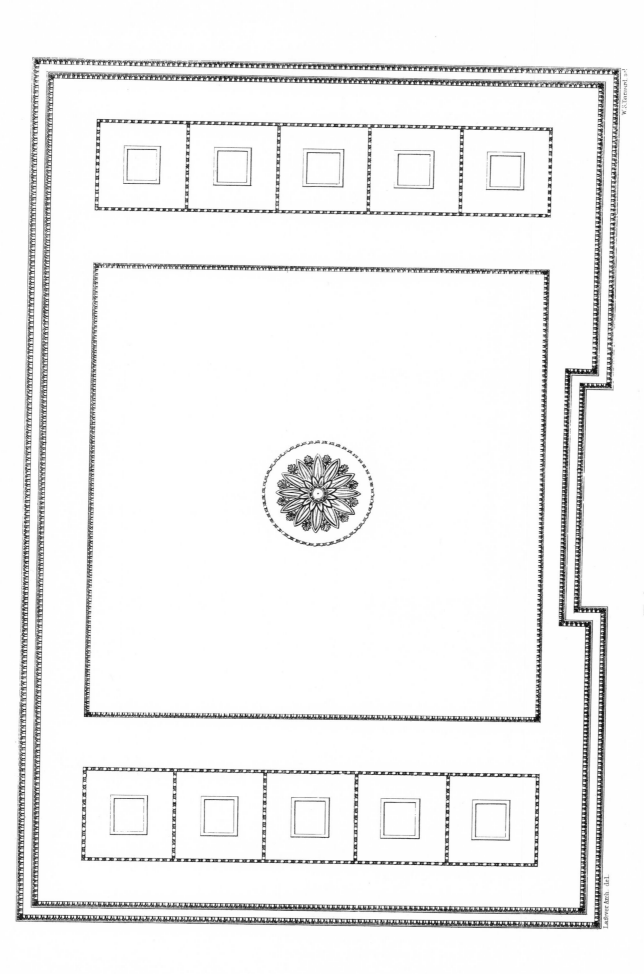

Pl. 71.

W.S.Barnard, sc.

Lafever Arch. del.

PARLOUR CEILING.

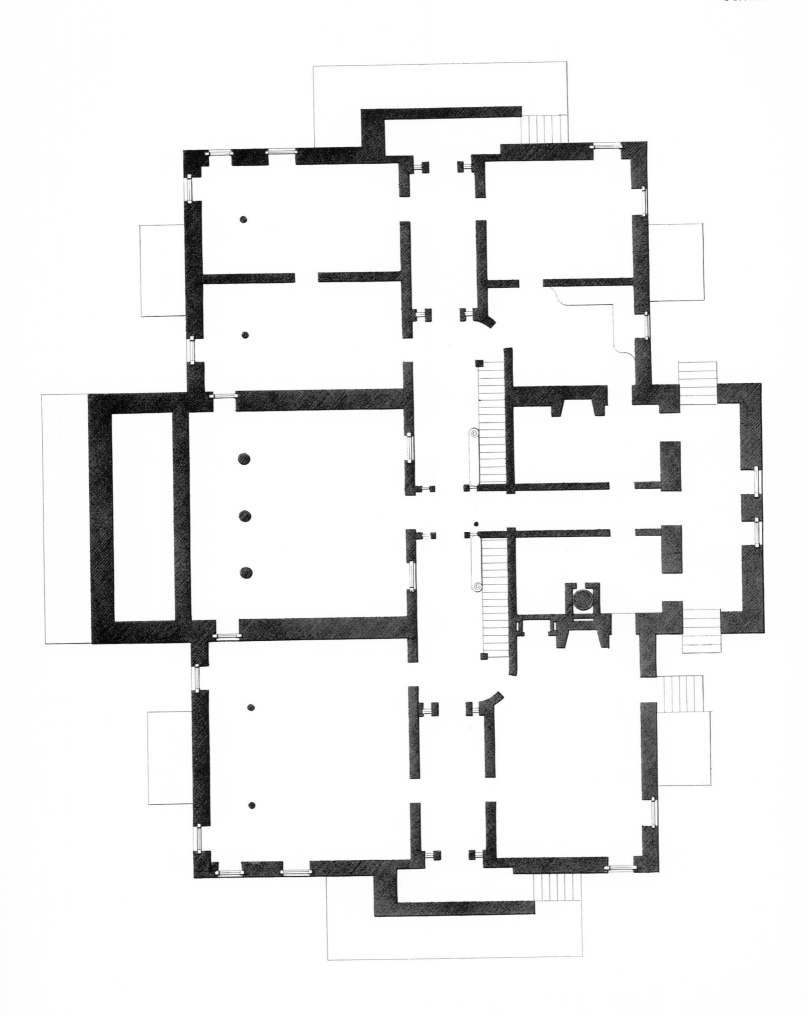

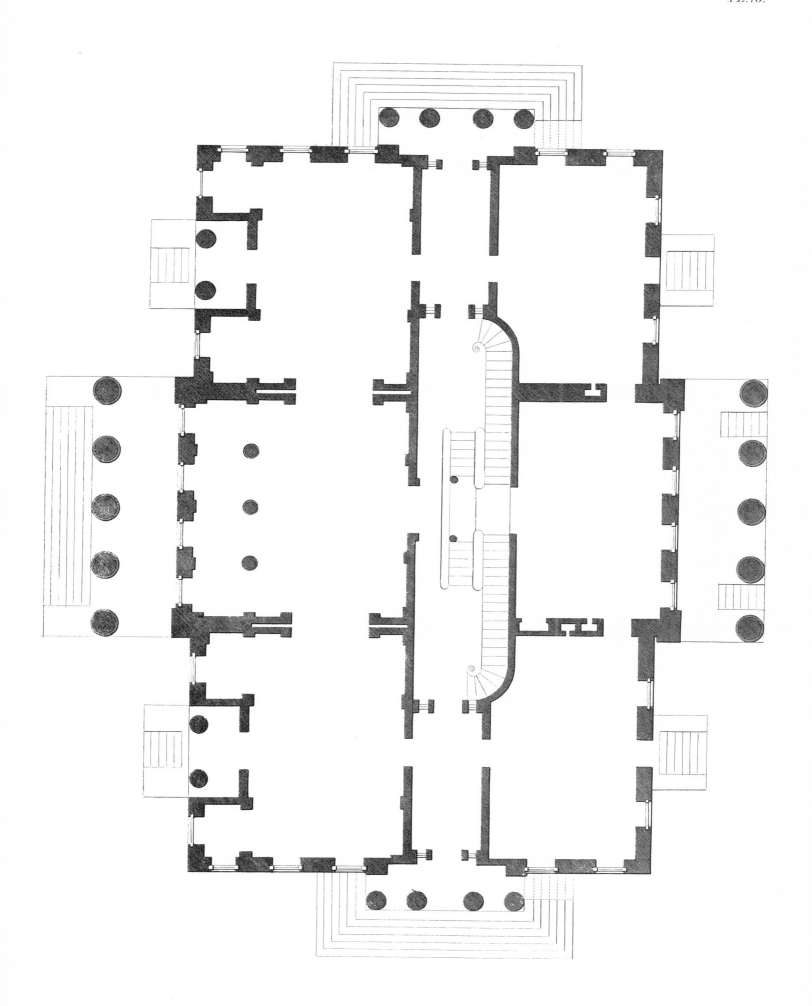

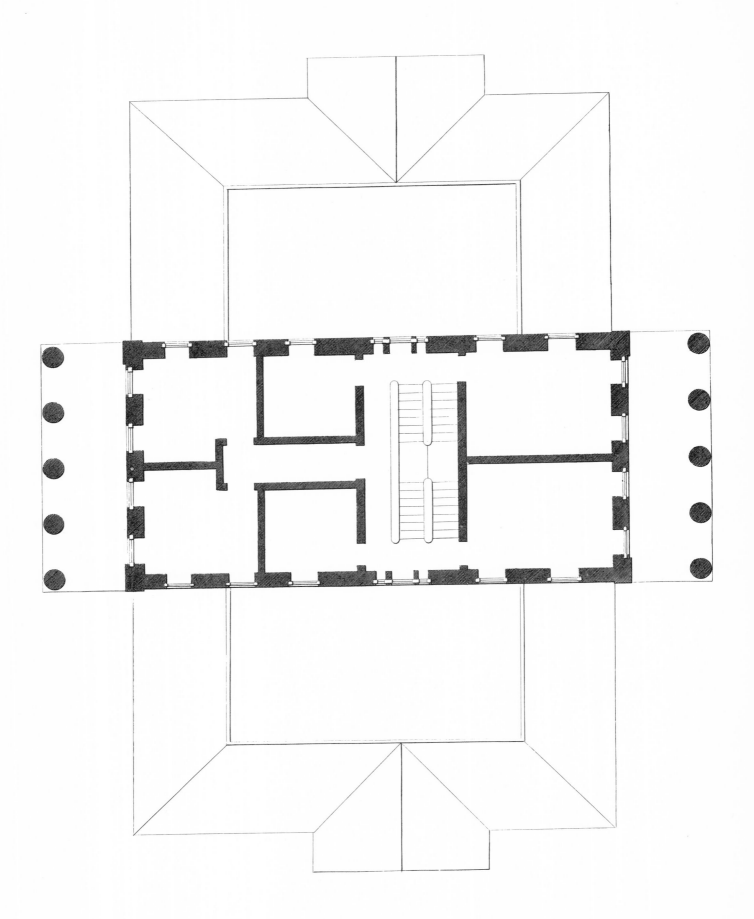

Designed & Drawn by Lafever.

Eng.ᵈ by Wm.D. Smith.

FRONT ELEVATION FOR A COUNTRY RESIDENCE.

Designed by Lefever.

Drawn by Bellangé.

& Engraved by H.Vejette.

SECTION OF THE PARLOUR & CONSERVATORY

OF PLATES 75 & 76

LOOKING THROUGH THE WINDOWS

Designed by Lafever. Drawn by Retheaft.

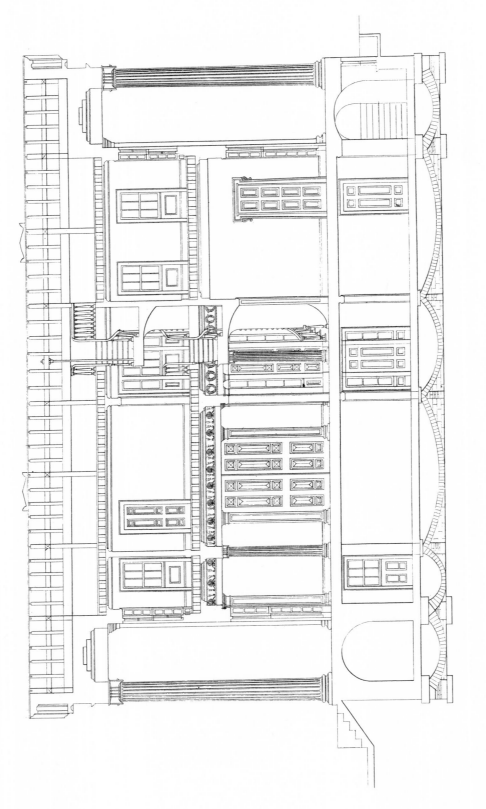

PL. 78.

SECTION OF PLATE 75 & 76.

Eng.d by Wm.D.Smith.

Designed by M.Lafever.

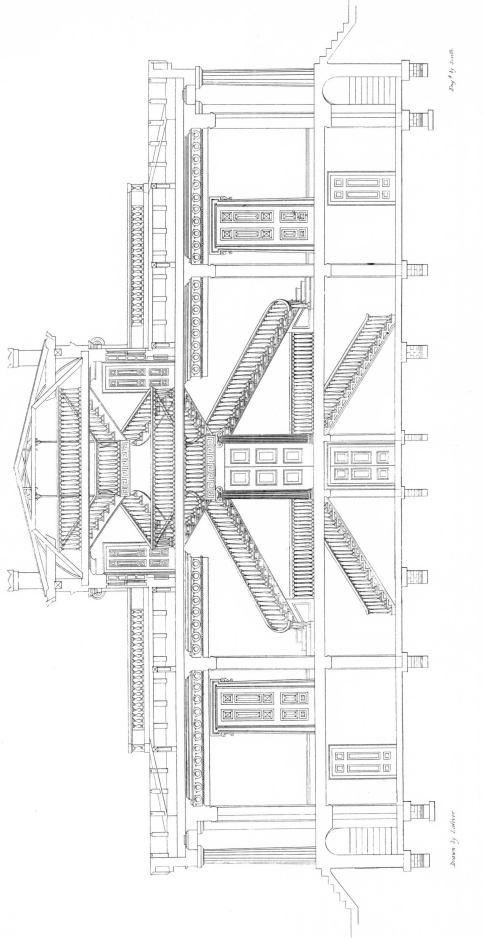

Drawn by Lefever

Engᵈ by Smith

LONGITUDINAL SECTION OF PLATE 75 & 76.

THROUGH THE HALL.

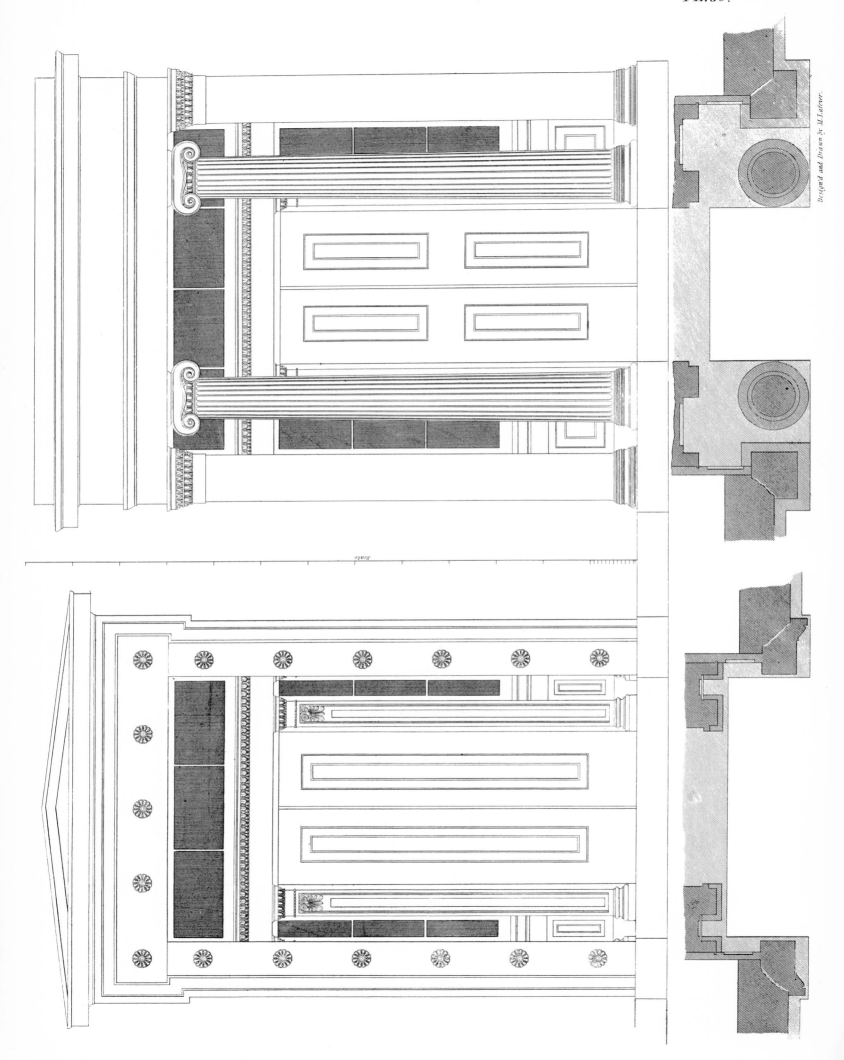

PL. 80.

Scale

Design'd and Drawn by M.Lafever.

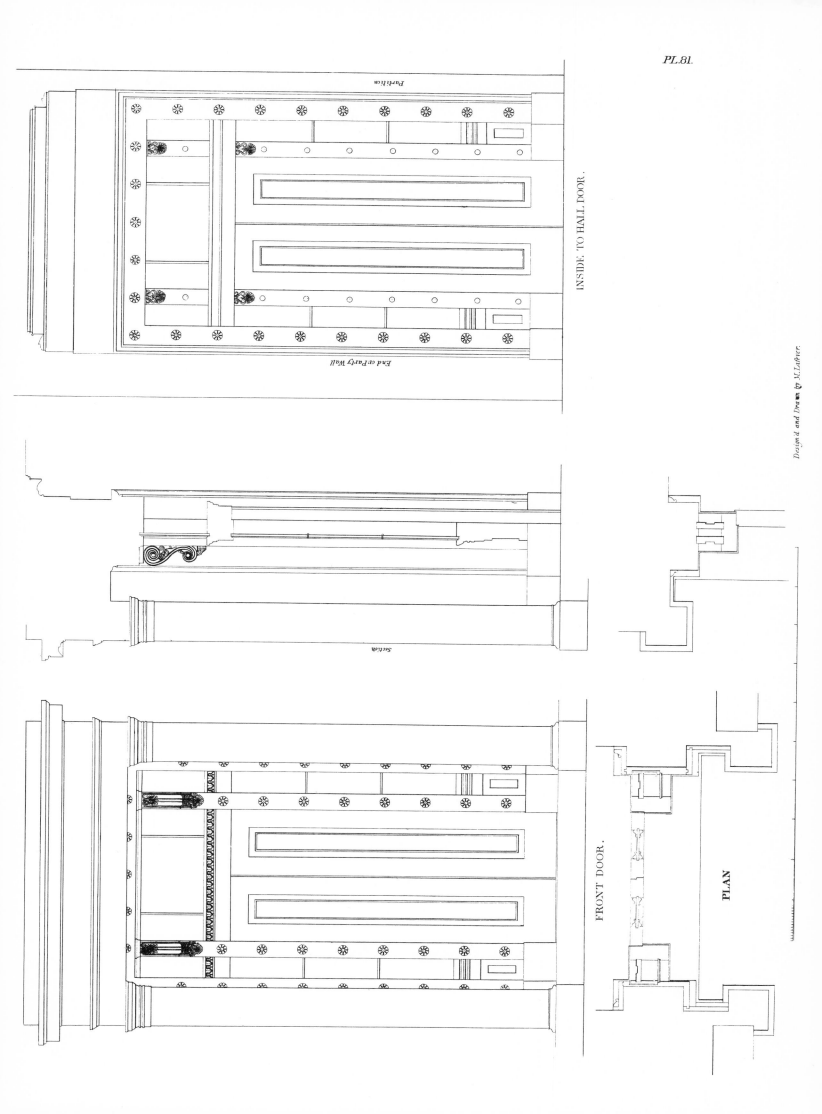

INSIDE. TO HALL DOOR.

Partition

End or Party Wall

Section

Design'd and Drawn by M.Lafever.

FRONT DOOR.

Partition

PLAN

ELEVATION OF PARLOUR DOOR.

Designed and Drawn by Lafever.

Wm. D. Smith Sc.

Antæ caps and bases full size for doors or other places admitting small projections. These antæ are remarkeably neat, and applicable to exterior and interior doors, windows, chimney pieces. &c.

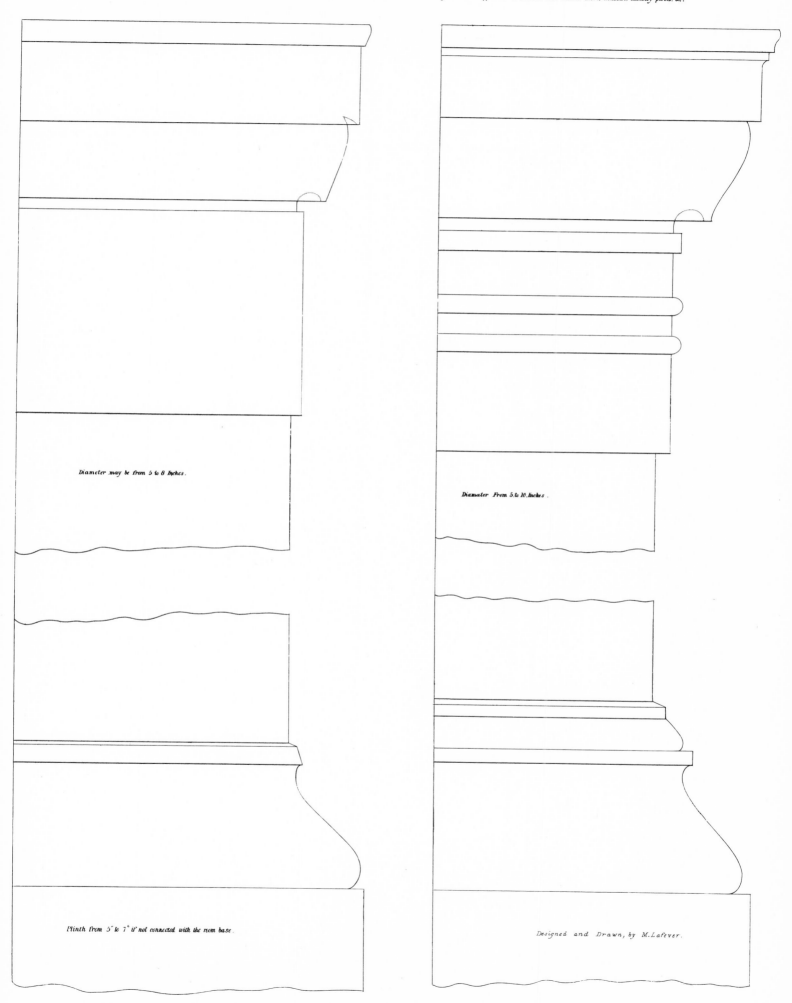

Diameter may be from 5 to 8 Inches.

Diamater From 5.to 10. Inches .

Plinth from 5″ to 7″ if not connected with the room base.

Designed and Drawn, by M.Lafever.

Fig.1.

A   B   C

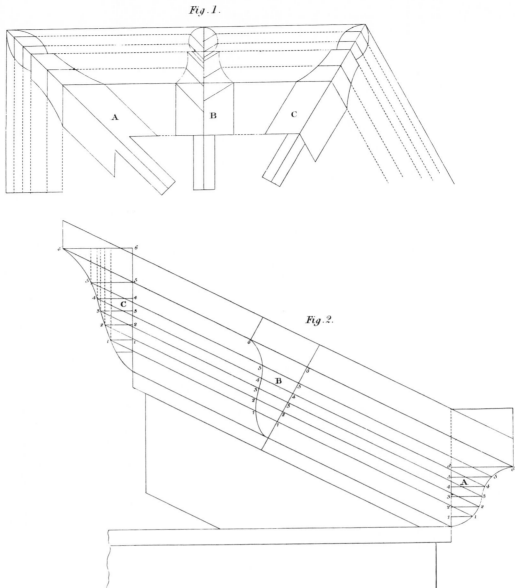

Fig.2.

Fig.3.

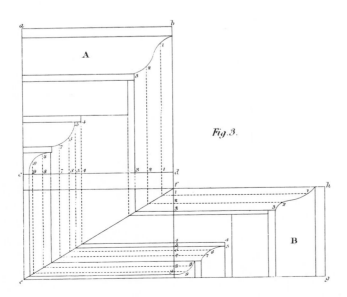

Pl. 85.

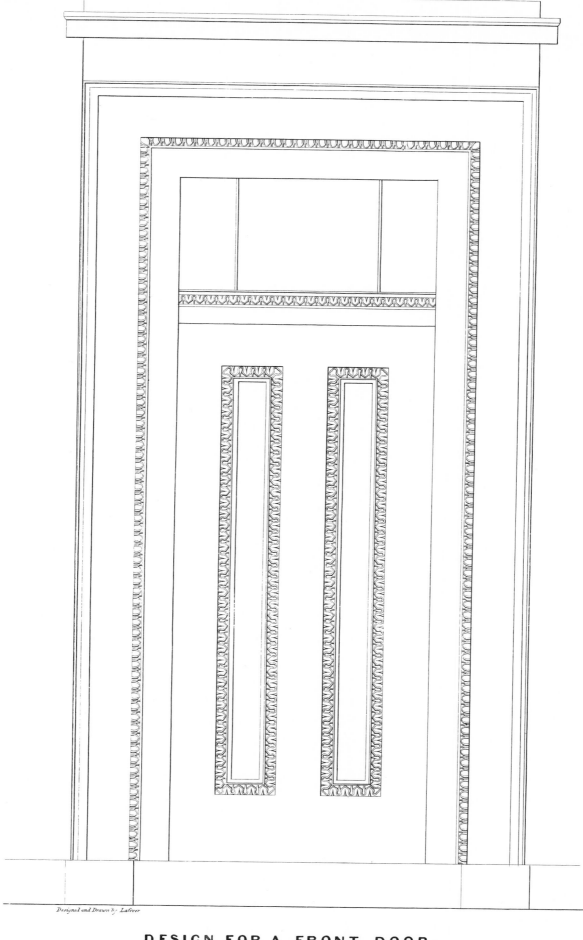

In small apertures or halls.

Designed and Drawn by Lafever

DESIGN FOR A FRONT DOOR
In small apertures or halls.

12   2   3   4   5   6   7   8

Pl. 86.

Wall

1 4 5/8   1 1

2 10   1 1 1/2

DESIGN for A FRONT DOOR

12'''   1   2   3   4   5   6   7   8

A. MANTLE.

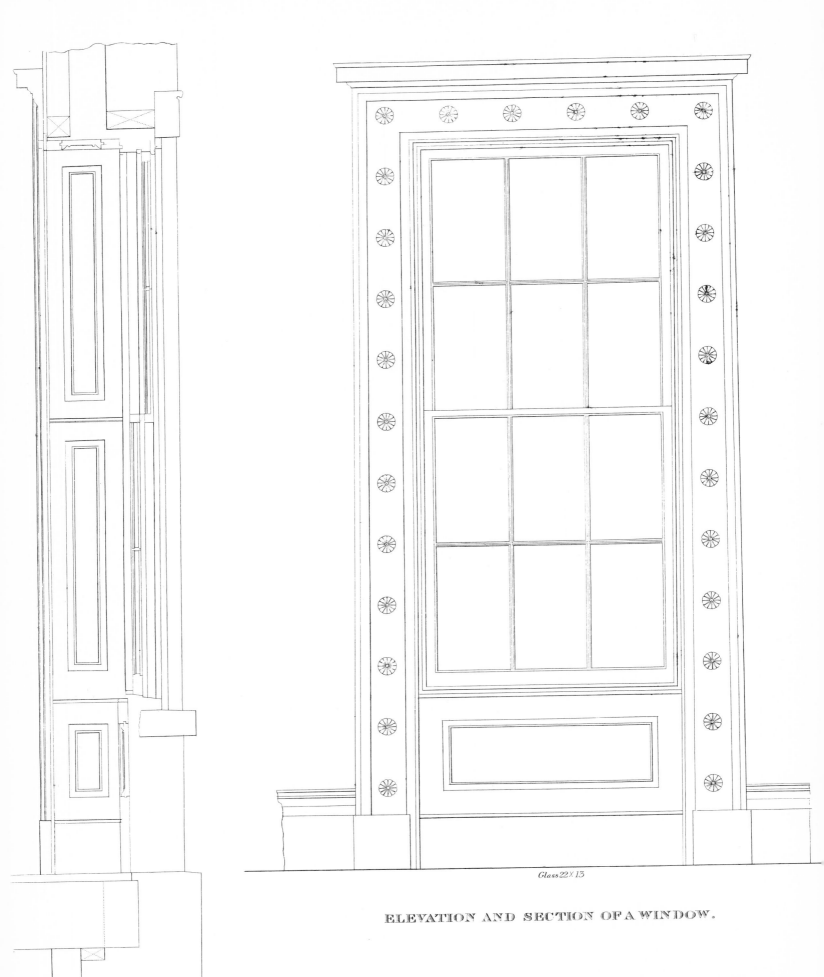

Glass 22 × 13

ELEVATION AND SECTION OF A WINDOW.

Eng? by Wm H Tolfree.

COUNTRY RESIDENCE.

Kitchen. Piazza.

Pantry. Private Stairs.

Dining Room. Living Room.

Pass-way.

Bath. Bed Room.

Stairs

Library. Green Room.

Receiving Room. Hall. Parlour.

10   30   50   70